Risk Management for
Pensions, Endowments,
and Foundations

Founded in 1807, John Wiley & Sons is the oldest independent publishing company in the United States. With offices in North America, Europe, Australia, and Asia. Wiley is globally committed to developing and marketing print and electronic products and services for our customers' professional and personal knowledge and understanding.

The Wiley Finance series contains books written specifically for finance and investment professionals as well as sophisticated individual investors and their financial advisors. Book topics range from portfolio management to e-commerce, risk management, financial engineering, valuation, financial instrument analysis, as well as much more.

For a list of available titles, visit our web site at www.WileyFinance.com.

Risk Management for
Pensions, Endowments,
and Foundations

SUSAN M. MANGIERO

WILEY

John Wiley & Sons, Inc.

Dedication

I want to thank my husband, George, who combines intellect with humor and makes every new day a delightful adventure. To Bridget, Alan, and Melissa: know how much I appreciate your words of wisdom and witty repartee.

Acknowledgments

I would like to thank attorney Kathleen Ziga for her review of the chapters on regulation and corporate governance. Her insightful comments reflect her experience as partner of Dechert LLP, specializing in the area of employee benefits. I owe a special thanks to the editors at John Wiley & Sons who provided guidance and advice.

Moreover, I want to express my appreciation of the many people who generously gave me their time and knowledge during the research phase of the book. Though some people preferred to speak anonymously, their assistance was nevertheless a big help.

On a personal note, my family and friends remind me everyday of my good fortune.

Contents

Just as the twig is bent the tree's inclined.

—Alexander Pope

TWO GIANTS MEET

Financial markets are undergoing massive changes, not the least of which is the role played by institutional investors, a group that includes endowments, foundations, and pension funds. The facts speak for themselves. Institutional assets worldwide now exceed $13 trillion.[1] About half of every dollar of U.S. corporate equity is in the hands of nonhousehold investors and their ownership of bonds is similarly impressive.[2] What, how, and when they trade can dramatically influence market prices and volume. Not surprisingly, business managers, policy makers, and individual market participants pay attention when institutions speak.

A second giant, the mushrooming interest rate derivatives market, now exceeds $123.90 trillion.[3] Add in other types of derivatives and total market size is impossible to overlook. Taken together, the use of derivative instruments by endowments, foundations, and pensions has the potential to roil markets if they are improperly used. In some situations, derivatives are being used directly to manage risk, transform cash flows, synthesize financial positions, or enhance returns. In other cases, institutions expose themselves indirectly by investing in leveraged funds or securities with embedded derivatives.

Besides their sheer size, endowments, foundations, and pension funds play a vital role in the lives of individuals who depend on commitments made by employers or grant-making institutions. Absent good financial habits, endowments, foundations, and pension funds may find themselves in the unfortunate position of being unable to keep promises. This means that others pick up the tab—taxpayers, shareholders, students on scholarship, community groups, and often the fund beneficiaries themselves. With so much at stake, ignoring if and how these investing giants manage risk is foolhardy and makes little sense.

ABOUT THIS BOOK

Fine books have been written about derivatives, but they often intimidate unless the reader has some understanding of finance, especially when the information is presented with lots of equations and in an overly technical manner. This book provides intuitive and straightforward information about risk management for persons involved with or affected by endowment, foundation, or pension fund investment decision making and performance assessment. That defines a wide audience of readers.

- *Plan sponsors, trustees, and anyone with a fiduciary responsibility.* In an era of increased concern about corporate governance, there is a compelling need to demonstrate the due diligence that leads to an informed decision. This includes senior executives and board members who are responsible for policy creation and approval, but who lack the expertise to tackle risk management issues at an excessively detailed level.
- *Regulators and auditors.* Compliance evaluation is complex. A nononsense guide to derivatives and risk management issues helps gatekeepers know what questions to ask and why.
- *Consultants and investment managers.* Knowing what clients need to properly diversify or meet other investment goals is a cornerstone of customer relationship building. Financial salespeople, consultants, and money managers can do a lot for institutional investors when they are comfortable enough to compare the impact of derivative use with alternatives that do not employ leverage.
- *Analysts, employees, and investors.* Understanding an organization's financial well-being requires knowing how derivatives can potentially impact earnings, cash flow, and capital structure. This is especially critical in the current era of myriad bankruptcies and material loss of shareholder wealth.
- *Investor relations specialists and fund-raisers.* Pension plan performance can affect the bottom line in non-trivial ways. To the extent that derivative usage affects pension plan results, persons who interface with Wall Street need to understand their influence on earnings. Fundraisers must likewise be able to answer donors' questions about investment performance and related spending ability.
- *Financial journalists.* Reporting about companies or nonprofit organizations that use derivatives is difficult without a rudimentary knowledge about how and why they are used.
- *Students and jobseekers.* Individuals seeking to work for or with an endowment, foundation, or pension fund that employs derivatives can improve their chances for career development by understanding financial risk management basics.

HOW THIS BOOK IS STRUCTURED

This book is organized into four parts. Part One provides a corporate governance rationale for risk management education and describes why a tax-exempt investor might consider using derivative instruments. Part Two examines the basics of risk, futures, options, and swaps, including case studies specific to endowments, foundations, and pensions. Part Three addresses the risk management process from start to finish, with special emphasis on its dynamic nature. Part Four ties together earlier parts of the book with comments about the current operating environment that is changing, even as this book goes to press.

Part One lays the foundation for risk management from a leadership perspective. Chapter 1 furnishes compelling reasons to support risk management education apropos to endowments, foundations, and pension funds. Chapter 2 provides an overview of corporate governance issues that supports a close relationship between risk management and investment policy making. Chapter 3 addresses the legal and regulatory landscape from a fiduciary perspective. Chapter 4 describes reporting requirements, along with requisite information for proper risk management.

Part Two presents building block concepts about risk and the three major derivative instrument groups—futures, options, and swaps. Chapter 5 introduces financial concepts that are critical to investing and therefore to risk management. Chapter 6 looks at financial futures. Chapter 7 explains options, and Chapter 8 talks about swaps. Chapter 9 discusses risks associated with derivative instrument use.

Part Three looks at various elements of the risk management process. Understanding basics about derivative instruments is important but represents only one part of the overall risk management process. Chapter 10 introduces the risk management process, where to start, the role of the Chief Risk Officer, and the importance of technology. Chapter 11 addresses different ways to measure risk and the significance of monitoring positions over time, including a discussion of stress testing and risk budgeting.

Part Four includes Chapter 12, which looks ahead at the risk management challenges for endowments, foundations, and pension funds.

WHY THIS BOOK

Few books about derivatives have been written exclusively for institutional investors. Books that rely on a solid knowledge of mathematics add to readers' anxiety about a topic that is already viewed by many as arcane and complex. Factor in the seemingly infinite amount of information about the topic and reading about derivatives quickly takes on the appeal of having a tooth pulled. Avoiding the topic is the wrong answer. Fiduciaries need to know enough about derivatives and risk management to justify either their use or prohibition. They have little time or inclination to tackle a book that is long on formulas and short on intuition. Examples, checklists, and end-of-chapter summaries in this book seek to simplify the learning process.

This book is written as a gentle introduction to assist individuals at the top who are responsible for a host of investment and risk management issues—(1) whether to use derivatives, (2) how to use them, (3) how much to use, (4) who can trade, and (5) what safeguards to implement to detect misuse. Unlike the detail a trader needs to know before executing a trade, a managerial decision maker must look at the big picture. In addition to laying out risk management essentials, this book focuses on the broader aspects of risk management as they relate to endowments, foundations, and pension funds.

BOOK HIGHLIGHTS

The challenge is to create a useful reference guide that (1) informs without overwhelming, (2) describes key concepts in an easy-to-understand manner, and (3) can be read in a short period of time. The reader should come away with a basic understanding of the following concepts:

- *General description* of derivative instruments
- *Various benefits* owing to derivative instrument use
- *Basic features* of futures, options, and swaps
- *Comparison* of different derivative instruments
- *Different types of risks* related to derivative instruments
- *Indirect exposure* to derivatives from various investment strategies
- *Common derivative strategies* used by endowments, foundations, and pensions
- *Risk measurement*
- *Risk management considerations* for institutional investors
  And much more.

No book can possibly provide a complete overview of the risk management topic, and this work is no different. The book should be a springboard for further action. This could mean holding in-depth interviews with external money managers, taking an internal assessment of current policies and procedures, or making a commitment to training in the areas of investing and risk management. Whatever happens, any action is one of many required steps in implementing an effective risk management program or improving an existing system.

List of Abbreviations

Abbreviation	Description
ABS	Asset-Backed Security
AICPA	American Institute of Certified Public Accountants
AIMR	Association for Investment Management and Research[*]
ASPA	American Society of Pension Actuaries
BIS	Bank for International Settlements
CBOT	Chicago Board of Trade
CFTC	Commodity Futures Trading Commission
CME	Chicago Mercantile Exchange
COSO	Committee of Sponsoring Organizations of the Treadway Commission
DB	Defined Benefit
DC	Defined Contribution
D&O	Directors and Officers
DOL	U.S. Department of Labor
EBSA	Employee Benefits Security Administration
ERISA	Employee Retirement Income Security Act
FASB	Financial Accounting Standards Board
GFOA	Government Finance Officers Association
HLI	Highly Leveraged Institution
HLIWG	Highly Leveraged Institutions Working Group
IAS	International Accounting Standards Board®
ICC	Independent Consultants Cooperative
IOSCO	International Organization of Securities Commissions
IRS	Internal Revenue Service
ISDA	International Swaps and Derivatives Association, Inc.
LIBOR	London Interbank Offer Rate
MBS	Mortgage-Backed Security
MPT	Modern Portfolio Theory
MOSERS	Missouri State Employees' Retirement System
NACUBO	National Association of College and University Business Officers
NCCUSL	National Conference of Commissioners on Uniform State Laws
NYMEX	New York Mercantile Exchange
OCC	Office of the Comptroller of the Currency
OECD	Organization for Economic Co-operation and Development

(*continued*)

*Renamed the CFA (Chartered Financial Analyst®) Institute as of mid 2004.

Abbreviation	Description
OTC	Over-the-Counter
PBGC	Pension Benefit Guaranty Corporation
PSLRA	Private Securities Litigation Reform Act
PWBA	Pension and Welfare Benefits Administration
RFP	Request for Proposal
SEC	U.S. Securities and Exchange Commission
SPAN®	Standard Portfolio Analysis of Risk
UPIA	Uniform Principal and Income Act of 1997
VaR	Value at Risk

Operating Environment

CHAPTER 1

Why Focus on Risk Management?

There is nothing more frightful than ignorance in action.

—Johann Wolfgang von Goethe

FIDUCIARY EDUCATION—THE BIG PICTURE

A fiduciary is paid to make intelligent decisions about other people's money, something that is difficult to do without full information. Fiduciary responsibility is more than common sense. Volatile market conditions, plunging asset values, and an ever-growing variety of investment choices are heavy-duty challenges for the estimated 3 million persons in the United States with fiduciary responsibility. "The overwhelming majority of these investment decision makers want to do the right thing, but lack the education and training on the practices that constitute a prudent investment process."[1]

As shown in Exhibit 1.1, decisions made by those in power have a dramatic effect on a number of constituencies. One flawed choice sets off a domino effect, potentially drawing the sponsor into litigation, using up precious resources along the way. In some cases, taxpayers may be required to make up the loss, and all the while, beneficiaries feel the pinch. Effects may vary. Fewer scholarships are granted or a community center has to shut down or retirement is postponed until it is more affordable.

Current events tell the tale well. Poor managerial decisions that lead to bankruptcy are particularly hard for employees with a 401(k) concentration in company stock, especially if unemployment follows. Even though individuals determine asset allocation with these self-directed plans, management determines the possible choices, and sometimes the choices are just too limited to permit effective diversification.[2] The renewed focus on 401(k) plan choices is only one of many recent reminders that sponsor vigilance is critical, even when investment decision making is shifted to individuals.[3]

EXHIBIT 1.1　Fiduciary Decision-Making Matters

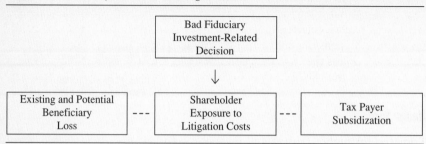

HIDDEN RISKS

As if fiduciary education was not already serious business, add derivatives to the mix and the challenge looms large. Like any financial tool, derivative instruments are a double-edged sword. Used properly, they can transform a financial exposure in ways otherwise not available to the investor or deemed too expensive without them. Used incorrectly, they can wreak havoc, causing monetary loss, missed opportunities, and legal damage. The problem is that derivatives-induced leverage may go unnoticed until too late, especially if no one knows it exists. As shown in Exhibit 1.2, a fund can easily be exposed to derivatives-related risk without an investor explicitly buying or selling a derivative instrument.

Three common examples are hedge funds, embedded derivatives, and use of outside managers. Hedge funds, a popular choice with many institutional investors, often employ derivative instruments. This choice may be good or bad but at the very least, their effects on portfolio risk and return should be

EXHIBIT 1.2　Direct and Indirect Sources of Derivative Exposure

Direct Use of Derivatives	Indirect Use of Derivatives
Employ futures	Allocate money to hedge funds that use derivative instruments
Use options	Allocate money to private equity funds that use derivative instruments
Execute swaps	Hire external money managers that use derivatives
Enter into combination of derivative instruments	Invest directly in securities with embedded derivative-like features.
	Assume liabilities with embedded derivative-like features
	Execute vendor contracts with embedded derivative-like features

considered. Convertible bonds and other complex securities include derivative-like features that alter the way they behave as market conditions change. Money managers, selected directly or by outside consultants, can use derivatives and the pension, endowment, or foundation investors are completely in the dark unless they ask the right questions and are given complete information. Risks may be lurking out of view but present a danger nevertheless.

Hedge Funds

Potential for higher returns and diversification benefits has attracted many new entrants to the $500 billion global hedge fund market.[4] Surprisingly, there is no legal definition of a hedge fund though most people agree that the term refers to a pool of money that is largely unregulated. A few definitions are shown in Exhibit 1.3. The name itself says little about the fund's investment strategy and, as shown in Exhibit 1.4, the style can range considerably. Funds that are highly leveraged in nature are recommended only for more sophisticated investors and are restricted to certain conditions. According to Mark R. Szycher, Director of Research & Chief Risk Officer of Weston Capital Management, some hedge funds "initiate positions using derivatives. Others use protected puts or write covered calls, etc. In general, fixed income and direction strategies such as global macro/managed futures use lots, equity managers use fewer."[5]

Hedge fund investors include tax-exempt organizations, such as endowments and foundations.[6] Until recently, pension funds had taken to hedge funds in smaller numbers, due in large part to opaque reporting that makes it difficult to evaluate a fund's inherent risk.[7] Anemic returns from traditional asset classes, the prospect of comparatively better returns, and

EXHIBIT 1.3 Selected Definitions of a Hedge Fund

Definition

A hedge fund is a private investment limited partnership that invests in a variety of securities.[a]

A fund, usually used by wealthy individuals and institutions, which is allowed to use aggressive strategies that are unavailable to mutual funds, including selling short, leverage, program trading, swaps, arbitrage, and derivatives. Since they are restricted by law to less than 100 investors, the minimum investment is typically $1 million. The general partner usually receives performance-based compensation.[b]

[a]*Source: Hedge Fund Center.* Copyright © 2001, Fund-Investors, LLC. Reproduced with permission. All rights reserved.
[b]*Source:* InvestorWords.com. Copyright © 2002, InvestorGuide.com. Reproduced with permission. All rights reserved.

EXHIBIT 1.4 Some Hedge Fund Strategies

Strategy	Subtype	Comment/Description
Event-Driven: Investment theme is dominated by events that are seen as special situations or opportunities to capitalize from price fluctuations.	Distressed securities	Focused on securities of companies in reorganization and/or bankruptcy, ranging from senior secured debt (low risk) to common stock (high risk).
	Risk arbitrage	Manager simultaneously buys stock in a company being acquired and sells stock in its acquirers. If the takeover falls through, traders can be left with large losses.
Global	International	Manager pays attention to economic change around the world (except U.S.); bottom-up-oriented in that they tend to be stock-pickers in markets they like. Use index derivatives much less than macro managers.
Market Neutral: Manager attempts to lock-out or neutralize market risk. In theory, market risk is greatly reduced but it is difficult to make a profit on a large diversified portfolio, so stock picking is critical.	Long/short	Net exposure to market risk is believed to be reduced by having equal allocations on the long and short sides of the market.
	Convertible arbitrage	One of the more conservative styles. Manager goes long convertible securities and short underlying equities, profiting from mispricing in the relationship of the two.
	Stock arbitrage	Manager buys a basket of stocks and sells short stock index futures contract, or reverse.
	Fixed income arbitrage	Manager buys bonds—often T-bonds, but also sovereign and corporate bonds—and goes short instruments that replicate the owned bond; manager aims to profit from mispricing of relationship between the long and short sides.

Source: MAR_FAQ. Copyright © 2001, Managed Account Reports, Inc. Reproduced with permission. All rights reserved.

less volatility has prompted some pension funds to take a fresh look at hedge funds, "something they may not have been comfortable with even a few months ago."[8] Study after study indicates continued institutional investor interest in the hedge fund market with no decline in sight.[9] As things stand right now, this translates into an estimated 7 percent of total hedge fund assets from investments made by endowments and foundations and 9 percent from retirement funds.[10]

So what's the big deal? The answer is leverage, leverage, and more leverage. Fiduciaries who fail the hedge fund I.Q. test may find themselves in hot water, trying to explain away losses if a strategy sours. It's easy to forget that a financial position that goes way up has the potential to fall precipitously. In his speech to the Public Funds Symposium, Securities and Exchange Commission (SEC) director Paul Roye urged caution, noting that

> *The funds are relatively unregulated, which allows the managers to use derivatives or debt to gear up returns and to be more secretive. High debt and secrecy have become parts of the hedge fund culture. Many hedge fund managers make money because they are privy to information others do not have. Demands for regular disclosure and transparency from investors can hinder this process—if your competitor knows what you are up to, he might get a leg up on you. As a result, it is harder for hedge fund investors to know how their funds are being managed, much less exert control over the manager. Managers can change investment strategies and their investors would never know. Moreover, it is more difficult for hedge fund investors to vote with their feet. Many hedge funds only allow investors to cash in their holdings on a few days a year.[11]*

On the plus side, some hedge funds are opening their books to more clients and making a point to thoroughly disclose their use of derivatives and related risk control policies. After all, the low transaction costs, ease of market entry, and relative liquidity are compelling reasons that favor use of some of the more common derivative instruments.[12] Moreover, using derivatives to take offsetting positions in bonds, commodities, currencies, or stocks is certainly different from using them to speculate.

Investing in hedge funds is not a question of right versus wrong but rather that investors are weighing potential risks against expected returns, a task that is virtually impossible without knowing whether and how a hedge fund employs derivatives and manages risk. At the very least, the hedge fund should disclose data about the type and amount of derivatives used, if any, their purpose, and the fund's ability to liquidate positions in short order.

Securities with Embedded Derivatives

The value of a compound security, sometimes called a complex security, also depends on factors that drive the value of the derivative instrument. These may or may not be the same factors that determine the value of the underlying host stock or bond. Ignoring the more complicated structure of a complex security makes no sense because the derivative cannot be stripped out and sold separately.

There are many kinds of compound securities. A mortgage-backed security (MBS) is one example. It can be thought of as a straight bond paired with an option on the underlying assets. Specifically, the MBS bond takes the prepayment option associated with the underlying mortgagee into account. The key is to accurately value the derivative-like feature embedded within the security.

Ownership by pensions, endowments, and foundations merits discussion for several reasons. First, as shown in Exhibit 1.5, two types of complex securities—asset-backed and mortgage-backed bonds—represent large markets. Second, relaxed rules invite pension plan participation. As of August 23, 2000, employee benefit plans covered by the Employee Retirement Income Security Act (ERISA) can now choose from an expanded list of permitted asset-backed and mortgage-backed securities, including bonds with "eligible interest rate swap" features.[13] Third and very importantly, the risk-return trade-off of these bonds differs from the attributes of more straightforward structures.

Similar to investments in leveraged hedge funds, derivative-like features of complex securities, liabilities, or other financial arrangements expose an

EXHIBIT 1.5 Bond Market Size (Billions of Dollars)

Year	Mortgage-Related	Asset-Backed
1991	1,636.9	129.9
1992	1,937.0	163.7
1993	2,144.7	199.9
1994	2,251.6	257.3
1995	2,352.1	316.3
1996	2,486.1	404.4
1997	2,680.2	535.8
1998	2,955.2	731.5
1999	3,334.2	900.8
2000	3,564.7	1,071.8
2001	4,125.5	1,281.1

Source: The Bond Market Association.

investor to a broader, but more subtle, mix of risk factors. Later chapters in this book will look at these issues in greater detail.

Consultants and External Money Managers

According to the *Pension Fund Consultant Survey 2001,* "47.1% of surveyed plan sponsors, with assets over $100 million, use the services of pension fund consultants."[14] Endowments and government entities report even higher numbers. As shown in Exhibit 1.6, a whopping 78.7 percent of large public and government sponsors use consultants for a variety of investment-related services, including but not limited to crafting official investment policies, recommending how to allocate assets, and selecting money managers and/or evaluating their performance. Having expert help can prove invaluable, particularly for organizations with limited staff or expertise. The flip-side is a cost in terms of information-gathering and oversight.

Fiduciaries must ask intelligent questions about the use of derivatives by outsiders, especially if a large chunk of the investment work is contracted out via consultants or direct hiring of external money managers. Everyone should be very clear about what constitutes a proper usage of derivatives or whether their use is even logical. The pension, endowment, or foundation plan should create policy guidelines that explicitly list permitted instruments, applications, limits, and reporting frequency.

One example is the "Statement of Derivatives Investment Policy for External Money Managers," posted on the web site of the California Public Employees' Retirement System. The document lays out the rules for permitted and banned derivative strategies along with a requirement that external money managers "prepare, maintain, and periodically review a

EXHIBIT 1.6 Excerpts from "Pension Fund Consultant Survey 2001: Consultant Use among Plan Sponsors—2001"

Type of Sponsor	Number of Sponsors Over $100M	Number Using Consultants	Percent Using Consultants
Public/government	478	376	78.7%
Endowments	358	247	69.0%
Hospitals	268	131	48.9%
Unions/Taft-Hartley	618	289	46.8%
Corporate/ERISA	2,333	980	42.0%
Foundations	536	138	25.7%
Total	4,591	2,161	47.1%

Source: Nelson Information's 2001 Survey of the pension, endowment, and foundation investment consulting industry. Copyright © 2001, Nelson Information, a Thomson Financial company. Reproduced with permission. All rights reserved.

written derivatives policy." Major components of the prescribed policy are shown in Exhibit 1.7 and reflect an effort to exchange information between external managers and the pension plan sponsor.

In the absence of an established communications policy or question-naire, the request for proposal (RFP) is a good place to include questions about derivative instruments, notably how their usage is likely to affect performance outcome and what metrics are used to validate their contribution. Some of these can be quite long, but length is not the issue. No one can afford to buy the services of an outsider without a proper vetting. Play the

EXHIBIT 1.7   Excerpts from "Statement of Derivatives Investment Policy for External Managers"

Policy Components

1. Specifies the philosophy and prescribed use of derivatives for client accounts;
2. Establishes limits to derivative exposure within a client account expressed in terms of a percentage of notional amount of derivatives exposure as a percent of market value;
3. Establishes a standard of care concerning the following areas:
   a. Back office and systems capabilities,
   b. Internal audit and review of derivatives use,
   c. Separation of responsibilities,
   d. Senior management supervision,
   e. The required expertise of those permitted to engage in the use of derivatives, and
   f. The authority of those permitted to use derivatives.
4. Establishes and describes the following criteria:
   a. The accounting and valuation procedures in the use of derivatives,
   b. The counter-party exposure credit limit policy,
   c. The value-at-risk analysis regarding the impact to a client's portfolio caused by the use of derivatives,
   d. Reconciliation procedures with the client's master custodian bank,
   e. Reporting requirements to clients, and
   f. The frequency of the policy review and the names of individuals conducting the review.
5. Establishes and describes the monitoring procedures for the following issues:
   a. Policy implementation, and
   b. Risk exposures
6. Describes the compensation of traders, portfolio managers, and other individuals involved in the use of derivatives to avoid inappropriate, fraudulent, or non-compliant behavior.
7. Specifies the periodic review of the written derivatives policy.

role of a financial detective and employ the RFP to ferret out the facts about risk management policies of the external manager(s).

RISK MANAGEMENT AND DERIVATIVES

The discussion so far has used the terms *derivatives* and *risk management* without much explanation. When it comes to headlines, derivatives tend to be a key focus, but the reality is that risk management encompasses a broader array of concerns. What is risk management? That's the "$64,000 question"—one that begs a more fundamental question: What is risk in its most basic sense? Simply put, risk relates to uncertainty. No one has a lock on the future. Bad things can happen.

In the case of pensions, endowments, and foundations, the risk that really matters is the possibility that projected funds will be unavailable for whatever reason. Managing risk is the process of containing any negative surprises. Put another way, risk management represents the policies and controls put in place to ensure—to the extent possible—that beneficiaries will get what they are promised. Where do derivatives fit in? Futures, options, swaps, and combinations of this trio are tools that, if properly used, can minimize risk. Derivative usage is just one part of the dynamic risk management process that repeats itself over and over again. As shown in Exhibit 1.8, identifying risks is a natural starting point, followed by techniques to control them. This process of risk identification and control must be reviewed on a regular basis and revised as needed.

EXHIBIT 1.8   Risk Management Cycle

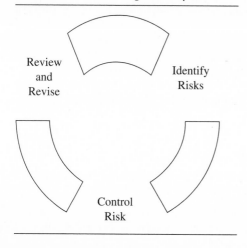

Review and Revise

Identify Risks

Control Risk

Learning about derivative instruments is a necessary but insufficient step. Fiduciary education must include information about many facets of risk. This point is often given short shrift. Noteworthy is the fact that many companies and colleges offer courses with names like "Futures and Options" or "Derivative Securities Markets" as opposed to "Risk Management Basics."[15] Although product knowledge is essential, it is a poor substitute for understanding broader risk management principles well enough to apply them.

More fundamentally, risk management is not an exercise in and of itself. It should be an integral part of the overall investment process. "Incorporating derivatives into a risk management strategy can benefit institutional investors, particularly public and corporate pension funds, so long as fund officials look carefully at the risks and rewards and determine exactly how derivatives fit into an overall investment strategy."[16]

SUMMARY

1. Fiduciaries make decisions that affect multiple groups. These include fund beneficiaries, shareholders, donors who may fear imprudent management, and anyone who benefits from the trickle-down effect of fund disbursement.
2. Those in charge may not realize if and how funds are exposed to derivative usage.
3. Exposure to derivatives may stem from explicit use of derivative instruments or an indirect exposure.
4. Investing in hedge funds that use derivatives or buying securities with derivative-like features are two ways a fund can be indirectly exposed to derivative instrument market movements.
5. A fiduciary must ask detailed questions of consultants and external money managers regarding the use of derivatives.
6. Fiduciaries have a responsibility to learn about the risk management process. Focusing on derivative instruments alone is insufficient.
7. Risk management is an ongoing process that includes the identification and control of risk, followed by a review of policies and procedures.

CHAPTER 2

Corporate Governance and Risk Management

You cannot escape the responsibility of tomorrow by evading it today.

—Abraham Lincoln

WATCH OUT FOR THE ALLIGATORS

A fiduciary's work is fraught with challenges and probably no more so than today. States face tighter budgets, charitable giving is down, liability insurance costs are skyrocketing, pension fund accounting is under the microscope, and investment litigation appears poised to rise. What does that have to do with derivatives and overall risk management? Simply put, a lot. Weak economic conditions and lower returns encourage unwarranted leverage in anticipation of higher future returns. Corporate governance is today's watchword and behaving badly can lead to lawsuits or worse. Exploring the link between the two—corporate governance and risk management—puts things in perspective.

LITIGATION WORRIES

Employee Retirement Income Security Act (ERISA) civil cases filed in federal district courts "jumped 12.8% to 10,292 during the 12-month period ended September 30, 2001, from 9,124 in the prior 12-month period—a level not seen in almost a decade."[1] Plan design, weaker market conditions and demographic changes all factor into the picture. "Past fiduciary mistakes are being masked by years of superior market performance. As the market stalls and employees become more disgruntled, they will increasingly vent their frustration through the courts."[2] Rising litigation is a clear and present danger for anyone in a fiduciary role or a position that is viewed as functionally the same. Post-Enron, "a broader category of persons could face breach-of-fiduciary duty claims,"[3] and board members may find themselves in the hot seat for pension fund problems despite never having directly participated in plan design or operations. By having the authority to designate and then retain or dismiss plan fiduciaries, directors "have ultimate supervisory responsibility, and that is a fiduciary duty in itself."[4]

Education

At a time when fiduciaries confront greater legal liability, they are also asked to make informed decisions on behalf of trust beneficiaries about an assortment of issues ranging from mundane to sublime. Education is essential but may be a concern even when it relates to fundamentals. Consider that only a handful of the executives who attended a recent seminar for directors demonstrated a decent grasp of accounting basics, despite the fact that some of them sat on the audit committee of their respective organizations.[5]

Imagine the outcome with more complex decision making and an ill-informed leadership. In *Brane v. Roth,* ignorance proved to be a futile defense for the directors who were found to have breached their duties "by retaining a manager inexperienced in hedging; failing to maintain reasonable supervision over him; and failing to attain knowledge of the basic fundamentals of hedging to be able to direct the hedging activities and supervise the manager properly. . . ."[6]

Exhibit 2.1 showcases the current sentiment about financial leadership, something without which a system of trust inevitably crumbles. The idea is that effective decision making is simply not possible without understanding business basics. With respect to risk management, a rudimentary knowledge of derivative basics precedes all else and is not just confined to folks at the top. The quiz in Exhibit 2.2 is a modest start. (Answers are provided in Exhibit 2.3.) A failing grade signals a need to learn more—and the sooner the better.

Even when organizations employ derivatives, there is always room for improved knowledge-sharing. First, original decision makers may have moved on, leaving little or no documentation about trades. Second, supervisors may be unaware of hidden derivatives that are part of their portfolios even when traders are comfortable with the risks. Finally, management may feel that they understand the inherent risk–return characteristics of derivative instruments when in fact they do not.

For those just considering their use, education is a *sine qua non*. Thinking otherwise is folly, especially with new mandates such as the Sarbanes-Oxley Act of 2002 and heightened pressure for accountability. Compliance

EXHIBIT 2.1   Focus on Financial Leadership

Notable Quotes

By its terms, Sarbanes-Oxley applies only to public companies—businesses that issue publicly traded stock. However, although Sarbanes-Oxley does not apply to them, some charities are asking whether they should adopt similar rules to bolster public confidence in their financial integrity.[a]

—Excerpted from "Recent Reforms in Corporate Governance: Should Foundations Change Too?"

Senior management identifies and manages the risks that the corporation undertakes in the course of carrying out its business. It also manages the corporation's overall risk profile.[b]

—Excerpted from "Principles of Corporate Governance," May 2002.

[a]Copyright © 2002, the Council on Foundations, www.cof.org. Reproduced with permission. All rights reserved.
[b]Copyright © 2002, The Business Roundable. Reproduced with permission. All rights reserved.

requires knowledge, and knowledge requires commitment. Even organizations with modest budgets can and should establish a cost-effective risk management training program. Beyond compliance, organizations should concern themselves with avoiding a tarnished reputation. Evidence that leadership is informed and vigilant goes a long way to assure the various parties that things are in good shape.

EXHIBIT 2.2   Risk Management Literacy Quiz

Questions

1. What is a derivative instrument?
2. Do a lot of organizations use derivative instruments?
3. What are the major types of derivative instruments?
4. How are derivative instruments priced?
5. How can derivatives be properly used?
6. When might derivatives be considered risky instruments?
7. Are derivative instruments costly to use?
8. Is it possible to be exposed to derivative instruments without knowing it?
9. Does derivative usage relate to risk management?
10. Is price movement the only concern?

Source: Seminar handout. Copyright © 2003, BVA, LLC. Reproduced with permission. All rights reserved.

EXHIBIT 2.3 Quiz Answers

1. A derivative instrument is generally thought of as something that *derives* its value from an underlying asset. For example, gold futures have a value that is directly related to the price of traded gold in the cash market.
2. Countless companies, financial institutions, and government agencies use derivative instruments in a variety of ways. The market size is huge and, with few exceptions, continues to grow.
3. Futures, options, and swaps are often referred to as the primary family of derivative instruments, though there are numerous hybrid combinations.
4. Various theoretical and empirical models are used to price derivative instruments, often taking into account the behavior of the inputs that determine their value. No one model is perfect or always exact. Model risk looks at problems associated with determining derivative instrument value.
5. The key to proper usage depends on first and foremost understanding how the investment profile of a fund changes when derivative instruments are used. Is it more risky? Less risky? The same?
6. Derivative instrument users get into trouble when their actions speculatively increase their organization's exposure to changes in financial market conditions or when they make an uninformed judgment in error. Lack of oversight often leads to problems.
7. The cost of derivatives depends on many factors including market conditions, deal structure, and the creditworthiness of the two counterparties involved. In many cases, derivative instruments can reduce an endowment, foundation, or pension fund's costs or they can increase return.
8. Many investors own derivative instruments without knowing it, for several reasons. First, the investor may not be knowledgeable enough to know that a financial instrument is properly classified as a derivative. Second, the derivative instrument may be embedded in a security's structure and not clearly visible to the buyer. Third, an investor may have indirect exposure to derivatives if the pension, endowment, or foundation puts money with outside managers who actively use derivatives.
9. Risk management goes well beyond derivative usage alone if derivatives are part of the process at all. It is the systematic identification, measurement, and control of risk.
10. Price movement of derivative instruments is one concern. Other aspects of derivative usage include legal uncertainties, possibility of default of the counterparty, computer system malfunctioning, incorrectly specified valuation model, and missed payments, to name a few.

Source: Seminar handout. Copyright © 2003, BVA, LLC. Reproduced with permission. All rights reserved.

Training

Often, an organization will decide to train in increments with each module building on earlier ones. Simplicity and applicability are the hallmarks of a successful program. Anyone with a fiduciary responsibility can ill afford to waste time and money on training that is overly complicated and irrelevant. The person in charge of putting together training or hiring an outside consultant to develop a program must insist on a nuts-and-bolts presentation, especially when so many boards or oversight committees consist of people without a finance background. In fact, many times the audience will have no business background at all yet nevertheless be compelled to make key decisions on investment—and related risk management—issues.

Training should extend beyond people at the top because risk management necessarily cuts across different functions, including systems, legal, auditing, and operational support staff. Consider a pension plan with a nearly perfect risk management system by most standards. Hardware and software work together to capture real-time market data that is used to update risk levels and adjusted security returns. Exposure to various counterparties is closely watched and warnings are issued when outstanding amounts get close to limits. Policies are clearly documented and only authorized traders execute. It sounds too good to be true until someone in the back office misses an option exercise or swap payment. How could this happen? A post-audit reveals that staff members were excluded from training because of the high cost of seminars for persons not considered integral to the risk control process. More will be said about training in Chapter 10.

This kind of mistake is expensive, often outweighing the incremental amount of adding a few more support staff to the training roster. Ensuring that everyone benefits from risk management education goes a long way in preventing avoidable and costly mishaps. As shown in Exhibit 2.4, the American Institute of Certified Public Accountants (AICPA) tackles the issue of product familiarity on the part of directors with a simple list of questions about derivative use.

EXHIBIT 2.4   Derivatives: The AICPA's Six Questions for Directors

---

Questions

---

1. Has the board established a clear and internally consistent risk management policy, including risk limits (as appropriate)?
2. Are management's strategies consistent with the board's authorization?
3. Do key controls exist to ensure that only authorized transactions take place, and that unauthorized transactions are quickly detected and appropriate action is taken?
4. Are the magnitude, complexity and risks of the entity's derivatives commensurate with the entity's objectives?
5. Are personnel with authority to engage in and monitor derivative transactions well qualified and appropriately trained?
6. Do the right people have the right information to make decisions?

Source: Copyright © 1994, by the American Institute of Certified Public Accountants, Inc. Reprinted with permission. All rights reserved.

Role of Institutional Investors

Knowledge is vital, especially when its absence or misuse leads to legal action. Institutional investors are somewhat unique because their involvement could be as plaintiff or defendant, depending on the case at hand. As the defendant, doing lots of financial management homework beforehand can minimize the likelihood of incurring big monetary damages. As the plaintiff, institutional investors that own large amounts of an issuer's stocks or bonds may find it necessary to recoup losses or otherwise remedy a wrong through legal action. Their role has changed over time, due in part to their extensive and growing holdings and to legislative imperatives such as the Private Securities Litigation Reform Act of 1995 (PSLRA), an initiative that redefined the lead plaintiff as the party with the greatest damage, not necessarily the first to file.[7]

That certainly applies today. With several large financial debacles writ large in the headlines, institutional investors are making a beeline to the courthouse. The University of California was recently cited as lead plaintiff, aggregating multiple actions into a unified class action case against Arthur Anderson and Enron.[8] The West Virginia Investment Management Board filed suit against WorldCom, following those filed by New York, several Californian pension funds, and the Illinois Teachers' Fund.[9] As of fall 2001, the Florida State Board of Administration was considered an active institutional litigation participant, involved in several hundred securities fraud lawsuits and classified as lead or co-lead plaintiff in eight of them.[10]

The role of institutional investors in litigation is still evolving. Some welcome institutional plaintiffs because their ownership interest means they are less likely to seek large damages that imperil a company's ongoing existence.[11] Though not explicitly stated as part of the PSLRA, some argue that institutions have a fiduciary responsibility to litigate owing to their investment oversight responsibilities as implied by various governing regulations such as the Employee Retirement Income Security Act.[12]

Litigation has undeniably been affected by institutional involvement in the post-PSLRA era, particularly in cases with unprecedented large settlements like *In re Cendant Corporation Litigation* whereby Cendant agreed to a settlement of almost $3 billion.[13] Despite the uncertainty of what role institutions will play in future litigations, their control of huge amounts of money—and the public's attention—continues to grow.[14]

Legal Action Costs Money

Litigation is costly whether a settlement occurs or not. Consider the case of Enron. Its bankruptcy filing has already resulted in $64 million in legal fees and expenses, and the end is nowhere in sight.[15] Try explaining huge litigation costs to shareholders, taxpayers, and regulators, especially in a down economy when so many people are barely getting by. Some of these costs are laid out in Exhibit 2.5 and show up whether the institution wears the

EXHIBIT 2.5 Litigation Is Costly

| *Before the Problem:* Due diligence costs of identifying risks plus cost of taking steps to begin managing risks | → | *Problem Uncovered:* Investment loss due to no or poor risk management | → | *Costs Associated with Litigation to Recoup Losses:* Reduced time and attention of fiduciaries plus legal fees plus reduced confidence in fiduciaries | → | *Corrective Action:* Explicit cost of making up for loss plus cost to put risk management controls in place (or improve existing ones) plus cost to hire new experts |

Source: Seminar handout. Copyright © 2003, BVA, LLC. All rights reserved. Reproduced with permission.

hat of defendant or plaintiff. The burden is especially heavy when the pension, endowment, or foundation assumes responsibilities not otherwise shared by related parties, such as when it is the lead plaintiff. In addition to time, money, and damaged reputation, litigation can have a long-lasting effect if it signals problems regarding the ability of fiduciaries to manage judiciously the money in their care. In that sense, it has a cascading effect by inviting further scrutiny and additional legal claims.

Even corrective action—rebalancing, hiring a new consultant, or augmenting the trust with additional monies—requires an outlay of cash. A prudent approach mandates putting controls in place long before anything can go wrong. The goal is to minimize legal costs by being proactive.

Insurance Costs

Managers rarely have the luxury of making mistakes. Insurance for directors and officers (D & O) is skyrocketing with no cap in sight. Premiums have gone up by as much as 300 percent in addition to which some companies are required to contribute part of the costs of settling shareholder lawsuits. In the case of criminal liability, the insurer may walk away altogether, leaving the defendant to pay for his or her own defense.[16] Some sectors are harder hit than others and may not be able to get insurance at any price as insurers become more cautious about the kinds of risk they are willing to assume.[17]

The rising severity of claims is tied in part to class actions against U.S. companies, often involving huge claims.[18] To complicate things further, legal opinions are mixed regarding legal fees that directors incur in defending themselves against shareholders' allegations of wrongdoing. Specifically, the Delaware Supreme Court ruled that "directors are entitled to 'fees on fees' when they sue for indemnification and win."[19] Before executives breathe a sigh of relief, they may want to evaluate seriously whether contrary decisions made by the New York Court of Appeals and the Delaware Court of Chancery are a harbinger of changed attitudes toward fiduciaries. Essentially, the issue is cost. How much does someone in a fiduciary role have to personally pay if things go awry?

Applicable to Everyone?

The Sarbanes-Oxley Act of 2002, Public Law 107-204, has kept executives busy as they work to meet rigorous standards for reporting, one of many requirements now imposed on publicly traded companies. Hiring financial experts is another feature of this law, an attempt to have more informed decisions made on behalf of shareholders. Though technically exempt from the Sarbanes-Oxley Act, many nonprofits wonder whether it makes sense to adopt this new law as their own and comply as if it is a mandate for tax-exempt organizations as well as for public firms. As shown in Exhibit 2.6,

EXHIBIT 2.6 Sarbanes-Oxley Act of 2002 and Nonprofit Organizations

"Enron, Nonprofits and the New York Attorney General" by John M. Horak, Esq.

The Enron debacle led to Congress' passage of the Sarbanes-Oxley Act. The Act creates, for publicly owned for-profit corporations, new rules concerning accounting oversight, board responsibility, corporate counsel ethics, and criminal penalties. Is any of this relevant to nonprofit organizations? If so, is it limited only to "large" nonprofits—or should "small" nonprofits be concerned as well? Recent statements by New York Attorney General Eliot Spitzer may give us some indication of what the future will bring.

Relevance to Nonprofit Sector
It is easy to overlook the governance similarities between nonprofits and for-profits. In the case of a for-profit, the shareholders/owners elect a board of directors which (i) oversees management, and (ii) has so-called "fiduciary" duties of care (to be prudent and informed) and loyalty (to avoid conflicts of interest) to the shareholders. The word "fiduciary" is a legal term that simply means "trust"—as in one person being "entrusted" with responsibility for managing property owned by another. If you invested your money in Enron, the Enron board was "entrusted" with your money.

Things work in a surprisingly similar way in the nonprofit sector. The board of a nonprofit oversees management, and has the same fiduciary duties of loyalty and care. The primary difference is in the persons to whom the duties are owed. In the case of a for-profit, the duties clearly are owed to the shareholders. However, the concept of "ownership" is more diffuse in the nonprofit world—the closest we can come is to say that the nonprofit is "owned" by the public, the community, or the charitable class being assisted.

Because "ownership" is more diffuse in the nonprofit sector, nonprofit directors often are under the impression that they are not as "answerable" for their actions as for-profit directors. Other variations on this theme are (i) the "ignorance is bliss" defense—the belief that nonprofit directors cannot be held responsible for what they do not know; and (ii) the belief that under so-called "volunteer protection" statutes directors cannot be sued. The "ignorance is bliss" argument does not necessarily hold water because boards are increasingly seen as having affirmative obligations to ask questions and obtain information—especially where there is some reason to suspect that something is wrong. Moreover, volunteer protection statutes do not prevent suit from being brought—they make it more difficult for the plaintiff to win—and do not apply to actions taken outside of a director's policy making functions.

At any rate, the point we're getting at is that the same governance and ethical principles implicated in Enron are relevant to the boards of nonprofit organizations.

Does Size Matter?
The next question is whether "small" nonprofits need to be concerned about this. Our response is that the applicability of the Enron lessons does not turn on size (the annual budget or the amount of net assets) as much as it does on how the

(continued)

EXHIBIT 2.6 *Continued*

organization is funded and what it does. To state it simply, if your nonprofit is in the nature of a "foundation" that essentially manages an endowment and makes charitable grants, then the governance questions are still relevant but less likely to pop up on anyone's radar screen. On the other hand, (i) if the nonprofit receives monies from outsiders (private donations or, more importantly, under government grants or contracts), and (ii) if it runs a charitable activity or program (provides facilities or services), then size does not matter and the Enron lessons apply.

The reason is simple—the board has been entrusted with both the proper use of someone else's funds, and the proper management of the organization's charitable activities. While the misuse of $50,000 of a government grant may not sound as egregious as the misuse of $500,000, the principle is the same. If a nonprofit is administering medications without the proper licenses to a relatively small population—as opposed to the population served by a hospital—the results will be pretty much the same if a patient dies. And remember—even if (and it can be a big "if") individual directors may avoid legal liability, significant damage can still be done to the reputations of the individuals on the board and of the organization itself.

What to Do?
One area where size matters is in the extent of the prophylactic measures to consider taking. The actions taken by a small social services provider need not be as extensive as those taken by a hospital or university. Nevertheless, there are two common threads to keep in mind.

First, nonprofits should have a set of written policies that address: (i) the mandatory flow of information from management to the board; (ii) regular board review of management performance; (iii) the "core" duties and expectations of board members; (iv) an enhanced perspective on conflicts of interest and how they can be resolved; (v) a code of ethics; (vi) compliance with state and federal regulatory and licensure requirements; and (vii) the relationship of the organization's financial officers and outside auditors. Second, we cannot overemphasize good board recruitment and education practices.

What Does Eliot Spitzer Have to Say?
In January of this year, New York Attorney General Eliot Spitzer called for the extension to nonprofits of many of the key governance reforms in the Sarbanes-Oxley Act—to ensure that charities are "held accountable" for the funds they receive. We believe that this is a sign of a growing national trend, and, in closing, suggest to nonprofits that they keep in mind the old adage that "an ounce of prevention is worth a pound of cure."

Source: This article originally appeared in the *Connecticut Law Tribune.* Copyright © 2003, Law Tribune Newspapers. All rights reserved. Reproduced with permission.
*John M. Horak is Chairman of the Nonprofit Organization Practice Group of Reid and Riege, P.C. in Hartford, Connecticut.

Attorney John Horak suggests that for-profits and nonprofits have a lot in common and offers suggestions for what every nonprofit should be doing at a time when outsiders are asking hard questions.

PERCEPTION VERSUS REALITY: RISK MANAGEMENT AND CORPORATE GOVERNANCE

Taking pre-emptive action to ward off costly mistakes goes beyond good business practice. According to one school of thought, risk management is an integral part of effective investment oversight and therefore a legal imperative. Statistics suggest otherwise, indicating a low priority for an independent risk management function. In its "2002 Defined Benefit Survey," PLANSPONSOR found that 38 percent of respondents had an independent risk management function in place in 2002, up slightly from 35 percent in 2001 but still less than half of all respondent firms.[20] As shown in Exhibit 2.7, things are not much better for any particular size category except for very large funds, those with more than $10 billion in assets.

Pension Fund Problems

Inattention to an important issue is bad enough but especially dangerous when fiduciaries and their money managers are under pressure to make up for losses or simply to earn enough to stay adequately funded. Weak economic conditions are hammering investment returns, and uncertainty about the future provides new meaning to the term "dismal science."[21, 22] "To put this into perspective, the last time three-quarters of public plans were underfunded was in 1993, in the wake of a recession."[23] Private companies fare

EXHIBIT 2.7 Independent Risk Management/Control Function Survey Question Responses

Defined Benefit Assets (Dollars)	YES Responses (Percent)	NO Responses (Percent)
<10 million	25	75
10 million to 49 million	38	62
50 million to 199 million	51	49
200 million to 499 million	33	67
500 million to 999 million	31	69
1 billion to 9.9 billion	28	72
>10 billion	60	40

Source: "2002 Defined Benefit Survey," *PLANSPONSOR.* Copyright © 2002, *PLANSPONSOR.* All rights reserved. Reproduced with permission.

similarly. The Pension Benefit Guaranty Corporation estimates unfunded private company pension liabilities in the neighborhood of $111 billion at year-end 2001, "four times the total at the end of 2000, and nearly double the previous high of $58 billion" in 1995.[24]

Endowments and Foundations Struggle, Too

For endowments, the picture is just as gloomy. University endowments averaged a loss of 3.6 percent on investments in 2001 according to a study done by the National Association of College and University Business Officers (NACUBO).[25] "Public universities face a double whammy: shrinking endowments and less support from state legislatures" with most colleges facing a "dismal" 2004 and inevitably forced to reduce their spending as 3-year average assets fall.[26]

Foundations and charities have their own problems. "Overall, philanthropic foundations, which last year managed a 5.1% increase in giving, to $29 billion, are unlikely to be able to afford any increase this year in the face of a second year of losses in their portfolios."[27] Like endowments, foundations typically look at asset value as a rolling 3-year average so losses today directly affect future spending as a percent of assets. Giving in 2001, a 2.3 percent decline from 2000, "marks the first time in seven years that contributions have dropped in inflation-adjusted terms, and is a decline that is somewhat sharper than in typical recession years."[28]

Temptation Beckons

In the past, investors have sought enhanced returns by taking on more risk, sometimes with disastrous consequences. Even as individual investors are shying away from the stock market, pension funds are increasing their holdings in an attempt "to prop up their depleting equity portfolios to levels called for by their long-term investment policy."[29] Though rebalancing is relatively commonplace, it may not be a panacea and problems can still exist, especially when the issuer's financial health is less than robust. For example, companies can inflate their bottom line by using an unrealistic pension-return assumption. Companies "where pension income accounts for more than 50% of corporate net income" are deemed "highly risky investments" according to then California State Controller Kathleen Connell, and evidence backs her up.[30] A recent study issued by Milliman USA revealed that "fifty of the largest U.S. corporations have continued to employ high return assumptions for their pension funds despite the battering markets took in 2001."[31]

Diane Mix, president of Chicago-based Horizon Cash Management LLC, puts it this way: "Institutional investors have purchased complex securities to boost returns without fully understanding the inherent risks. Sometimes, the investments have involved derivative instruments, often embedded within the asset's structure."[32] The danger of investing in something not well understood should be obvious. The message that is screaming "HEAR ME" is simple. Careful risk management is important when times are good and especially when times are bad. When fiduciaries choose to look the other way—accepting higher returns without acknowledging the higher accompanying risks—calamity is inevitable. This is exactly why fiduciaries must listen and act now to ensure their understanding of the risks at hand.

SUMMARY

1. Fiduciaries face many challenges in the current environment, not the least of which is an increase in litigation.
2. Besides contributing to fiduciaries acting in an informed manner, education can be a cost effective way to minimize legal vulnerability.
3. Institutional investors play the role of both defendant and plaintiff in class-action cases. On the corporate governance front, their presence affects decisions made by companies and other financial institutions.
4. Soaring insurance costs and limited availability of insurance compel fiduciaries to behave prudently.
5. When weak economic conditions bode poorly for the foreseeable future, fiduciaries must exercise care in not adding too much risk to the trust as a way to bolster sagging returns.

CHAPTER 3

Legal and Regulatory Considerations

No question is so difficult to answer as that to which the answer is obvious.

—George Bernard Shaw

REGULATORY IMPERATIVES

The literature on fiduciary duty is vast. Entire books are written on this topic alone, although seldom in the context of risk management. This chapter tries to bridge the gap between responsibility and action with a specific view to endowments, foundations, private pension plans, and their public equivalents. Start with basic concepts of diversification and suitability as part of the fiduciary's duty regarding investments. Add supervisory guidance, corporate governance mandates, and industry best practices and what emerges is a strong case that risk management is appropriately part of a fiduciary's responsibilities. As shown in Exhibit 3.1, fiduciaries are subject to a variety of influences. On a continuum, regulatory agency mandates and existing state and federal laws are hard to ignore because noncompliance triggers its own set of problems. Industry association guidelines and market-based pressures to reform are likewise important, especially if the public equates inaction with irresponsibility. The goal of this chapter is to provide a general overview of the operating environment for pensions, endowments, and foundations. Despite differences in the rules each investor type must follow, the common theme is a focus on fiduciary duty that goes way beyond providing a perfunctory stamp of approval.

Pension Plan Design

Pension plan benefits and regulations of pension plans depend on the type of plan. With a defined benefit (DB) plan, a formulaic approach based on

EXHIBIT 3.1   Some Prevailing Influences on Fiduciary Behavior

Mandatory	Voluntary
Federal law: pensions, trusts	Industry associations: best practice guidelines
Legal precedents: federal, state, local	Market-focused: public pressure for reform, reputation of organization, shareholder wealth maximization
Regulatory agencies: DOL, IRS, state agencies	
State law: pensions, trusts	

salary, years of service, and other variables is used to determine retiree payout. The sponsor bears the risk of investing wisely to ensure adequate funds when needed. In contrast, a defined contribution (DC) plan asks the employee to determine how much to set aside—within statutory and organizational limits—and how the funds will be invested—given specified choices. As shown in Exhibit 3.2, the former accounts for about 75 percent of the approximately $5 trillion of pension plan assets in 2001.

As Exhibit 3.3 points out, the trend in number of plans tells a different story, favoring DC plans due in part to greater employee mobility, changing demographics, and a need for flexibility not typically available with a DB plan. High costs to administer DB plans likewise play a role.[1] A June 2002 Congressional hearing points out the magnitude of the shift as approximately 44 million people participate in DB plans.[2] Both types of plans, DC and DB, require fiduciary care, but the nature of who bears the investment risk is a significant factor with respect to what constitutes a proper discharge of responsibility.

EXHIBIT 3.2   Pension Plan Design Statistics

Type of Plan	Asset Amount (billions of dollars)	Asset Amount (% of total)
Defined benefit	3,611.2	75.3
Defined contribution	1,184.0	24.7
Total	4,795.2	100.0

Source: Excerpted from "P&I 1000 Statistics at a Glance, Top 1000 Assets: Defined Benefit & Defined Contribution, *The P&I 1,000,* January 21, 2002. Reprinted with permission by *Pensions & Investments.* Copyright © 2002, Crain Communications, Inc.

Note: Data reported in the January 26, 2003, issue of *Pensions & Investments* suggests a similar breakdown by type of plan.

EXHIBIT 3.3   Trends in Number of Plans, by Type

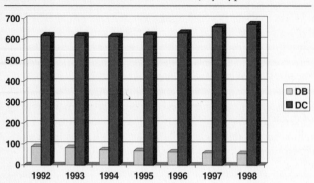

Notes:

DB, defined benefit.

DC, defined contribution.

Source: Private Pension Plan Bulletin: Abstract of 1998 Form 5500 Annual Reports, U.S. Department of Labor, Pension and Welfare Benefits Administration, Winter 2001–2002.

ERISA Pension Law

Assets controlled by large private pension plans are considerable, and the regulations that govern them are just as imposing. The Employee Retirement Income Security Act of 1974 (ERISA), part of Title 29, Chapter 18 of the U.S. Code, lays out the guidelines for asset management of nongovernment pension plans, another name for private plans, with oversight from the U.S. Department of Labor, Pension Benefit Guaranty Corporation, and the Internal Revenue Service.

As shown in Exhibit 3.4, an ERISA plan fiduciary is associated with control or authority over the plan and its assets. A fiduciary can be an individual, corporation, or other type of organization as defined by law. A plan must have at least one identified fiduciary. Under federal law, a plan fiduciary

> *shall discharge his duties with respect to a plan solely in the interest of the participants and beneficiaries (A) for the exclusive purpose of providing benefits to participants and their beneficiaries; and defraying reasonable expenses of administering the plan; (B) with the care, skill, prudence and diligence under the circumstances then prevailing that a prudent man acting in a like capacity and familiar with such matters would use in the conduct of an enterprise of a like character and with like aims; (C) by diversifying the investment of the plan so as to minimize the risk of large losses, unless under the circumstances it is clearly prudent not to do so; and (D) in accordance with the documents and instruments governing the plan*

EXHIBIT 3.4 Who Is a Plan Fiduciary?[a]

The Employee Retirement Income Security Act defines a plan fiduciary as a person who (1) exercises any discretionary control or authority over management of the plan, (2) exercises any authority or control over the management of plan assets, (3) renders direct or indirect investment advice with respect to assets of the plan, or has authority to do so, for a fee or other compensation, or (4) has any discretionary authority or responsibility in the administration of the plan.

The employer and its officers and directors may be considered plan fiduciaries to the extent they act or serve in a capacity by performing functions that are covered in ERISA's definition of a plan fiduciary. Plan fiduciaries generally include plan trustees, plan administrators, investment managers, and members of a plan's investment committee.

---

[a]Both individuals and organizations can be fiduciaries.
Source: Excerpted from *Answers to Key Questions about Private Pension Plans,* U.S. General Accounting Office, September 18, 2002.

> *insofar as such documents and instruments are consistent with the provisions of this subchapter and subchapter III of this chapter.*[3]

These few words speak volumes, in part reflecting the Prudent Man Rule, which dates back nearly two centuries to *Harvard College v. Armory.*[4] At that time, the Massachusetts court required a trustee "to observe how men of prudence, discretion and intelligence manage their own affairs, not in regard to speculation, but in regard to the permanent disposition of their funds, considering the probable income, as well as the probable safety of the capital to be invested."[5]

The more modern Prudent Investor Rule differs from the Prudent Man Rule in four ways:

> *(A) a trust account's* entire *investment portfolio is considered when determining prudence. Under this approach, a fiduciary would not be held liable for individual losses, so long as an account's investment portfolio, as a whole, appreciates. (B) Diversification is explicitly included as a duty for prudent fiduciary investing. (C) No category or type of investment is deemed inherently imprudent. Instead,* suitability *to the trust account's* purposes and *beneficiaries'* needs *is considered the* determinant. *As a result, junior lien loans, investment in limited partnerships, derivatives, futures and similar investment vehicles, are not automatically considered imprudent merely due to the type of asset involved. However, while the fiduciary is now permitted, even encouraged, to develop greater flexibility in overall portfolio management, speculation and outright risk taking is not sanctioned by the rule either, and they remain subject to criticism and possible liability. (D) Delegation of fiduciary investment and other management functions to other fiduciaries and agents is sanctioned.*[6]

Where do derivatives come in? Besides their explicit mention, one can argue for their use as a diversification tool. Consider the example of a pension fund that owns airline stock that could drop in value if oil prices rise. Buying oil company stock is one way to hedge against this risk. The idea is that higher energy prices benefit an oil supplier but increase costs for an airline company. Ideally, the two stocks would move in opposite directions but by the same magnitude and provide a type of natural investment offset. Use of derivatives is another approach. Taking a proportionate short position in a suitable derivative instrument provides an offset if airline company stock values drop. More is said about diversification in this chapter and in Chapter 5. Although ERISA standards seem to implicitly condone consideration of derivatives, the U.S. Department of Labor provides explicit guidance about their use in its March 21, 1996, letter to the Comptroller of the Currency. Reproduced as Exhibit 3.5, the intent of the letter is clear. "Investments in derivatives are subject to the fiduciary responsibility rules in the same manner as are any other plan investments. Thus, plan fiduciaries must determine that an investment in derivatives is, among other things, prudent and made solely in the interest of the plan's participants and beneficiaries."[7] The letter goes on to say that use of a derivative requires the same exact due diligence that is done when making any other investment decision. This would include, but not be limited to, a "consideration of how the investment fits within the plan's investment policy, what role the particular derivative plays in the plan's portfolio, and the plan's potential exposure to losses."[8]

Acknowledging that not all derivatives represent the same balance between risk and return, the U.S. Department of Labor offers that some derivatives, "such as structured notes and collateralized mortgage obligations" require investors to have "a higher degree of sophistication and understanding."[9] This guidance extends to derivative use when they are part of a pooled fund managed by an outside firm. Included are managers such as "banks (as defined in the Investment Advisers Act of 1940), insurance companies qualified under the laws of more than one state to manage, acquire and dispose of plan assets, or persons registered as investment advisers under the Investment Advisers Act of 1940."[10] Each manager is required to identify and abide by the plan's goals and constraints. This is the not the same as preapproval of every trade made on behalf of the managers' clients.[11] The message is that managers and plan fiduciaries must work together in carrying out their duties to beneficiaries.

Public Pension Guidance

According to the National Governors Association, "state and local governments administer approximately 2,300 retirement systems that cover about 15 million employees" and "hold nearly $3 trillion in assets for the payment

EXHIBIT 3.5 U.S. Department of Labor Letter about Derivatives

---

PWBA[a] Office of Regulations and Interpretations

March 21, 1996

Honorable Eugene A. Ludwig
Comptroller of the Currency
250 E Street, S.W.
Washington, D.C. 20219

Dear Mr. Ludwig,

At our last meeting we discussed the Department of Labor's views with respect to the utilization of derivatives[b] in the management of a portfolio of assets of a pension plan which is subject to the Employee Retirement Income Security Act of 1974 (ERISA). This letter is to provide you with an update of our views in a format which may be of use to you and your staff.

ERISA governs private-sector sponsored employee welfare and pension benefit plans and provides a general framework within which plan fiduciaries are expected to conduct their investment activities. Under ERISA, a fiduciary includes anyone who exercises discretion in the administration of an employee benefit plan; has authority or control over the plan's assets; or renders investment advice for a fee with respect to any plan assets.[c] Thus, any entity, including an institution such as a bank, that meets this functional test with respect to an employee benefit plan sponsored by a private-sector employer, employee organization, or both, would be considered a fiduciary under ERISA.

ERISA establishes comprehensive standards to govern fiduciary conduct. Among other things, fiduciaries with respect to an employee benefit plan must discharge their duties with respect to a plan solely in the interest of the plan's participants and beneficiaries, and with the care, skill, prudence and diligence under the circumstances then prevailing that a prudent person acting in a like capacity and familiar with such matters would use in the conduct of an enterprise of a like character and with like aims.[d]

Investments in derivatives are subject to the fiduciary responsibility rules in the same manner as are any other plan investments. Thus, plan fiduciaries must determine that an investment in derivatives is, among other things, prudent and made solely in the interest of the plan's participants and beneficiaries.

In determining whether to invest in a particular derivative, plan fiduciaries are required to engage in the same general procedures and undertake the same type of analysis that they would in making any other investment decision. This would include, but not be limited to, a consideration of how the investment fits within the plan's investment policy, what role the particular derivative plays in the plan's portfolio, and the plan's potential exposure to losses. While derivatives may be a useful tool for managing a variety of risks and for broadening investment alternatives in a plan's portfolio, investments in certain derivatives, such as structured notes and collateralized mortgage obligations, may require a

(continued)

EXHIBIT 3.5   *Continued*

higher degree of sophistication and understanding on the part of plan fiduciaries than other investments. Characteristics of such derivatives may include extreme price volatility, a high degree of leverage, limited testing by markets, and difficulty in determining the market value of the derivative due to illiquid market conditions.

As with any investment made by a plan, plan fiduciaries with the authority for investing in derivatives are responsible for securing sufficient information to understand the investment prior to making the investment. For example, plan fiduciaries should secure from dealers and other sellers of derivatives, among other things, sufficient information to allow an independent analysis of the credit risk and market risk being undertaken by the plan in making the investment in the particular derivative. The market risks presented by the derivatives purchased by the plan should be understood and evaluated in terms of the effects that they will have on the relevant segments of the plan's portfolio as well as the portfolio's overall risk.

Plan fiduciaries have a duty to determine the appropriate methodology used to evaluate market risk and the information which must be collected to do so. Among other things, this would include, where appropriate, stress simulation models showing the projected performance of the derivatives and of the plan's portfolio under various market conditions. Stress simulations are particularly important because assumptions which may be valid for normal markets may not be valid in abnormal markets, resulting in significant losses. To the extent that there may be little pricing information available with respect to some derivatives, reliable price comparisons may be necessary. After entering into an investment, a plan fiduciary should be able to obtain timely information from the derivatives dealer regarding the plan's credit exposure and the current market value of its derivatives positions, and, where appropriate, should obtain such information from third parties to determine the current market value of the plan's derivatives positions, with a frequency that is appropriate to the nature and extent of these positions.

If the plan is investing in a pooled fund which is managed by a party other than the plan fiduciary who has chosen the fund, then that plan fiduciary should obtain, among other things, sufficient information to determine the pooled fund's strategy with respect to use of derivatives in its portfolio, the extent of investment by the fund in derivatives, and such other information as would be appropriate under the circumstances.

As part of its evaluation of the investment, a fiduciary must analyze the operational risks being undertaken in making the investment. Among other things, the fiduciary should determine whether it possesses the requisite expertise, knowledge, and information to understand and analyze the nature of the risks and potential returns involved in a particular derivative investment. In particular, the fiduciary must determine whether the plan has adequate information and risk management systems in place given the nature, size and complexity of the plan's derivatives activity, and whether the plan fiduciary has personnel who are competent to manage these systems. If the investments are made by outside investment managers hired by the plan fiduciary, that fiduciary should consider whether the investment managers have such personnel and controls and whether the plan fiduciary has personnel who are competent to monitor the derivatives activities of the investment managers.

EXHIBIT 3.5 *Continued*

Plan fiduciaries have a duty to evaluate the legal risk related to the investment. This would include assuring proper documentation of the derivative transaction and, where the transaction is pursuant to a contract, assuring written documentation of the contract before entering into the contract. Also, as with any other investment, plan fiduciaries have a duty to properly monitor their investments in derivatives to determine whether they are still appropriately fulfilling their role in the portfolio. The frequency and degree of the monitoring will, of course, depend on the nature of such investments and their role in the plan's portfolio.

We hope these comments have been helpful. However, if you should have any further questions or if we can provide any further assistance, please feel free to contact Morton Klevan at (202) 219-9044 or Louis Campagna at (202) 219-8883.

Sincerely,

Olena Berg

[a]*Note:* In 2003, the PWBA changed its name to the Employee Benefits Security Administration.
[b]We refer to derivatives in this letter as financial instruments whose performance is derived in whole or in part from the performance of an underlying asset (such as a security or index of securities). Some examples of these financial instruments include futures, options, options on futures, forward contracts, swaps, structured notes, and collateralized mortgage obligations.
[c]See ERISA section 3(21).
[d]See ERISA section 404(a).
Source: U.S. Department of Labor.

of benefits and cover virtually all full-time employees."[12] State programs typically consist of a DB plan and a DC plan, funded "by revenues from state and local government taxpayers, contributions by employees themselves, and earnings from assets in the retirement fund."[13] If supplemental DC plans exist, they tend to be funded largely by the employees directly. They are frequently "administered by an independent agency covering multiple jurisdictions or third party administrators and are separate from the employer."[14] A board of trustees with employee representation is common. Their duties vary, but can generally be classified as policy making and oversight. Exhibit 3.6 is the statement of duties for the Kansas Public Employees' Retirement System.

Whereas private pension plans are exempt from state laws and instead regulated at a federal level, public pension plans are almost entirely regulated by the states, although efforts are afoot to take a second look at the situation.[15] In the aftermath of large corporate bankruptcies in the last few years, the U.S. Congress is considering legislation that would require pension

plan sponsors, "including state pension plan sponsors, to ensure employees
receive full disclosure regarding retirement plan assets and investment decisions and information about the importance of diversification."[16]
   Investment policy statements are in place for many public pension plans.
The rationale for having a formal policy is fivefold. A policy (1) codifies an
investment goal, (2) creates a method for assessing the trade-off between risk
and return, (3) exhibits due diligence on the part of pension caretakers, (4)
establishes checks and balances, and (5) informs and documents plan strategy.[17] Of the 40 investment policies examined by the Government Finance
Officers Association (GFOA), 68 percent included a statement about "limitation on derivatives," although nearly all the policies included a statement
about risk management via diversification.[18] Exhibit 3.7 provides more
detail.
   Use of derivatives in an investment vacuum makes no sense. Consider
the Missouri State Employees' Retirement System (MOSER). According to
its web site, as of June 30, 2001, MOSER was "one of the 200 largest
defined benefit plans in the United States with total assets of just over $5.4
billion."[19] Selected by the GFOA, the MOSER pension investment policy
received praise for its "depth, breadth, and clarity."[20] Derivative instruments are discussed in several places, but their use is always tied to investment goals. Securities with embedded derivatives such as mortgage-backed
securities and convertible stocks and bonds are permitted as "diversification
pool investment vehicles."[21] As shown in Exhibit 3.8, MOSER uses derivatives internally for rebalancing purposes and only with senior-level approval.

EXHIBIT 3.7 Risk Management Inclusion in Investment Policies of Public Pension Funds

Category/Element	Statement on Managing Risk in the Overall Portfolio	Frequency (%)
C1.	Asset allocation target (adds to 100%)	68
C2.	Guidelines on alternative assets	37
C3.	AA range	76
C4.	Rebalancing guidelines	59
D1.	Allowable investment types/strategies listed	76
D2.	Prohibited investment types/strategies listed	66
D3.	Limitation on derivatives	68
D4.	Limitation on market timing	7
D5.	Diversification within asset classes	88

Source: "Exhibit 4, Frequencies for Investment Policy Elements—Pension Investment Policies: The State of the Art," *Government Finance Review,* February 2002. Reprinted with permission of the Government Finance Officers Association, publisher of *Government Finance Review,* 203 N. LaSalle St., Suite 2700, Chicago, IL 60601-1210; phone: 312-977-9700; fax: 312/977-4806; e-mail: GFR@gfoa.org; web site: www.gfoa.org. Annual subscriptions: $30.

EXHIBIT 3.8 Missouri State Employees' Retirement System Statements about Derivatives Use

Statement Number	Section VIII. General Investment Restrictions and/or Guidelines
1.	No leverage will be used with any investment strategy. The use of futures to rebalance the fund as provided in this document is not considered to be leverage.
3.	Derivative securities and synthetic products including futures, options, swaps, and forward contracts (and/or combinations of these instruments), and pooled, mutual or segregated funds that employ derivative and synthetic products may not be used by any investment manager without the written authorization of the Director, CIO and the Consultant.

Source: Excerpted from "Missouri State Employees' Retirement System, Adopted by the Board of Trustees in June 1995 and last revised on September 20, 2001, Section VIII, General Investment Restrictions and/or Guidelines, Statement Numbers 1 and 3, pages 14 and 15." Copyright © 2002, Missouri State Employees' Retirement System.

According to Gary Findlay, executive director of MOSER,

Rather than attempt to anticipate every possible future circumstance in a comprehensive document, we elected to go with an outright prohibition and then allow for specific exceptions to that policy based on discussions with our money managers. When we retain a new manager, we work with them to develop mutually acceptable implementation guidelines. If we are persuaded that facts and circumstances will warrant the use of derivatives, we craft language that is very specific regarding the latitude the manager has in that regard. The primary problems with derivatives in the past stemmed from the heavy use of leverage and/or the use of products that were extremely interest rate sensitive. We believe we have been able to mitigate those risks through implementation guidelines with our managers.[22]

Not surprisingly, there is no "one size fits all" model for public plans any more than there is for private plans, endowments, or foundations. Nevertheless, looking at what others have done is instructive. For example, the state of Florida documents its use of derivatives—asset- and mortgage-backed securities—"to improve yield," recognizing their sensitivity to "prepayments by mortgagees caused by changing market conditions."[23] The state also reports mid-year 2000 fair value of futures, options and swaps in which the "Defined Benefit Pension Plan had investments."[24] The Texas State Auditor's Office publishes an entire appendix to their financial manual devoted to derivatives, citing public concern over public fund losses related to derivatives.[25]

A collaborative effort by members of the Association of Public Pension Fund Auditors and several pension fund chief investment officers led to the July 2000 publication of *Public Pension Systems: Statements of Key Investment Risks and Common Practices to Address Those Risks*. Meant as guidelines for public pension funds and other funds, the publication has been endorsed by the GFOA, the National Association of State Retirement Administrators, and the National Council of Teacher Retirement. Importantly, its focus is on the broader topic of risk management and not derivatives alone. Excerpts are shown in Exhibit 3.9, although an unnamed source describes plans to update and revise the publication within the next year to ensure relevancy. In addition, the Association of Public Pension Fund Auditors has posted information about operational risks on its web site.

While many organizations recognize the importance of risk management, many do not. Therefore, finding information is sometimes arduous. According to Greg Kaza, executive director of the Arkansas Policy Foundation, "transparency through public disclosure is crucial to effective market discipline and can reinforce supervisory efforts to promote high standards in risk management."[26] Public funds need something analogous to the

EXHIBIT 3.9 Derivative Securities and Public Pension Systems

Managers of Derivative Securities

Typically, public pension systems do not have significant exposure to derivative instruments that could swiftly change the risk profile of the fund. Many derivative exposures are simple and direct substitutes for the underlying instrument. For example, the use of certain futures and forwards markets, such as the S&P 500 Futures Market, is practically interchangeable for holdings in the underlying security or securities. As a result, the risk management procedures for managers with publicly traded portfolios would suffice for tracking those positions if they could materially impact the portfolio.

The concern is with exotic instruments that have express or hidden leverage features or significant elements of optionality. These features could make the standard characteristic measurements (such as duration, beta, etc.) inapplicable for large market moves or, through express or implied leverage, result in a cascading effect from relatively small or marginal market moves. The task for a public pension system is to determine if those types of instruments are in the portfolio and, if they are, whether the aggregate exposure to the overall portfolio is such that additional and more detailed tracking mechanisms and other risk control measures are required.

Source: Excerpted from *Public Pension Systems: Statements of Key Investment Risks and Common Practices to Address Those Risks,* July 2000, pages 21 and 22. Copyright © 2000, Association of Public Pension Fund Auditors, Inc.

derivative reporting rules put in place by the Financial Accounting Standards Board for publicly traded companies. As Michigan State Representative, he wrote legislation that permitted public access to information about government use of derivative instruments and hopes that other states will follow suit.[27] Nasty surprises about the oft-hidden use of derivatives remind investors, regulators, and taxpayers alike that good information is everything. More is said about reporting in Chapter 4.

U.S. Trust Law

The world of tax-exempt organizations is a complex one, particularly with respect to rules and regulations. Although Section 501(c) of the Internal Revenue Service Code exempts many philanthropic organizations from paying federal income taxes, their specific structure determines the way they should operate. For example, a private foundation differs from a public charity. Funding for a private foundation typically comes from a single source such as a corporation or family donor. In addition, the private foundation must file a tax return known as the 990-F that includes financial information along with the names of trustees.[28] This form is discussed in Chapter 4.

There are many types of nonprofit organizations.[29] They typically follow relevant trust laws. Although state laws can and do vary throughout the United States, the National Conference of Commissioners on

EXHIBIT 3.10   Some Changes in U.S. Trust Law

Name of Act	Changes	Year
Uniform Prudent Investor Act:	Focus on portfolio performance	1994
	Enhanced variety of permitted investments	
	Delegation of investment management duties	
Revised Uniform Principal and Income Act	Focus on total return	1997
	Defines derivative instruments	
	Addresses synthetic securities	

Source: "Uniform Prudent Investor Act (UPIA) and Revised Uniform Principal and Income Act: States Nationwide Need to Adopt Both Acts to Bring Trust Law Into Line with Modern Portfolio Theory," *National Conference of Commissioners on Uniform State Laws Press Release,* January 2000. Copyright © 2000, National Conference of Commissioners on Uniform State Laws.

Uniform State Laws (NCCUSL) drafts guideline legislative proposals that can be adopted or modified by individual states.[30] In January 2000, the NCCUSL released a statement about both the Uniform Prudent Investor Act and the Revised Uniform Principal and Income Act that led to updated trust legislation by a majority of the 50 states. Exhibit 3.10 summarizes some of the changes that affect trust investment policy and the role of the trustees.

As stated earlier, trust law in many areas incorporates the notion of diversification and other tenets of Modern Portfolio Theory (MPT) to guide trustees in their duties regarding investments. As of the January 2000 press release date, Arkansas, California, Connecticut, Iowa, North Dakota, Oklahoma, and Virginia had adopted revisions to former principal and income allocation rules to reflect

> *total return rather than a certain level of "income" as traditionally per-ceived in terms of interest, dividends, and rents. The revised act, for example, helps the trustee who has made a prudent, modern portfolio-based investment decision that has the initial effect of skewing returns from all the assets, viewed as a portfolio, as between income and prin-cipal beneficiaries. The Act gives that trustee a power to reallocate the portfolio return suitably. To leave a trustee constrained by the tradi-tional system would inhibit the trustee's ability to fully implement mod-ern portfolio theory.*[31]

The Uniform Principal and Income Act of 1997 (UPIA) advanced trust law in another important way. It recognizes derivatives and other new financial instruments, not in place in 1962, when the act was last revised.

The commissioners provide a definition for derivative instruments while also making a distinction between stand-alone derivatives and those that are embedded in other securities. The UPIA explicitly mentions derivatives, but some assert that trust law in general goes further. Allowing that derivatives can diversify a portfolio and, focusing on the need for balance, "[t]he legal community has begun to accept the idea of a fiduciary duty to hedge; therefore, a requirement that directors and money managers be knowledgeable and understand basic hedging strategies has evolved. Additionally, direct legal challenges will arise against trust fiduciaries who fail to manage corpus risk with derivatives when appropriate."[32]

Related Authorities

Augmenting regulatory agency guidance, several organizations have taken the lead in the area of industry best practices. *Derivatives: Practices and Principles,* published in 1993 by the Group of 30—a group that includes academicians, practitioners, and public sector officials—offers advice to end users and dealers alike, focusing on standards that have the potential to prevent a market mishap from doing irreparable damage to global capital markets.

In 1994, the Bank for International Settlement (BIS) addressed oversight by similarly emphasizing the crucial role played by both the board of directors and senior management. As shown in Exhibit 3.11, BIS recognizes that management must prioritize risk management enough to supply adequate resources to ensure a successful implementation of policies and procedures.

In 1996, the Risk Standards Working Group published risk standards that could be used by institutions and their managers, emphasizing the need for an independent third-party review of the risk management process, if affordable, or at the very least, a separation of responsibilities.[33] Other industry standards are mentioned in Chapter 12.

What should be abundantly clear from these guidelines, and a concept that is repeated throughout this book, is that investing and risk management go hand in hand. Treating them as separate functions makes no sense. To recap, fiduciaries must be informed well enough to establish—and regularly review—investment and risk control policies and procedures. Even if delegation occurs, the ultimate responsibility belongs to the fiduciaries. By creating the "big picture" standards, fiduciaries should at the same time understand that committing to an integrated investment–risk control process affects many parts of an institution's operations, from accounting to systems to traders. Moreover, the extent to which fiduciaries properly establish and execute a unified investment–risk management policy should be reflected in the procedures that govern anything from authorizing trades to setting up a reasonable compensation standard to hiring knowledgeable and experienced staff.

EXHIBIT 3.11 Basel Committee on Banking Supervision, Bank for International Settlements Risk Management Oversight Recommendations

1. As is standard practice for most banking activities, an institution should maintain written policies and procedures that clearly outline its risk management guidance for derivatives activities. At a minimum these policies should identify the risk tolerances of the board of directors and should clearly delineate lines of authority and responsibility for managing the risk of these activities. Individuals involved in derivatives activities should be fully aware of all policies and procedures that relate to their specific duties.

Board of directors
2. The board of directors should approve all significant policies relating to the management of risks throughout the institution. These policies, which should include those related to derivatives activities, should be consistent with the organisation's broader business strategies, capital strength, management expertise and overall willingness to take risk. Accordingly, the board should be informed regularly of the risk exposure of the institution and should regularly reevaluate significant risk management policies and procedures with special emphasis placed on those defining the institution's risk tolerance regarding these activities. The board of directors should also conduct and encourage discussions between its members and senior management, as well as between senior management and others in the institution, regarding the institution's risk management process and risk exposure.

Senior management
3. Senior management should be responsible for ensuring that there are adequate policies and procedures for conducting derivatives operations on both a long-range and day-to-day basis. This responsibility includes ensuring that there are clear delineations of lines of responsibility for managing risk, adequate systems for measuring risk, appropriately structured limits on risk taking, effective internal controls and a comprehensive risk-reporting process.
4. Before engaging in derivatives activities, management should ensure that all appropriate approvals are obtained and that adequate operational procedures and risk control systems are in place. Proposals to undertake derivatives activities should include, as applicable:
   - a description of the relevant financial products, markets and business strategies;
   - the resources required to establish sound and effective risk management systems and to attract and retain professionals with specific expertise in derivatives transactions;
   - an analysis of the reasonableness of the proposed activities in relation to the institution's overall financial condition and capital levels;
   - an analysis of the risks that may arise from the activities;
   - the procedures the bank will use to measure, monitor and control risks;
   - the relevant accounting guidelines;
   - the relevant tax treatment; and
   - an analysis of any legal restrictions and whether the activities are permissible.

EXHIBIT 3.11 *Continued*

5. After the institution's initial entry into derivatives activities has been properly approved, any significant changes in such activities or any new derivatives activities should be approved by the board of directors or by an appropriate level of senior management, as designated by the board of directors.
6. Senior management should regularly evaluate the procedures in place to manage risk to ensure that those procedures are appropriate and sound. Senior management should also foster and participate in active discussions with the board, with staff of risk management functions and with traders regarding procedures for measuring and managing risk. Management must also ensure that derivatives activities are allocated sufficient resources and staff to manage and control risks.
7. As a matter of general policy, compensation policies—especially in the risk management, control and senior management functions—should be structured in a way that is sufficiently independent of the performance of trading activities, thereby avoiding the potential incentives for excessive risk taking that can occur if, for example, salaries are tied too closely to the profitability of derivatives.

Independent risk management functions
8. To the extent warranted by the bank's activities, the process of measuring, monitoring and controlling risk consistent with the established policies and procedures should be managed independently of individuals conducting derivatives activities, up through senior levels of the institution. An independent system for reporting exposures to both senior-level management and to the board of directors is an important element of this process.
9. The personnel staffing independent risk management functions should have a complete understanding of the risks associated with all of the bank's derivatives activities. Accordingly, compensation policies for these individuals should be adequate to attract and retain personnel qualified to assess these risks.

Source: Reproduced with permission of the Basel Committee on Banking Supervision, Bank for International Settlements from *Risk Management Guidelines for Derivatives: Section II. Oversight of the Risk Management Process,* 1994.

LEGAL ISSUES

Case Law

The challenge of examining case law for guidance about derivative use lies in knowing what legal precedents to evaluate, a task best left to attorneys. Absent legal training, the best that anyone can do is research the topic for a general understanding of the relationship between fiduciary duty and risk management tactics.

Because many cases do not explicitly address derivative instruments, those that do tend to address the broader issues of loyalty, obedience, and care merit review, while recognizing that what constitutes breach depends on organizational type and authoritative venue. Another limitation is the evolving nature of relevant case law about derivatives markets.

Fiduciary Breach

As shown in Exhibit 3.12, the Revised Model Nonprofit Corporation Act of 1987 sets out standards for directors of nonprofit organizations and demonstrates adherence to care, loyalty, and obedience. Duty of loyalty forbids use of confidential information for personal profit. Duty of care "requires a director to exercise independent judgment," and to: "(i) be reasonably informed, (ii) participate in decisions, and (iii) do so in good faith and with the care of an ordinarily prudent person in similar circumstances."[34] Duty of obedience requires directors to "fulfill the particular purposes for which the organization was created" or know that they may "be liable to the corporation for any harm it suffers as a consequence, or for any amounts expended if the transaction cannot be unwound."[35]

Personal liability is likewise an issue. As shown in Exhibit 3.13, the implications are far-reaching. "Regardless of whether a director is familiar with the nitty-gritty of a sophisticated risk analysis, she must make sure that it is being carried out," so that "a director need not second guess the results of an analysis, but should assure himself that (a) it is tailored to the company's actual business (as opposed to something off the shelf) and (b) it covers all of the company's operations—which many analyses fail to do."[36] Applied to financial management, fiduciaries must have a well thought-out plan in place. They don't have to become rocket scientists, but they do have to learn enough to make informed decisions.

Delegation

A decision made by the U.S. Court of Appeals for the Ninth District in a recent case goes to the heart of the matter regarding delegation and fiduciary responsibility. Ruling in favor of several pension funds, the court found that the delegated investment manager had "breached the fiduciary duties required under the Employee Retirement Income Security Act and failed to conduct a thorough, independent investigation before investing the Plans' assets in complex derivative securities, known as inverse floaters, which later plummeted in value."[37] The court also found that "The ERISA duty to investigate is not fulfilled simply by hiring an expert; a fiduciary may rely on expert advice only if the fiduciary make[s] an honest, objective effort to read the [expert's opinion], understand it, and question . . . the methods and assumptions that do not make sense."[38]

EXHIBIT 3.12 Duties of Directors of Nonprofit Organizations

(a) A director shall discharge his or her duties as a director, including his or her
duties as a member of a committee:
  (1) in good faith;
  (2) with the care an ordinarily prudent person in a like position would exercise
  under similar circumstances; and
  (3) in a manner the director reasonably believes to be in the best interests of
  the corporation.
(b) In discharging his or her duties, a director is entitled to rely on information,
opinions, reports, or statements, including financial statements and other
financial data, if prepared or presented by:
  (1) one or more officers or employees of the corporation whom the director
  reasonably believes to be reliable and competent in the matters presented;
  (2) legal counsel, public accountants or other persons as to matters the
  director reasonably believes are within the person's professional or expert
  competence;
  (3) a committee of the board of which the director is not a member, as to matters within its jurisdiction, if the director reasonably believes the committee
  merits confidence; or
  (4) in the case of religious corporations, religious authorities and ministers,
  priests, rabbis or other persons whose position or duties in the religious
  organization the director believes justify reliance and confidence and
  whom the director believes to be reliable and competent in the matters
  presented.
(c) A director is not acting in good faith if the director has knowledge concerning
the matter in question that makes reliance otherwise permitted by subsection
(b) unwarranted.
(d) A director is not liable to the corporation, any member, or any other person
for any action taken or not taken as a director, if the director acted in compliance with this section.
(e) A director shall not be deemed to be a trustee with respect to the corporation
or with respect to any property held or administered by the corporation,
including without limit, property that may be subject to restrictions imposed
by the donor or transferor of such property.

Source: Excerpted from Section 8.30, Sections (a), (b), (c), (d), and (e) from Chap-
ter 8: Directors & Officers, and Subchapter A: Board of Directors from *Revised
Model Nonprofit Corporation Act of 1987.* Copyright © 1987 by the American Bar
Association. Reprinted by permission.

Know What to Do

Despite the growing body of cases that make it to court, many cases settle.
This is partly driven by economics, but also by fear of admitting a mistake.
According to attorney Melvyn I. Weiss, "It will be hard for companies to
say the people who were in charge of investing in all these funds weren't

EXHIBIT 3.13 Breach of Fiduciary Duty Liability

Any person who is a fiduciary with respect to a plan who breaches any of the responsibilities, obligations, or duties imposed upon fiduciaries by this subchapter shall be personally liable to make good to such plan any losses to the plan resulting from each such breach, and to restore to such plan any profits of such fiduciary which have been made through use of assets of the plan by the fiduciary, and shall be subject to such other equitable or remedial relief as the court may deem appropriate, including removal of such fiduciary.

Source: Excerpted from U.S. Code, Title 29, Chapter 18, Subchapter I, Subtitle B, Part 4, Section 1109.

doing it under the aegis of senior management and weren't sophisticated enough to know what they were doing."[39] In today's climate of mistrust, business leaders are wise to take their fiduciary responsibilities seriously and perhaps more so than ever before.

SUMMARY

1. Risk management is an integral part of investment management responsibilities.
2. Plan design is a big consideration in determining proper investment policies. Asset allocation risk is not borne equally by the sponsor across plan designs.
3. ERISA mandates fiduciaries to diversify holdings unless inappropriate to do so. Derivative instruments, if used properly, provide one way to reduce risk.
4. State law determines use of derivatives by public pension funds, many of which are defined benefit plans.
5. Recent changes in U.S. trust law emphasize diversification in the context of a portfolio of investments. Derivatives are specifically mentioned in many legislative initiatives.
6. Guidelines issued by various industry and policy-making groups support the notion of a duty to consider hedging with derivatives as part of an institution's investment decision-making process.
7. Evolving case law suggests that fiduciaries need to inform themselves about derivatives as a risk management tool.
8. Delegation to outside parties does not absolve fiduciaries from their investment-related responsibilities.

CHAPTER 4

State of Reporting about Institutional Investors

What is food to one man may be fierce poison to others.

—Lucretius

INFORMATION IS EVERYTHING

Everyone agrees that information is important, but what kind of information? How often should it be provided? Should the data be provided in summary form or do trustees need detailed reports? The answers depend on purpose, availability, and cost of collection and maintenance. Many times information is simply not available on a regular basis or with enough particulars to make a difference.

Strange as it sounds, too much information can likewise be a problem, especially when it comes to complex transactions or a perception of complexity. Many otherwise knowledgeable people tremble at the thought of reading detailed reports concerning the use of derivative instruments, in large part because of the notion that anything involving their use must require some time and effort on the part of the reader.[1] A report left unread, however detailed and otherwise informative, is of little use. Cynics add that bankers have done little to demystify transactions involving derivatives, possibly fearing a reduced role and lower fees as a result. On the flip side, educating executives can be a costly undertaking and banks may not want to be the first to bear the cost, especially if there is lukewarm interest on the part of their clients in learning about derivatives.

Moreover, an abundance of data is no guarantee of ongoing profitability. As shown in Exhibits 4.1 and 4.2, the Federal National Mortgage Association (Fannie Mae) provided the public with what many would agree is a lot of information about its use of derivative instruments. At the same time, it ended up with a 24.7 percent decline in second quarter 2003

EXHIBIT 4.1 Fannie Mae's Disclosure Initiatives

Description

1. Periodic Issuance of Subordinated Debt—Fannie Mae will issue publicly traded and externally rated subordinated debt in an amount that, together with core capital, will equal or exceed four percent of on-balance sheet assets.
2. Liquidity Management and Contingency Planning—Fannie Mae will maintain at least three months of liquidity to ensure the company can meet all of its obligations in any period of time in which it does not have access to the debt markets. Fannie Mae will also comply with the Basel Committee on Banking Supervision's 14 principles for sound liquidity management.
3. Interim Risk-Based Capital Stress Test—Pending the Office of Federal Housing Enterprise Oversight's (OFHEO) publication of a final risk-based capital rule, Fannie Mae will implement and disclose the results of a risk-based capital stress test based on the standards in the 1992 Act. *(September 2002 update: OFHEO published a final rule in September 2001 and announced that the rule would become effective in September 2002. As a result, Fannie Mae will no longer make this interim disclosure. Please see OFHEO's quarterly risk-based capital classifications of Fannie Mae for more information.*
4. New Interest Rate Risk Disclosures—Fannie Mae will disclose monthly the effect on its mortgage portfolio of a 50 basis point change in interest rates and a 25 basis point change in the slope of the yield curve, and enhance existing disclosures consistent with Basel Committee guidance.
5. New Credit Risk Disclosures—Fannie Mae will disclose quarterly the financial impact of an immediate five percent decline in U.S. home prices, and enhance existing disclosures consistent with Basel Committee guidance.
6. Public Disclosure of an Annual Rating—Fannie Mae will obtain and disclose annually a rating that will assess the risk to the government or the independent financial strength of Fannie Mae.

Source: Excerpted from the Fannie Mae web site. http://www.fanniemae.com. Copyright © 2003, Fannie Mae. All rights reserved. Reprinted with permission.

earnings, despite an increase of 18.2 percent in core business earnings. Their news release describes a nearly $1.9 billion loss from "the mark to market of the time value of Fannie Mae's purchased options during the second quarter of 2003."[2]

There is also the often overlooked reality that disclosure, regardless of how ample or sparse, may fail as a litmus test for determining whether derivatives are suitable for an organization or if they are being effectively employed. Be that as it may, information can be a powerful tool in making choices. When it is unavailable or opaque in form, fiduciaries have a difficult time knowing where things stand and how to make improvements accordingly.

EXHIBIT 4.2   Fannie Mae and Use of Derivatives

Derivatives are securities that many financial companies use to reduce the risk of investing. They're called derivatives because their cash flow is derived from that of other instruments. Fannie Mae uses derivatives to reduce the risk and cost of investing in mortgages, which we buy to expand homeownership.

As Federal Reserve Chairman Alan Greenspan has said, derivatives have made our financial system "far more flexible, efficient, and resilient."

Here's how derivatives work at Fannie Mae. To raise capital for home buyers, we sell debt securities to investors on Wall Street and globally. We use the proceeds to purchase mortgage assets from lenders, so they can make more loans. Then we hold those mortgages assets in our investment portfolio.

As a disciplined portfolio manager, Fannie Mae chooses to use a "matched" portfolio strategy. That is, unlike some mortgage investors that purchase long-term mortgages using short-term funding (such as bank deposits), Fannie Mae tries to match the expected life of the mortgages we buy and the debt we issue to fund them. That way, the cash flow in and the cash flow out remain relatively in balance and stable from quarter to quarter even when interest rates become volatile.

We can match the initial duration of our assets and liabilities by issuing bullet debt of different maturities. Or we can issue short-term debt and lengthen its maturity by entering into derivative contracts that swap the short-term interest payments for fixed long-term payments.

However, the life of our mortgage assets can change at any time. Why? Homeowners always have the option to "call," or refinance, most long-term, fixed-rate mortgages anytime they want to. When interest rates fall, the refinancing increases and the mortgages on our books prepay and leave our books. This shortens the overall duration of our mortgage assets. Or when interest rates rise, the expected duration of our assets increases. In order to maintain a "matched" portfolio, we need the ability to adjust the overall duration of our debt as well. We do that by attaching options to the debt that allow us to "call" in the debt early.

We have two ways to obtain options on our debt:

First, we issue callable debt, which allows us to call back our debt securities and reissue debt at lower interest rates.

Second, we use derivatives to create synthetic callable debt. These give us the flexibility to create the funding we want at the time of the mortgage purchase, or to adjust the funding later in response to changing market conditions.

It is important to understand several things about the way Fannie Mae uses derivatives:

1. Fannie Mae uses only the most straightforward types of derivatives—e.g., interest rate swaps, swaptions, and interest rate caps—whose values are easy to obtain and predict.
2. We also act only as an end-user of derivatives—we do not trade, take positions, or speculate in derivatives.
3. Our derivative counterparties are highly rated financial institutions, and we require them to post collateral to secure their obligations to Fannie Mae.

(continued)

EXHIBIT 4.2   *Continued*

4. Fannie Mae has far less derivatives exposure than other large financial institutions. At the beginning of 2002, the largest commercial bank dealer in derivatives had $42 billion in net exposure, while Fannie Mae had only $200 million in net exposure. Even in the unlikely event that all of our derivative counterparties failed simultaneously it would have cost Fannie Mae less than 3 percent of our pre-tax income in 2001.

Source: Excerpted from "Answers from the CEO," Fannie Mae web site. http://www.fanniemae.com. Copyright © 2003, Fannie Mae. All rights reserved. Reprinted with permission.

SIZE MEANS DIFFERENT THINGS

The large size of the derivatives market, however defined, continues to be newsworthy, especially when compared with other financial statistics. For example, the International Swaps and Derivatives Association (ISDA) reports an approximate market size of $100 trillion in terms of notional amounts outstanding.[3] By most counts, this is about 15 times the size of monies invested by endowments, foundations, and pensions. So what does this mean? It depends on who is asking the question and why.

The outstanding notional amount approximates the aggregate use of derivative instruments.[4] These statistics are readily available and are often updated by derivative instrument type and for selected user groups such as banking institutions.[5] Logic suggests that product acceptance is reflected in large and growing notional amounts. Although that sounds reasonable, notional amounts offer limited insight about any one sector or individual institution's risk exposure by asset class, maturity, counterparty, country, or currency.

As Kathryn E. Dick, Deputy Comptroller for Risk Evaluation with the Office of the Comptroller of the Currency (OCC), points out,

> *the risk in a derivatives contract is a function of a number of variables, such as whether counterparties exchange notional principal, the volatility of the currencies or interest rates used as the basis for determining contract payments, the maturity and liquidity of contracts, and the creditworthiness of the counterparties in the transaction.*[6]

If available, contract terms tell a more complete story. For example, will two counterparties net what they owe each other? This can reduce exposure considerably. If a derivative is being used to hedge an investment or liability, the risk of the entire package is reduced considerably. As shown in Exhibit 4.3, knowing more than notional principal amount goes a long way toward knowing how much is at stake as market conditions change.

EXHIBIT 4.3   Notional Principal Amount Statistics Can Be Misleading

Counterparty	A	B	C
Notional principal amount	$20 million	$20 million	$20 million
Transaction type	Interest rate swap	Interest rate swap	Interest rate swap
Obligation	Pay fixed, receive floating	Pay fixed on $10 million swap with counterparty D and received fixed on $10 million with counterparty E	Pay fixed, receive floating
Purpose	Hedge against rising rates	Middleman fee	Anticipates rising rates
Background	Company issues commercial paper		Trades derivatives

The notional principal amount is the same in all three cases but the exposure differs. Each case reflects a different level of risk. Counterparty A employs an interest rate swap to lock in a fixed cost of funds. Essentially, the company issues commercial paper and uses the floating rate receipts from the swap to service its variable debt. In contrast, Counterparty B collects a fee for standing in the middle of two counterparties. Its outstanding notional amount is $20 million, twice the face value of each $10 million swap. Structured properly and assuming no defaults, the interest inflow from one swap should be an outflow for the second swap with a net zero cash outlay for Counterparty B. Counterparty C uses interest rate swaps to take advantage of its expectation of rising interest rates. If correct, Counterparty C will receive more and more on the variable stream or sell the swap at a profit. Of the three hypothetical swap parties, C has the most to lose, having taken a speculative position, something not immediately obvious if notional principal amount is the sole metric.

WHERE THINGS STAND NOW

General Situation

Information quality and amount is not equal across institutions. Endowments, foundations, and pensions, unlike banks and publicly traded companies, disclose little about derivative use in their public documents. Some of this is changing, but slowly.

Private Foundations

Assets in 2001 for independent foundations accounted for more than 80 percent of the nearly $500 billion reported in *Foundation Growth and Giving Estimates, 2003.*[7] Knowing how foundations invest in the aggregate can be helpful. Other times, a focus on the individual foundation is important. For this purpose, one source of information is the Form 990-PF, *Return of Private Foundation,* required for "all private foundations exempt under 501 (c) (3)."[8] States may have their own requirements as shown in Exhibit 4.4, in addition to any reporting requirements imposed by the trustees.

Prior to rules that took effect in March 2000, obtaining a Form 990 was "an arduous process, traditionally requiring a written request to the IRS or individual charity, and typically involving many weeks or months of waiting to receive the return."[9] The change in rules required a foundation to provide its Form 990 upon demand. About the same time, an organization called GuideStar®, which was already posting public charities' 990s, made online accessibility a reality by posting images of private foundations' Forms 990-PF. Today, GuideStar gathers and disseminates "financial information for 61,000 private foundations."[10] According to Director of Communications Suzanne E. Coffman,

> *We're a 501(c)(3) public charity (we're in our own database). We're not a watchdog—instead, we strive to provide a neutral platform of information about U.S. charitable organizations. We don't rate the organizations*

EXHIBIT 4.4 Reporting Requirements for Private Foundations

Federal	State
All private foundations must file a federal tax return, Form 990-PF. In addition to information about the foundation's assets, income, and expenses, this form requires that the foundation list its substantial contributors, foundations managers, and highly compensated employees as well as all payments made to these persons.	Copies of the federal tax return (Form 990-PF) must be filed with the attorney general's office in most states in which a private foundation is located. Some states may impose additional reporting requirements on private foundations, and advice concerning these should be sought from an attorney or certified public accountant.

Source: Excerpted from "Starting a Private Foundation: Reporting and Record keeping," Forum of Regional Associations of Grantmakers, http://www.givingforum. org/giving/starting_reporting.html, 1999. Copyright © 1999, Forum of Regional Associations of Grantmakers. Reprinted with permission.

in our database. Again, we want to be neutral; our goal is to make information about specific nonprofits available so that people can make their own decisions about the organizations. We invite charitable organizations to update their respective reports in our database. There's no charge for updating.[11]

Notwithstanding the free availability of data, Form 990 is less than complete on several fronts.[12] Although it

can provide a snapshot of the financial health and expenditures of an organization at a specific time, they are virtually useless in comparing one organization to another unless the organizations are of similar size, age, geography, and field of activity. Further, they tell us nothing about the ultimate or relative effectiveness of an organization with respect to meeting its objectives.[13]

Specific to derivatives, the form is silent about an organization's use of derivatives, if they were used at all. As Chuck McLean, Vice President of Research, Philanthropic Research, Inc./GuideStar® puts it,

Foundations and endowments are required to report such investments on Form 990-F on Part IV, if the net result of such an investment is a capital gain or loss. They should also probably be reported on Part II if held at the close of the fiscal year. Traditionally, these instruments have been frowned upon and are probably not used much. However, standards have evolved. It was more or less the case in the past that each investment made was subject to the standard of prudence, without regard to the overall portfolio of investments. Under the Uniform Prudent Investor Act, which was approved in 1994 and has been adopted by many states, no investment is per se imprudent, but is viewed in the context of the diversified portfolio. The IRS is vague on the matter.[14]

Improvement is unlikely to occur any time soon. According to the Forum of Regional Associations of Grantmakers,

private foundations have been reticent about publicizing their activities. While many foundations sincerely feel that it would be inappropriate to sing the praises of their own good works, this silence has sometimes been mistaken for aloofness. In an effort to promote better understanding of private foundations and their endeavors, individual foundations should develop effective ways of communicating with the general public.[15]

Private Pension Plans

According to the Internal Revenue Service (IRS), "all pension benefit plans covered by ERISA are required to file a Form 5500."[16] The few exceptions are spelled out in IRS documents. According to the U.S. Department of Labor Employee Benefits Security Administration web site,

> the Form 5500 Series is an important compliance, research, and disclosure tool for the Department of Labor, a disclosure document for plan participants and beneficiaries, and a source of information and data for use by other Federal agencies, Congress, and the private sector in assessing employee benefit, tax, and economic trends and policies.[17]

Besides the Form 5500 itself, there are many attachments, including a financial form for "large" plans, Schedule H. Part I is an asset and liability statement. Part II is an income and expense statement for these bigger plans that have more than 100 participants.[18] Snapshot valuations are provided for corporate debt and equity securities, other than those issued by the plan sponsor.

Similar to foundations, government-required documents offer limited help regarding use of derivatives. Vital questions that should be asked are nowhere to be seen. Exhibit 4.5 describes this dilemma in more detail.

A U.S. government official familiar with ERISA-required reports acknowledges the need for further revisions.

> Right now, the Form 5500 series prescribes a format—not an actual form—that filers should use to list the assets held for investment at the end of the plan year. That list should include any derivative investments and their value but is not always the case. Valuation details and more timely reports are two improvements that would go a long way to improve transparency, not just derivatives but all investments made by a particular pension fund.[19]

As with foundations, reform may be slow in coming because "major changes to the forms are difficult and infrequent due, in part, to the need to coordinate the concerns of the four agencies involved (IRS, EBSA, PBGC, and SSA)."[20] In late 2003, the Financial Accounting Standards Board increased reporting requirements for defined benefit plans, recognizing the need for more transparency.

Public Pension Plans

Public pension plan reporting requirements for investment and risk management activities vary by state. Many of the larger funds post their investment

EXHIBIT 4.5 Pension Fund Risk Management Reporting

While pension fund finance has always been important, it is especially important now. Headlines express concern about under-funding, unrealistic rate of return assumptions, growing liabilities and the possible need for cash flow infusions. Add to the mix the sheer size of pension funds and readers pay close attention. Unfortunately, only a select few individuals have enough information to gauge a pension fund's true risk, leaving others to speculate what dangers may loom ahead. Without information, it is virtually impossible to know how a pension fund's financial health affects the well-being of the plan sponsor, shareholders and beneficiaries. This is especially true when trying to ascertain if, and the extent to which, a pension plan uses derivative instruments.

Transparency is vital. Knowledge about a plan's investments—and related risk management activities—sheds light on market sensitivities. Where is the plan exposed? Is a position in a particular asset class or sector too large given market conditions and expectations about the future? These and other "must know" questions are shown in Exhibit One. The obvious next step is to seek out answers from publicly available data.

Exhibit One: Basic Pension Risk Management Questions

1. Does the pension fund employ derivative instruments? (If the answer is "yes", proceed to other questions.)
2. What is the primary goal of derivative instrument use? Risk minimization? Return enhancement? Cash flow synthesis? Benefit payment scheduling? Other reason?
3. What derivative instruments are used, by category? Futures? Listed options? Over-the-counter options? Swaps? Hybrid?
4. What derivative instrument are used, by asset class? Equity? Fixed income? Currency? Credit? Hybrid?
5. Is short-selling permitted?
6. What is the permitted maximum size, by instrument type, asset class and percent of plan assets?
7. Who directs the use of derivatives? Individual? Committee? Mathematical rule?
8. What is the oversight process for pension fund use of derivatives?
9. How often are derivatives valued?
10. How are derivative instrument values accounted for? Do changes in value show up in the footnotes to FAS 133? Someplace else?
11. What is the creditworthiness of large counterparties, by rating? How often are credit lines reviewed? Who makes the final decision?
12. How often are derivatives transactions reviewed for effectiveness? What are the benchmarks? Who reviews them?
13. When does re-balancing occur? Is the decision based on a mathematical rule?
14. Is risk management for the pension fund completely separate from risk management done by treasury?
15. What systems are in place to capture risk management information?

Source: Excerpted from "Derivatives Use Unclear When Diagnosing a Pension Fund's Financial Health," *AFP Exchange,* January/February 2003. Reprinted with permission from the Association for Financial Professionals. Copyright © 2003, Susan Mangiero. All rights reserved.

policy on the Internet, along with statements about the use of derivatives. This might include a statement that they are prohibited. When allowed, the policy typically includes information about instrument type, scope of use, and limits. Examples are included later in this book.

According to an anonymous public pension plan auditor,

> *public pension funds tend to do a better job of making information about risk management more available to the public. For one thing, we are accountable to the taxpayers who fund municipal defined benefit pension programs. Then there is the budget approval process required by law. When money is tight, a lot more attention is paid to cutting costs. This includes the amount of money going to plan beneficiaries. Additionally, there is a fair amount of uniformity in public pension plans and that makes it easier to work together in creating best practice guidelines for both investing and risk management.[21]*

Not everyone is happy. Greg Kaza, executive director of the Arkansas Policy Foundation, favors a requirement for comprehensive disclosure by state pension funds. He advocates detailed quarterly reports about investments, which would arguably be an improvement for all types of private pension plans as well.[22] His point is that oversight is impossible without full information.

Common Themes

Field interviews and survey results suggest that when derivative instruments are used, they tend to be employed for one of several reasons as shown in Exhibit 4.6, including but not limited to equity enhancement, currency overlay, and fixed-income portfolio management. For example, a pension fund might hire a money manager to use derivatives to manage the currency risk associated with its non-U.S. dollar stocks.[23]

Notwithstanding the common goal of investing wisely on behalf of beneficiaries, institutional investors will vary in the way they achieve their objectives. Part of this is driven by regulation. Some of it stems from the trustees and their divergent knowledge of and comfort levels with derivative instruments. Those who choose to avoid derivative instruments may do so by design or because their staff resources preclude a thorough vetting. According to Andrew S. Lang, National Director for Nonprofit Services with BDO Seidman, "Some nonprofits do not see any revenue potential. Others may simply be too strapped, staff-wise, to make the time to evaluate the economics of using derivatives as part of their investment activity."[24]

For example, correcting a duration mismatch can be done with any one of the available fixed-income products. Analyzing the alternatives requires

EXHIBIT 4.6   Common Uses of Derivatives by Private Pension Plans[a]

Application	Asset Class
Treat derivatives as separate asset class in allocation mix	Currency, commodity, equity, fixed income
Hedging market risk[b]	Equity, fixed income
Duration matching of assets with liabilities	Fixed income
Return enhancement	Currency, equity, fixed income

[a]*Derivatives Primer*, authored by the Association for Financial Professionals' Committee on Investment of Employee Benefit Assets, includes survey results about the use of derivatives by private pension plans, December 2001.
[b]Some might classify duration matching as a type of hedging and not list it separately. Copyright © 2001, Association for Financial Professionals. All rights reserved. Reprinted with permission.

time, skill, and experience. Beyond that, external money managers play a role in what happens. They may avoid pitching derivative instruments to their clients if there is a question about suitability that could land them in trouble down the road. Certainly, any unfamiliarity with derivative instruments on the part of managers will make them reluctant to propose their use. When managers do bring up derivatives, they must have the ability to clearly communicate their potential impact on performance.

As the managing director of a large university endowment fund stated,

> *transparency is a deal breaker. We may choose not to hire an outside money manager if their intended use of derivative instruments is not clearly and explicitly spelled out in the interview process. For our part, we use S&P 500 futures to equitize our cash position. The goal is to enhance returns without taking on too much risk. Occasionally, we use zero cost collars to protect the value of stock positions that have been committed but not yet donated. The benefits are twofold. There is no cash outlay for the option fees and the value of the stock is protected within a range until such time that formally becomes part of the university endowment's assets.*[25]

INITIATIVES

A review of disclosure requirements for all types of endowments, foundations, and pension funds is beyond the scope of this book. Needless to say, the topic is complicated and made more so because the operating environment itself is very much in flux. Rating agencies, accounting standards organizations, and tax authorities are each giving information requirements a lot of thought.[26] While they do their work, fiduciaries must likewise ferret out whatever information helps them do their job more effectively. Waiting is not an option. If they don't have the information they need to perform their fiduciary duties, they must ask for it. Time marches on, and the task of gathering and assimilating information cannot be postponed.

SUMMARY

1. Detailed information about derivative instrument use is not necessarily a predictor of profitability or effective use.
2. Notional principal amount is a misleading indicator of risk exposure associated with derivative instruments.
3. Explicit information about derivative instrument use is not part of Form 990-PF, the report most private foundations must file on a regular basis.
4. Derivative instrument use is not included as a specific item on Form 5500, the form many private benefit plans must file on a regular basis.
5. Return enhancement, currency overlay, and duration matching are common applications of derivative instrument use.

PART TWO

Toolbox

CHAPTER 5

Basic Concepts

Knowledge is power.

—Francis Bacon

BUILDING BLOCKS

Every field has its own language and risk management is no different. The topic is broad and multifaceted. As discussed in Chapter 10, some organizations hire risk management specialists to implement and run this function. Does that let fiduciaries off the hook? The answer is "absolutely not." While fiduciary persons may not need the same technical expertise as a risk management specialist, they need to at least be familiar with the six basic concepts described in Exhibit 5.1. Beyond that, striking the delicate balance between "must know" and "nice to know" is often addressed as a legal or regulatory matter, something best left to legal counsel.

THE THREE Rs

Choosing the "best" investment or deciding on the optimal risk management strategy is virtually impossible without understanding how alternatives compare when both risk and return are taken into account. This point bears repeating. Focusing on one attribute and ignoring the other makes no sense. Hence the emphasis on the three Rs—risk, return, and ranking.

Consider the four stocks shown in Exhibit 5.2. Using returns alone, security D is the most appealing because it offers the highest return, 20 percent. When risk is considered, things change. A traditional risk measure, the standard deviation of returns, is helpful only when returns are the same for each security being compared. Because none of the stocks shown in Exhibit 5.2 have the same return, the standard deviation is no good. Another measure, the coefficient of variation, scales risk by return. Values close to

EXHIBIT 5.1 Building Block Concepts

Concept	Purpose	Application	Comments
Beta	Measure of market risk	Can be used to determine the hedge ratio when trying to minimize equity price risk	S&P 500 Index is frequently used as the gauge of equity market performance
Coefficient of variation	Measure of risk, relative to expected return	Used when two or more investments each have different expected returns	Computed as standard deviation divided by expected return
Correlation coefficient	Pairwise measure of linear association	Required to evaluate portfolio risk	Falls within [−1, +1] interval
Duration	Measure of market risk	Can be used to determine the hedge ratio when trying to minimize interest rate risk	Not appropriate for large interest rate changes
Expected return	Forward-looking measure of performance	Often used in lieu of historical average return	Depends on accurate forecasts of possible outcomes that affect return, such as states of the economy or competitive position within the industry
Leverage	Measure of amount of debt used to finance a transaction	More leverage magnifies return but increases risk	Derivative usage can induce leverage because a large exposure can typically be created at little cost

EXHIBIT 5.2 Risk–Return Example

Stock	Expected Return (%)	Standard Deviation*a* (%)	Coefficient of Variation*b* (unit-free)	Ranking by Return, with No Focus on Risk	Ranking by Risk, Adjusted for Return
A	10	7	0.70	3	3
B	5	2	0.40	4 (Worst)	1 (Best)
C	15	10	0.67	2	2
D	20	16	0.80	1 (Best)	4 (Worst)

*a*The standard deviation is used to rank investments when the expected return is the same for each one.

*b*The coefficient of variation is found by dividing the standard deviation by the expected return. This risk measure is used to rank investments with different expected returns, as is the case here. Though not shown here, the coefficient of variation can also be found by dividing the standard deviation by the historical average return.

zero suggest a low level of risk. Large numbers indicate higher risk.[1] Coefficient of variation numbers are frequently presented in absolute value form, making it unnecessary to include a positive or negative sign.

Instead of topping the list, security D now ranks at the bottom of the list in terms of attractiveness. To earn the higher 20 percent return, the investor must assume an additional 0.80 percent of risk for every 1 percent of return. In contrast, the risk–reward ratio for security B is 0.40, one half that for security D.[2] What this means is that return alone is insufficient for investment selection purposes. Worse yet, ignoring risk can lead to an incorrect investment choice with long-term adverse consequences.

CORRELATION

Given the importance of diversification, fiduciaries need to understand how the risk–return trade-off changes when a group of investments are considered rather than looking at each individual security. The correlation coefficient, a number that ranges from -1.0 to $+1.0$, is a popular metric for this purpose. It can be computed using either historical returns or forecasted returns, and is easy to compute using any one of the many available spreadsheet or statistical software programs.

Correlation coefficients are often presented in the form of a correlation matrix, as shown in Exhibit 5.3. Note the symmetry. The $+0.94$ correlation for the A, B pair is the same number for the B, A pair, so it is not necessary to complete the table. The interpretation of this number is based on both its

EXHIBIT 5.3 Sample Correlation Matrix

	A	B	C
A	1.00		
B	0.94	1.00	
C	-0.76	-0.70	1.00

Notes:
1. This table is based on hypothetical one-month returns for a one-year period.
2. A correlation matrix is symmetric. This means that the +0.94 correlation coefficient for the Security A and B pair is the same as the +0.94 correlation coefficient for the Security B and A pair. Therefore, the Row A, Column B, cell can be left empty.

sign and magnitude. A positive correlation coefficient suggests a direct movement in the two variables, but not necessarily in a cause-and-effect fashion. It may be that both variables are influenced by an outside factor. An oft touted example looks at the positive correlation between ice cream sales and number of thefts in a given locale. One interpretation is that ice cream consumption encourages law breaking. A second conclusion is that robbers eat ice cream after each new theft so sales rise in proportion to crime. A correct evaluation looks instead at a third variable such as temperature. People eat more ice cream in warmer weather. At the same time, felons do more damage when temperatures climb. Applied to investments, the same idea applies. Correlation is not a measure of cause and effect, but rather, it is a measure of association. How do the returns of two securities co-vary in response to a third factor such as inflation or credit risk premiums? Misinterpreting correlation coefficients limits their usefulness as a portfolio diversification or risk management tool.

Negative correlation indicates that two variables such as stock prices and gold prices should move in the opposite direction if past relationships prevail going forward. Negative correlation coefficients close to −1.00 reflect a strong inverse relationship, as is the case for the securities A, C pair with a coefficient of −0.76 in Exhibit 5.3. In contrast, a correlation coefficient of −0.1 indicates a weak indirect relationship.

Correlation is a powerful concept for investors and risk managers alike. On the investment front, correlation coefficients are used to construct well-diversified portfolios. This occurs when money is spent to buy securities that react to outside factors in different ways. Said another way, assembling a portfolio based on pairwise negative correlations offers significant risk reduction potential. Truly complete portfolio diversification—more a

EXHIBIT 5.4 Data for Portfolio Example

Stock[a]	Expected Return[b] (%)	Standard Deviation (%)
W	10	6
Z	10	2

[a]This table provides summary statistics for two hypothetical stocks.
[b]Expected return is the same 10 percent for each stock.

theoretical construct than an empirical reality—would result in a net change of zero dollars. No matter what happens, some securities would increase in value only to be offset by those that would drop in value by the same dollar amount.

Based on the data shown in Exhibit 5.4, Exhibit 5.5 illustrates the relationship between correlation and portfolio risk. As the correlation coefficient moves closer to -1.0, the risk of a two-stock, equally weighted portfolio shrinks, although not proportionately. With a correlation of -1.0, the standard deviation of Portfolio 5 is an enormous 33 percent lower than the case of no offset at all ($+1.0$ correlation), even though expected return is 8 percent for both portfolios.[3] Diversification is such a bedrock concept that it is often included as part of the investment policy statement and has been cited as a way to prevent large losses.[4]

When applied to risk management, correlation plays a critical role in determining the proper size of a derivative instrument hedge. Like an investment manager, the risk manager builds a diversified portfolio. However, as shown in Exhibit 5.6, there are several differences. First, an investor typically

EXHIBIT 5.5 Portfolio Risk and Correlation Example[a]

Portfolio No.	Correlation Coefficient	Return (%)	Standard Deviation (%)[b]
1	+1.0	8.0	6.0
2	+0.5	8.0	5.6
3	0	8.0	5.1
4	−0.5	8.0	4.6
5	−1.0	8.0	4.0

[a]These results are based on the Exhibit 5.4 summary statistics for Stocks W and Z, respectively.
[b]Only the portfolio risk measure changes as the correlation coefficient changes. The expected return for the portfolio is identical across portfolios.
Note: Each portfolio consists of Stocks W and Z in equal proportion. The only difference among Portfolio 1, Portfolio 2, Portfolio 3, and Portfolio 4 is the assumed correlation coefficient.

EXHIBIT 5.6 Correlation Wears Two Hats[a]

Portfolio Attribute	Investing[b]	Managing Risk[b]
Number of securities	Many more than two	Two
Types of components	Stocks, bonds, other	Derivative instrument and item being hedged
Correlation coefficient	Negative for each pair	Positive for the exposure-hedge pair
Position type	Long position in each security	Long position in exposure and short position in derivative instrument (or vice versa)
Quantification	Correlation used to determine portfolio risk	Correlation used to determine hedging instrument and size of hedge

[a]Diversification is the assumed goal of the investor.
[b]Investing and managing risk are herein treated as totally separate activities.

builds a portfolio of many more than two securities. Empirical studies suggest that a good mix of several dozen securities can materially reduce industry, company, and country risk.[5] In contrast, the risk manager creates a two-item portfolio, pairing together only the position being hedged and the derivative instrument used to hedge. Second, the investor looks for negatively correlated security pairs and takes a long position in each security. The risk manager looks for a derivative instrument that is positively correlated with the security being hedged and takes a short position. For example, a long position in bonds would be hedged with a short position in a bond derivative instrument, preferably one that exhibits high positive correlation with the cash bond holding. The goal of minimizing loss is the same, but the sign of the correlation coefficient differs in each case.[6]

Two advantages of correlation coefficients are that they are easy to compute and simple to interpret. On the downside, correlations change over time and are not always meaningful outside the range of values used to compute them. Furthermore, they are measures of linear association and are of little use if two variables are non-linearly related.

LEVERAGE

By definition, leverage refers to the extent to which debt is used to finance a transaction. The objective is to enhance investment returns by maximizing use of other people's money. Picture a heavy rock that few people are strong enough to lift on their own. When a lever is propped beneath the rock, the once unthinkable is now possible. Borrowed money has a similar magnifying effect. Exhibit 5.7 illustrates the point.

When no leverage is employed (Case One), a $100 gain on a $1,000 initial investment represents a 10 percent gain. In stark contrast, when the investor finances an investment largely with borrowed funds (Case Two), that same $100 gain represents a 100 percent gain because the investor's initial stake is only $100, having borrowed $900 from other sources. Even when borrowed funds cost something (Case Three), an initial outlay of $100 still yields a large return of 55 percent. On the face of it, leverage looks like a winning proposition—borrow money and enhance return, often many times over.

However, there are downsides that some mistakenly ignore. For one thing, few loans are available on a zero cost basis. Second, at some rate, leverage becomes prohibitively expensive. The break-even borrowing rate based on Exhibit 5.7 is approximately 11 percent. At this rate, interest on a $900 loan would equal $99, nearly erasing the $100 investment gain. At higher rates, the investor will lose money. For example, a 15 percent loan rate requires the investor to repay $135, more than the $100 investment gain.[7] Worse yet, the borrower may run into trouble if unable to make up the difference between interest owed and any investment gain. Default can trigger bankruptcy action by lenders, causing even more problems down the road.

Applied to derivatives, leverage is likewise a two-way street. When used effectively, leverage can improve returns. Improperly used, the leverage inherent in certain derivative transactions spells disaster. Margin calls, cash flow problems, bond rating downgrades, damage to reputation, and litigation are just a few of the possible consequences of excess leverage. Lessons learned from many of the publicized derivatives-related losses bear this out. On the global front, policy makers fear a collapse of the global financial system, starting with only one or two bad players who get in over their heads and pull others down with them.

One group, the Investment Performance Council of the Association for Investment Management and Research (renamed the CFA Institute in 2004), studies leverage through its Leverage and Derivatives Subcommittee. Its challenge is to define leverage as a precursor to measuring and managing associated risk, including the identification of transactions that give rise to leverage.[8] Related issues include whether to use a leveraged benchmark when evaluating the performance of a leveraged portfolio.

Combining forces, the Basel Committee on Banking Supervision and International Organization of Securities Commissions created the Highly Leveraged Institutions Working Group. Although it is hard to classify a highly leveraged institution with exact precision, the Basel Committee looks at large organizations that use leverage and "are subject to little or no direct regulatory oversight and limited disclosure requirements."[9] Work done so far suggests a continued focus on stress testing as a way to quantify vulnerabilities to adverse market conditions that worsen with leverage.[10]

EXHIBIT 5.7 Leverage Example

Funding	Initial Investment	Ending Investment	Investor's Return	Allocation of Proceeds
Case One: no leverage	$1,000 from individual	$1,100	10% $\rightarrow$ 100% × [($1,100 − $1,000) ÷ $1,000]	Individual investor receives entire $100 gain
Case Two: $900 borrowed at 0% interest	$900 borrowed funds, plus $100 from individual	$1,100	100% $\rightarrow$ 100% × [($200 − $100) ÷ $100] where $200 = $1,100 ending value − $900 loan amount	Individual repays $900 to lender and keeps $100 gain plus original $100
Case Three: $900 borrowed at 5% interest	$900 borrowed funds, plus $100 from individual	$1,100	55% $\rightarrow$ 100% × [($155 − $100) ÷ $100] where $155 = $1,100 ending value − $900 loan amount − $45 interest	Individual repays $900 to lender plus $45 interest, and keeps $55 net gain plus original $100

Assumptions:

1. The investment lasts for one period.
2. Time value of money is ignored.

Source: Copyright © 2001, Dr. George A. Mangiero. Reprinted with permission. All rights reserved.

BETA

Because risk means different things to different people, distinguishing among the various risk measures is critical to understanding what someone means when they describe the riskiness of a given security or group of securities. Correlation, earlier mentioned as an important concept for risk management purposes, provides one way to evaluate risk for a portfolio. Beta provides a second way to evaluate portfolio risk, but can also be used for individual securities. Beta measures something known as market risk and can be negative or positive. The two concepts are related since the mathematical formula for beta takes correlation as one of its inputs. (Remember that correlation is a pairwise measure. In the case of stock beta, returns on a market index and individual security returns comprise the pair.)[11]

The concepts supporting the use of beta as a risk measure are straightforward enough, but require a few explanatory comments. The standard deviation looks at variability of returns around an average and measures what is known as total risk. Total risk can be broken down into two components: market risk and unsystematic risk. Theory shows that *market risk*—sometimes referred to as *systematic risk*—cannot be diversified away, even when a portfolio consists of many different securities. It is simply the risk of being exposed to changes in market conditions. In contrast, *unsystematic risk*—sometimes referred to as *idiosyncratic risk*—can be nearly eliminated if an investor diversifies across countries, industries, and companies. Because a smart investor can diversify, the reward for assuming incremental risk should take into account only market risk because it is assumed that the right thing will be done.[12] Hence, beta is a more appropriate measure of risk than standard deviation.

When a method known as linear regression is used to estimate the relationship between market index returns and individual company stock performance, the beta shows up as the slope of the line of best fit.[13] The graph in Exhibit 5.8 shows a positively sloped regression line, pointing toward the northeast corner, and reflecting the notion that an individual stock return should move in the same direction as the general market. The opposite is true for a regression line that points southeasterly. Negative beta stocks should move up in value as the market index moves down or vice versa.

Beta coefficients for publicly traded companies are readily available from a wide source of vendors. They can be used to take a directional view, anticipating good news or bad. Like correlation, both the magnitude and sign play a role. Having one without the other is useless. A beta of $+0.65$ tells a completely different story than a beta of -0.65. If the sign is left out, the result is incomplete information and flawed decision making. Exhibit 5.9 looks at a variety of beta categories. An investor who anticipates a bearish market might buy stocks with negative betas because their respective

EXHIBIT 5.8   Beta as Slope of Regression Line

Market Index Returns

EXHIBIT 5.9   Beta Classifications

Beta Value	Interpretation	Stock Classification	Explanation
β < 0	Negative beta (example: −0.89)	Countercyclical	Investment value of stock should move in opposite direction of general market movement
0 < β < 1	Positive beta between 0 and 1 (example: +0.65)	Defensive	Investment value of stock should move in same direction of general market movement, but not on a percent-for-dollar basis
β = 1	Positive beta equal to +1.00	Market	Investment value of stock should move in same direction of general market movement and by the same amount
β > 1	Positive beta bigger than +1.00 (example: +1.50)	Aggressive	Investment value of stock should move in same direction of general market movement, but by more than one percent for every percent by which the market index value changes

prices ought to rise as the market tanks. Anecdotally, few stocks have neg-ative betas. In contrast, anyone who anticipates a strong equity market would be inclined to invest in stocks with beta coefficients exceeding +1.00. If the market climbs in value, these positive beta stocks should similarly rise but by more than the general market. On the risk management front, beta can be used to calculate hedge size. The sign of the beta coefficient would determine the nature of the position (long or short) in the derivative instrument.

Beta estimates tend to vary over time and across providers, and are ex-tremely sensitive to the choice of market index. Although beta has its share of critics, it is nevertheless used for both investing and risk management purposes.

EQUITY RISK MEASURE COMPARISON

Dealing with uncertainty is far from easy. As shown already, there are many ways to measure risk. Whether and when a particular approach is suitable depends on context. Consider the numbers shown in Exhibits 5.10 and 5.11. Using the standard deviation to assess risk, the market index compares

EXHIBIT 5.10 Performance Summary Information for Three Hypothetical Equity Securities

Variable	Individual Stock ABC	Individual Stock DEF	Market Index
Average return (%)	10	16	10
Standard deviation of returns (%)	8	8	6
Coefficient of variation	0.80	0.50	0.60
Correlation with market index	+0.56	+0.90	+1.00
Beta	+0.75	+1.20	+1.00

Notes:
1. The correlation of something with itself is mathematically and intuitively +1.00. This accounts for the +1.00 correlation of the market index returns with itself.
2. The beta coefficient measures the sensitivity of a stock's movement vis-à-vis the market index. That means that the beta of the market index has to be +1.00.
3. Mathematically, the beta value equals the product of market correlation times the standard deviation of an individual stock, divided by the standard deviation of the market index returns.
4. The coefficient of variation, correlation, and beta values are unit-free numbers, un-like the return and standard deviation numbers, which are expressed in percent form.

EXHIBIT 5.11   Risk Rankings for Three Hypothetical Equity Securities Described in Exhibit 5.10

Basis	Lowest Risk	Highest Risk	Comments
Standard deviation of returns (%)	Market index (6% standard deviation)	Stock ABC (8% standard deviation)	Only investments with identical means can be compared using standard deviation, so Stock DEF is not considered here.
Coefficient of variation	Stock DEF (0.50 coefficient of variation)	Stock ABC (0.80 coefficient of variation)	Stock ABC and Stock DEF both have 8% standard deviations but different means, so the coefficient of variation must be used to measure total risk.
Beta	Stock ABC (+0.75 beta)	Stock DEF (+1.20 beta)	Relative to the performance of the market index, Stock ABC is considered less risky because of its low beta.

favorably with Stock ABC. They both have the same expected return of 10 percent but the market index has a standard deviation of 6 percent, lower than the 8 percent standard deviation for Stock ABC. Using the coefficient of variation, risk-averse investors gravitate toward Stock DEF because it has the lowest relative risk measure of 0.50.

Evaluating systematic or market risk requires the use of beta and points to Stock DEF as the most sensitive to market movements, making it a riskier choice. In contrast, Stock ABC is the least sensitive with a beta of +0.75, even though its standard deviation puts it at the top of the risk rankings.

Complicating things further, risk measure names sometimes sound alike. The coefficient of variation measures risk relative to mean return. The correlation coefficient reflects the way returns for two securities ought to move in response to external factors. Then there is the beta coefficient just discussed. They are different metrics, even though they all share the word "coefficient" in their names.

DURATION

Standard deviation, coefficient of variation, and correlation coefficient can and are computed for stocks, bonds, and an assortment of other investment vehicles. However, market risk measured in the form of beta almost always refers to stocks. An analogous metric for bonds is known as duration. When applied to bonds, the notion of market risk refers to the impact of changes in interest rates on a bond's price. If the prevailing yield to maturity for similar risk-class bonds goes up, a bond's price will fall because its future expected cash flows have to be discounted at the now higher market interest rate. Like beta, duration is easy to compute and interpret and can be used either for investment selection or risk control. Another similarity is that the duration of a portfolio of bonds reflects proportional weighting of each item in the portfolio, much like finding the beta of a portfolio of stocks.

Keep in mind that stocks and bonds are different in many ways. When a company or government issues debt, it is in effect borrowing money from individuals and institutions who buy the bonds. However, a stock reflects pro-rata ownership in a firm, private or public. The standard bond pays regular dollar amounts, based on a fixed coupon rate, followed by a lump sum amount that reflects the amount borrowed. In contrast, a stock may or may not make short-term cash payments. If they are made, they take the form of cash dividends and management has discretion over the amount paid out. There is no assurance that the dollar amount will be the same every period, unlike fixed-coupon bonds.

Some experts posit that duration is best understood as a payback period that measures, in time-value terms, when a bond buyer can expect to recoup the initial price paid for the bond. Duration assumes that a bond is held to maturity, there are no missed payments or outright default by the issuer, and that interest is reinvested by the bond buyer at the bond's yield to maturity. Even though there are several other ways to measure and interpret duration that are not discussed here, a higher duration number reflects higher risk.

Bonds that are similar in every way but one are normally compared with each other on the basis of duration.[14] Consider the three bonds shown in Exhibit 5.12, each with a five-year maturity. For a zero coupon bond, the investor only receives an amount equal to its face value upon maturity. Because there is nothing to reinvest between purchase date and expiration, the duration of a zero coupon bond is the same as its time to maturity.[15] Bond GHI is a zero coupon bond so its duration is five years. In contrast, the other two bonds pay coupons, the effect of which is to shorten their duration. This is because the intervening coupons can be reinvested and therefore contribute to the recovery of the initial price paid for the bond.

EXHIBIT 5.12 Performance Summary Information for Three Hypothetical
Fixed-Income Securities

Variable	Individual Bond GHI	Individual Bond JKL	Market Index
Annual coupon (%)	0	6	6
Time to maturity (years)	5	5	5
Yield to maturity (%)	6	6	8
Standard deviation of returns (%)	4	6	7
Coefficient of variation	0.67	1.00	0.88
Correlation with market index	+0.50	+0.80	+1.00
Duration (years)	5.00	4.47	4.09

Notes:
1. The correlation of something with itself is mathematically and intuitively +1.00. This accounts for the +1.00 correlation of the market index with itself.
2. Duration measures sensitivity of a bond's movement vis-à-vis the market index and depends on coupon rate, time to maturity, and yield to maturity.
3. The duration of a zero coupon bond equals the number of years until it matures because there are no intervening coupon payments to reinvest that would shorten the payback period.
4. The coefficient of variation and correlation coefficient are unit-free numbers, unlike the return and standard deviation numbers, which are expressed in percent form. The duration measure used in this exhibit is expressed in terms of time.
5. The yield to maturity is divided into standard deviation to find the coefficient of variation.

Other factors such as yield and time to maturity affect duration. Everything else being equal, a high-yield bond has a lower duration, the assumption being that dollar coupon payments earn interest at a higher rate than low-yield bonds. Going back to the payback idea, more money made in earlier years accelerates the time it takes to recoup the initial price paid. Bond JKL and a market basket of bonds each reflect an annual 6 percent coupon and the same time to maturity, but differ in yield. The shorter duration of 4.09 years for the index reflects its higher yield.[16] The assumption is that each 6 percent coupon paid out by the bond market index portfolio is reinvested at the 8 percent yield to maturity rate, a number that is higher than the 6 percent yield to maturity for Bond JKL.

Although not shown here, the duration of two or more bonds with the same coupon and yield but dissimilar maturities will differ. Everything else being equal, longer-term bonds have higher durations.

As shown in Exhibit 5.13, duration and time to maturity move in the same direction. Coupon level and duration move in the opposite direction as is the case for yield to maturity and duration. Similar to beta, duration can be used to exploit an opinion about the market. If an investor predicts

EXHIBIT 5.13 Duration Factors[a]

Factor	Factor Increases	Factor Decreases
Annual percent coupon rate (annual dollar coupon payment)	Shorter duration as coupon rate increases	Longer duration as coupon rate falls
Time to maturity	Longer duration as time to maturity increases	Shorter duration as time to maturity decreases
Yield to maturity (assumed reinvestment rate)	Shorter duration as coupons are reinvested at higher rates	Longer duration as coupons are reinvested at lower rates

[a]Duration statements assume that only one feature at a time will change.

that rates will fall (prices will rise), a high-duration bond or portfolio of bonds is a good bet. If rates do indeed fall, the high-duration bond or portfolio of binds shoud rise in value by more than the increase in general bond market levels. Duration can be used to estimate the change in price for a small rate change and a host of other applications, including hedge size determination when seeking to manage interest rate risk.

Duration is a static measure of risk and reflects conditions only at a given point in time. Computing the duration of a bond after its issuance must necessarily reflect these changes. Whether used to determine hedge size, match asset–liability duration, or make an anticipatory investment, one duration calculation alone is ill advised. Duration should be recomputed on a regular basis to reflect changes in market conditions such as prevailing yields and the passage of time.

FIXED-INCOME MEASURE COMPARISON

As with equities, bond risk can be measured in different ways and rankings will vary by metric. As shown in Exhibit 5.14, a 4 percent standard deviation identifies Bond GHI as low risk, compared with Bond JKL with a 6 percent number. Because they each have the same yield of 6 percent, the coefficient of variation supports this ranking. Duration tells another story. Instead of ranking at the bottom as low risk, Bond GHI comes out on top. Its duration is 5 years, exceeding the 4.09-year duration for the market portfolio of bonds.[17] Which risk measure is the right one to use? It depends. Duration measures systematic risk, standard deviation measures absolute total risk, and the coefficient of variation measures total risk, relative to mean return. In practice, duration is employed more often than statistical measures of total risk. However, if any of its underlying assumptions are violated,

EXHIBIT 5.14   Risk Rankings for Three Hypothetical Fixed-Income Securities Described in Exhibit 5.12

Basis	Lowest Risk	Highest Risk	Comments
Standard deviation of returns (%)	Bond GHI (4% standard deviation)	Bond JKL (6% standard deviation)	Only investments with identical means can be compared using standard deviation, so the market index is not considered here.
Coefficient of variation	Bond GHI (0.67 coefficient of variation)	Bond JKL (1.00 coefficient of variation)	The market index ranks in between the two bonds. Its higher standard deviation is offset by a higher return, its yield to maturity.
Duration	Market index (4.09 years duration)	Bond GHI (5.00 years duration)	Relative to the performance of the market index, Bond GHI is considered more risky because of its higher duration.

duration may not be the best choice. Additionally, duration does not adequately reflect price changes for large rate moves. An extension of duration not described here is something known as convexity. Its use permits a more precise quantification of the relationship between bond price and interest rate levels.

DERIVATIVES AS FORWARD CONTRACTS

Broadly defined, a derivative instrument derives its value from something else, the asset underlying the derivative. There are three broad groups—futures, options, and swaps—and a large assortment of variations in between. Subsequent chapters address each major group. To the outsider, the topic of derivatives can be daunting, perhaps because of the math involved or the perceived complexity of use. In fact, derivative instruments share a common

EXHIBIT 5.15 Forward Arrangement Time Line

Agree on contractual terms now.	$\longrightarrow$	Take action later on.
Example:		
Buy right to purchase stock for $10 a share.	$\longrightarrow$	Buy stock if prevailing market price rises above $10.

trait in that they involve some kind of forward action. Two parties agree on terms today that characterize what can happen later on, as illustrated in Exhibit 5.15. The driving force is an expectation about future market conditions. Of course, investors anticipate the future all the time, but there are several differences. Leverage is one. Derivatives can be used to manufacture a large exposure at little cost. What's more, derivatives introduce risk that is not otherwise an issue with direct investing. Of course, derivatives also can minimize risk in a way not available through investing alone.

Much more will be said in later chapters about derivatives, their unique risks, motivation to use them, and the potential economic impact when used in conjunction with stocks and bonds.

SUMMARY

1. Risk and return are two key components of any investment plan and, by extension, the related risk management strategy.
2. Risk is measured in various ways. Standard deviation, coefficient of variation, and market risk measures are just a few of the ways to evaluate risk.
3. The appropriate risk metric depends on the investor's objectives and whether assumptions underlying the metric hold true.
4. Leverage describes the nonproportional relationship between investment outlay and expected returns.
5. Leverage is neither good nor bad, but rather depends on the potential loss if things go awry.
6. Beta is a frequently used risk measure for equities. It measures the sensitivity of a stock's performance to general movements in the equity market.
7. Duration is often used to measure the interest rate risk of fixed-income securities. More specifically, it looks at the behavior of a bond's price as a function of small changes in interest rates.
8. Risk rankings vary considerably, depending on how they are put together.
9. Derivative instruments and forward contracts are similar to each other in that two parties agree today on possible future action.

CHAPTER 6

Financial Futures

Ill-luck, you know, seldom comes alone.

—Miguel de Cervantes Saavedra

BACKGROUND

Futures, one type of derivative instrument, have been around for a long time. Each futures contract is uniquely determined by its standardized terms and conditions, including trading venue, face value, and description of the underlying asset from which the contract derives its value. Although commodity futures predate financial futures by more than a century, currency and interest rate contracts have quickly gained favor since their inception.[1] Popular contracts include futures on U.S. Treasury bonds, Eurodollars, and the S&P 500 Index. Exhibits 6.1 through 6.4 shed some

EXHIBIT 6.1 Futures Contract Turnover in Dollar Terms by Category in 2001

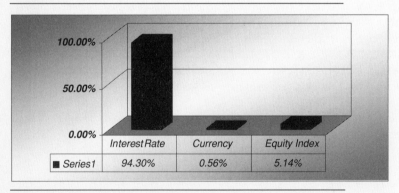

	Interest Rate	Currency	Equity Index
■ Series1	94.30%	0.56%	5.14%

Note: Some percentages are rounded.
Source: BIS Quarterly Review, December 2002. Copyright © 2002, Bank for International Settlements.

EXHIBIT 6.2 Futures Contract Turnover in Dollar Terms by Geographic Area in 2001

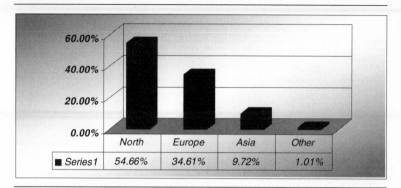

Note: Some percentages are rounded.
Source: BIS Quarterly Review, December 2002. Copyright © 2002, Bank for International Settlements.

insight on trading activity in terms of dollar amounts and number of contracts outstanding.

The futures market is large, with more than $446 trillion in futures turnover reported for 2001, due in large part to interest rate activity in North America and Europe.[2] Relatively low currency futures activity suggests that foreign exchange trading takes place instead in the sizeable over-the-counter (OTC) market.[3] Getting a detailed breakdown by user type is difficult. However, these statistics mirror results from a 1998 survey of U.S. institutional investors on their use of derivatives. When asked about use by type of

EXHIBIT 6.3 Futures Contract Turnover in Contract Number Terms by Category in 2001

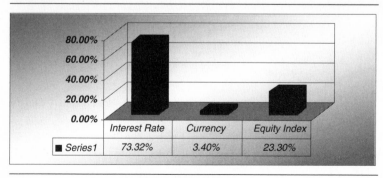

Note: Some percentages are rounded.
Source: BIS Quarterly Review, December 2002. Copyright © 2002, Bank for International Settlements.

EXHIBIT 6.4   Futures Contract Turnover in Contract Number Terms by
Geographic Area in 2001

	North	Europe	Asia	Other
■ Series1	33.52%	47.19%	10.45%	8.83%

Note: Some percentages are rounded.
Source: BIS Quarterly Review, December 2002. Copyright © 2002, Bank
for International Settlements.

derivative instrument, respondents cited a preference for OTC currency forwards, while favoring futures for interest rate and equity exposures.[4] Futures
and forwards share the fact that they each offer a way to decide today on a
later action, yet they differ from each other in several ways.

Forwards versus Futures

Technically speaking, futures are a type of forward contract, although they
are seldom referred to that way. Instead, the term *forwards* typically refers
to OTC forward contracts. Understanding the differences, as summarized in
Exhibit 6.5, goes a long way toward making an appropriate choice between
instrument types. An institutional investor with little flexibility may need to
trade a derivative instrument that exactly matches required terms, such as
size and underlying asset, rendering a standardized futures contract a poor
choice. Alternatively, an institutional investor may shy away from the higher
transaction fees that typically accompany customized OTC deals. Investor
risk tolerance, credit considerations, staff size, product knowledge, cash
availability, flexibility, and creditworthiness are a few factors that influence
the final decision. Another factor, margin, merits a more in-depth discussion.

Unlike OTC forwards, futures trading involves both margin and a daily
settlement of each position. The *initial margin* is the amount posted at the
inception of the trade. Depending on how far and how quickly a position
drops in value, a trader will thereafter post either maintenance or variation
margin. *Maintenance margin* is the amount needed to take the account balance back to the required minimum level. In the event that things get really
bad, a trader posts *variation margin,* which is an amount that takes the
account balance back to the higher initial margin levels.[5] Exhibit 6.6

EXHIBIT 6.5 Forwards Versus Futures

Attribute	Future	Over-the-Counter (OTC) Forward	Comments
Contract terms	Standardized	Customized	Contract specifications include information such as underlying asset type and quality, settlement, delivery, minimum price movement, and face value.
Credit risk	Exchange clearinghouse stands behind every trade	Either counterparty could default on obligation	Many OTC players trade in the name of separate derivative subsidiaries.
Margin	Required at outset of trade with additional margin required if position value drops below specified level	Typically none, but subject to requirements of individual broker	Initial, maintenance, and variation margin are the three types of margin associated with futures trading.
Mark to market	Mandatory daily settlement	No requirement	A reduction in position value below the level of maintenance margin triggers a margin call. This requires the trader to post enough money to take the balance back to the initial margin level.
Price transparency	Exists	Not always available	Sales and time information is available for futures trades.
Regulation	Commodity Futures Trading Commission and other regulators[a]	Largely self-regulated	Regulation varies across countries.
Trading venue	Exchange	Private negotiation between two parties	Each exchange has a set of rules regarding the listing and trading of various contracts.

[a]The promulgation of the Commodity Futures Modernization Act of 2000 changed the regulatory landscape for futures and some OTC derivative instruments. See "A Brief Overview of the Commodity Futures Modernization Act of 2000" by Kathryn Page Camp, *Derivatives Quarterly*, Spring 2001, pages 9–14.

EXHIBIT 6.6 Futures Margin Example

A hypothetical investor buys one futures contract on Asset X at a price of $100. An initial margin of 10 percent or $10 is required. Maintenance margin is $5. This represents a floor below which the margin account balance cannot fall without triggering a call for variation margin.

Day	Beginning of Day Position Value	End of Day Position Value[a]	Margin Account Balance	Change in Position
Inception date	$100	$100	$10	n/a
One day later	$100	$ 97	$ 7	–$3
Two days later	$ 97	$ 94.50	$ 4.50	(i) – $2.50 before margin call
			Balance below $5 triggers margin call:	(ii) $5.50 posted to bring balance to $10 after margin call

[a]A rise in position value increases the customer's equity. Exchange rules vary as to when and how an investor can withdraw surplus funds.

EXHIBIT 6.7   Futures Position Value and Margin

Original Position Type	Prices of Underlying Asset Drop	Prices of Underlying Asset Rise
Long: Buy futures	Original position value falls, additional margin may have to be posted if drop is large enough	Original position value rises
Short: Sell futures	Original position value rises	Original position value falls, additional margin may have to be posted if increase is large enough

illustrates how margin works. In a volatile and adverse market, an investor may have to make multiple bank transfers related to margin during the life of the trade. For some nonprofits, this daily settlement process could be tough to handle with a small staff and the cost of bank wires.

Exhibit 6.7 summarizes the role of margin with respect to position type. A long position goes down in value if prices fall because the trader has locked in a higher price with futures and loses the chance to buy at now lower levels. In contrast, lower prices benefit someone with a short position. The idea is that the investor could close an open short position by buying futures at lower levels and report a gain. Margin varies by exchange and by contract. Anyone working through a broker may pay margin amounts in excess of exchange minimums to reflect trading volume and creditworthiness of the client.

Margin varies by use as well. A hedger pays a lower amount than a speculator. Exhibit 6.8 illustrates this idea using performance bond minimums published by the Chicago Mercantile Exchange (CME) for selected

EXHIBIT 6.8   Margin for Selected Contracts

Contract (Ticker)	Trader Type	Initial Margin	Maintenance Margin
Nasdaq-100	Speculator	$11,250	$ 9,000
Index (ND)	Hedger or exchange member	$ 9,000	$ 9,000
Russell 2000	Speculator	$15,000	$12,000
Stock Index (RL)	Hedger or exchange member	$12,000	$12,000
S&P 500 Stock	Speculator	$17,813	$14,250
Index (SP)	Hedger or exchange member	$14,250	$14,250

Source: "SPAN® minimum performance bond requirements," Chicago Mercantile Exchange web site. © Chicago Mercantile Exchange.

equity index futures. The numbers are based on their proprietary Standard Portfolio Analysis of Risk® (SPAN®) model.[6]

A number of investors embrace margin as a good way to safeguard the financial integrity of the futures markets. Some find it deters their use of futures because it requires an active role in monitoring positions. Other institutions look at margin as a small cost to incur for the chance to gain exposure to a particular asset at a fraction of the face value. This is the leverage concept discussed in Chapter 5.

Contract Specifications

Endowments, foundations, and pensions can choose from a bevy of futures contracts and exchanges with more than a handful located in the United States.[7] Each contract is uniquely identified by its exchange and specifications. A ticker symbol identifies a particular contract as well as its delivery month and year. For example, USZ3 refers to the futures on U.S. Treasury bonds, traded at the Chicago Board of Trade and expiring in December 2003. Month codes are shown in Exhibit 6.9. If a contract is traded on two or more exchanges, the identifier could differ. For example, KW is the ticker symbol for the hard red winter wheat futures contract traded on the Kansas City Board of Trade. A similar contract, traded on the Chicago Board of Trade, goes by W.

Complicating things is the fact that different vendors may not use the same codes to identify a particular contract. This makes information collection more difficult. An analyst using historical data to determine hedge size or evaluate contract behavior must be careful to get prices for the right contract, specified by exchange, expiration, and month. Some vendors

EXHIBIT 6.9 Futures Month Codes

Month	Code
January	F
February	G
March	H
April	J
May	K
June	M
July	N
August	Q
September	U
October	V
November	X
December	Z

Source: Chicago Mercantile Exchange web site, http://www.cme.com. © Chicago Mercantile Exchange.

provide data for a currently traded, sometimes called "nearby," contract that changes over time as old contracts expire and new ones take their place. Data for this constant maturity instrument represents the next contract to settle. This is almost always the contract that is most actively traded and can therefore be used as a gauge of futures market interest.

Contract specifications are easy to find online. Exhibit 6.10 summarizes some of the futures contracts used by institutional investors. However, it is in no way an exhaustive list. For example, it does not include any contracts listed on non-U.S. exchanges. Moreover, because new contracts are always being added, no list will ever be permanently up to date.

Despite an abundance of choices, contracts are not available for all possible asset types. For hedgers, the substitute contract is referred to as a cross-hedge and entails additional risk in the form of basis. By definition, basis is the cash minus futures price difference. The precision of the hedge is inversely impacted by the size of the basis. Bigger basis tends to render a hedge less effective. This is true even for hedges that rely on a contract that is almost identical to the underlying exposure. Recall the discussion about correlation from Chapter 5. An appropriate cross-hedge instrument will track the movement of the security being hedged and reflect a correlation coefficient close to $+1.00$.

PRICE DISCOVERY

Some people never trade futures, but nonetheless pay attention to how they move. Their belief is that futures contract prices reflect new information quickly and, therefore, provide information about the market consensus for a particular stock, bond, currency, commodity, or index that defines the futures contract. As long as markets are deemed efficient, the price of a specified futures contract should reflect the prevailing opinion of both buyers and sellers about the ultimate value of the underlying asset. This process is known as price discovery, and is regularly used by companies, financial institutions, governments, and banks as part of their forecasting.[8]

HEDGING

Market conditions constantly change, putting the value of an institutional investor's portfolio at risk. A drop in value is bad for any investor, but has particular peril for a pension fund that is legally obliged to cover liabilities. The same holds true for an endowment that is required to distribute a certain percent each year or risk loss of its tax-exempt status. Hedging with futures provides one way to protect a portfolio from adverse changes in interest rates, equity prices, or currencies. Essentially, this means taking a position in futures that has the opposite sign of the financial exposure.

As shown in Exhibit 6.11, hedging can be used for many reasons. An investor with a long bond position will want a short position in futures to

EXHIBIT 6.10 Specifications for Selected Contracts

Specification	Eurodollars[a]	S&P 500[b]	30-Year U.S. Treasury Bond[c]
Contract months	March, June, September, December, and four serial months	March, June, September, December	March, June, September, December
Contract size	$1,000,000	$250 times price of S&P 500 futures	One U.S. Treasury bond with face value of $100,000 at expiration
Exchange minimum price fluctuation (tick)	CME, $6.25 CME per contract for spot-month contract and $12 per contract for others	CME, $25 per contract or 0.10 index points	CBOT, $31.25 per contract
Regular trading hours	7:20 A.M. to 2:00 P.M. (CST)	8:30 A.M. to 3:15 P.M. (CST)	7:20 A.M. to 2:00 P.M. (CST)
Underlying asset	U.S. dollar denominated time deposits that are placed in commercial banks outside the United States	S&P 500 Stock Index	U.S. Treasury bonds with maturity of 15 years or longer

[a]The Chicago Mercantile Exchange describes the Eurodollars contract as "the most actively traded futures contract in the world." See http://www.cme.com.

[b]According to the Chicago Mercantile Exchange web site, equity futures are used by both individual and institutional investors. See http://www.cme.com.

[c]The Chicago Board of Trade provides other details, including factors that convert different bonds to an equivalent price of a U.S. Treasury bond with a 6 percent yield to maturity that is either not callable or cannot be called for at least 15 years from the first day of the delivery month. See http://www.cbot.com.

EXHIBIT 6.11 Various Hedging Examples

Hypothetical Situation	Concern	Futures Hedge	Effect of Hedge If Cash Prices Rise	Effect of Hedge If Cash Prices Fall
Pension plan owns bonds	Interest rates rise, value of bonds falls	Sell bond futures today	Bonds go up in value, but gain is offset by futures position loss	Value of bonds falls, but is offset by futures position gain
Endowment fund will use new contributions to buy shares in an S&P 500 Index mutual fund	Equity index level rises, making it more expensive to wait to buy	Buy equity futures now	Futures position gain offsets higher cash amount paid later when new contributions are expected	Fund shares bought at lower price, but savings is offset by futures position loss
Foundation buys Japanese yen time deposit	Japanese yen weakens and fewer U.S. dollars can be purchased when time deposit matures	Sell Japanese yen futures on date deposit is made	Increased value of time deposit is offset by futures position loss if Japanese yen appreciates	Futures position gain offsets reduced value of time deposit if Japanese yen weakens
Pension plan allocates funds to invest in gold bullion	Gold prices peak, value of gold holdings fall	Sell gold futures immediately	Higher value of gold ownership is offset by futures position loss	Futures position gain offsets lower value of gold holdings

Notes:
1. The term *cash* refers to the underlying asset.
2. Margin, taxes, transaction costs, and basis are ignored.
3. Cash and futures position values are considered for only two dates, the beginning and end of the hedge time interval. Interim value changes are excluded for illustrative purposes.

offset the adverse impact of an interest rate rise. Conversely, an investor may not be ready to buy stock, but fears rising prices. Buying equity futures is one solution. An institution with investments abroad could sell currency futures now to stave off the ill effects of a depreciated foreign currency that forces repatriated profit, in U.S. dollar terms, downward.

Whatever the reason, the key is to construct a hedge that preserves the portfolio's original value regardless of what happens in the marketplace. If the worst-case scenario occurs, the hedge will serve its purpose. If things turn out fine, the hedge will have cost the investor an opportunity. After the fact, the hedge may look like a bad choice and that upsets investors. Without a crystal ball, decisions have to be made before market moves occur.

A good analogy is the purchase of auto insurance. At the beginning of the year, paying the premium makes sense given the likely higher cost associated with a car accident. At the end of the year, buying car insurance looks expensive after making it through 12 months without an accident. This ex-post conclusion is not really appropriate if the stated goal at the outset is to reduce risk. If financial managers know they will be penalized for failure to predict the future, however illogical that may be, they are unlikely to hedge because it commits the investor to a stated return or cost of funds.

Hedging is a complicated process. Besides choosing an appropriate hedge vehicle, an institutional investor needs to determine trade size, rules for rebalancing, and ways to measure hedge effectiveness. This is especially true in the aftermath of FAS 133 and related accounting rules for derivatives instruments.[9] Exhibit 6.12 provides a checklist of things to think about when hedging with futures. It should and can be customized to suit a particular investor's risk tolerance and return targets.

In the following examples, futures and the underlying asset are assumed to move in tandem, reflecting perfect positive correlation. Perfect positive correlation, reflected in a +1.00 correlation coefficient, is rare in practice. Ordinarily the hedger evaluates the statistical relationship between the futures instrument and what is being hedged. That helps to determine whether to buy more than or less than $1 in futures for every dollar of securities being hedged. There are many ways to compute the hedge ratio. Some techniques are more apropos than others.

Bond Hedge Example

Exhibit 6.13 looks at a hypothetical bond futures hedge for a pension fund that purchases $1,000,000 in long-term U.S. Treasury bonds at a price of 97-24 or $977,500.[10] Fearing rising rates, the pension fund decides to hedge with futures to avoid having to sell the bonds in 30 days at a lower price. The strategy is to sell futures because the pension fund is long cash bonds.[11] Nothing happens today regarding cash flow. The action occurs when the

EXHIBIT 6.12 Hedging with Futures Checklist

When to Take Action	What to Do
Before the hedge	1. Determine whether the investment policy permits use of futures.
	2. If allowed, identify considerations outlined in the investment policy statement, including the measurement and reporting of risk. Many investment policies preclude the short sale of futures or limit cross hedges.
	3. Write specific procedures for use of futures, if not done already.
	4. Identify the exact risk (nature and amount) to be hedged.
	5. Identify the best futures contract to use.
	6. Evaluate the hedge ratio to determine the size of the initial trade, using an appropriate methodology.
	7. Open a brokerage account to transact futures trades.
	8. Assign responsibilities to staff, including margin-based money transfers, and train staff.
During the hedge	1. Execute the initial hedge.
	2. Evaluate hedge effectiveness on prespecified dates.
	3. Rebalance if necessary (i.e., when the cash-futures basis changes or the underlying exposure shrinks or grows).
	4. Generate management reports for accounting, tax, and financial analysis use.
	5. Close out the futures position before expiration if delivery is not acceptable.[a]
After the hedge	1. Determine overall efficacy of hedge vis-à-vis investment goals during the entire life of the hedge.
	2. Identify ways to improve futures-related hedging procedures for later transactions.

[a]Many futures positions are reversed before the expiration date to avoid taking or making delivery of the underlying asset. Keep in mind that some contracts are cash settled, in which case offsetting the original trade may not be as much of an issue.

pension fund closes the futures position by buying a like amount of futures before the 30-day mark and selling the bonds in the open market. In between, margin posting may occur if rates fall far enough.[12] The pension fund does not have a choice in the matter of margin.

Jumping ahead one month later, the pension fund manager in this example was right to fear rising interest rates (lower bond prices). The cash bonds are sold at a $14,375 loss equal to the difference between the $977,500 investment cost and the $963,125 sale proceeds. In contrast, the short futures position is offset by buying an equal amount of bond futures

EXHIBIT 6.13 Bond Hedge Example

Date	Action	Price	Comments
Today	Buy bonds with a $1,000,000 face value	97-24 ($977,500)	Lower cash bond prices reduces the value of the pension's holdings
	Sell 10 futures contracts with a total $1,000,000 face value	99-12 ($993,750 price)	No cash outlay occurs until later
One month later	Sell bonds with a $1,000,000 face value	96-10 ($963,125)	Cash bonds are sold at a loss equal to $14,375 (i.e., $977,500 purchase price versus $963,125 sales price)
	Buy 10 futures contracts with a $1,000,000 face value to close out the initial short futures position	97-29 ($979,063)	Buying futures to close out position means a gain of $14,687 (i.e., $993,750 sales price versus $979,063 purchase price)
		Net effect	$312 gain

Notes:
1. Margin is ignored in this example, and a hedge ratio of 1.00 is assumed.
2. To avoid having to make delivery of bonds, the pension fund closes out the short futures position by buying futures before the delivery date.

at a lower price 30 days after the original trade. The result is a $14,687 gain; that is, the $993,750 short sales prices less the $979,063 purchase price. For all practical purposes, the hedge provides a perfect offset with a tiny $312 gain to the pension fund, stemming from the $14,687 futures gain less the $14,375 loss on the cash bonds.

Hedging equity, commodity, and currency price risk is similar in the sense that an investor takes a position in futures that is opposite of the existing security position. Futures can be used for a lot of reasons. In the case of transactions known as anticipatory hedges, futures are used to satisfy the investor's goal to buy or sell securities until such time that a cash transaction takes place. Futures can even be used as a means to enhance returns, as discussed shortly.

Equity Hedge Example

Following a successful fundraising campaign, an endowment fund expects to receive $1,000,000 in contributions within the next 90 days. Individual checks will be deposited into a general account until the full amount is available to buy 10,000 shares of a mutual fund that replicates the S&P 500 index. Each share currently costs $100. Concerned about a bullish market in the form of higher equity index levels, the endowment investment officer decides to buy S&P 500 futures today. Exhibit 6.14 illustrates what could happen if prices do indeed go up by the time all new contributions are available to invest.

In hindsight, the hedge in this example worked well. Rising equity prices led to a gain from buying futures at a low price and selling them later at a higher price. The gain was used to offset the increased cost of buying equity mutual fund shares. The net effect for the endowment fund was to lock in an investment cost, even though no cash was immediately available to purchase mutual fund shares. Note that the equity example differed slightly from the bond example in that no cash security was purchased when the hedge was put into place. Nevertheless, both examples illustrate the benefit of using futures as a mechanism to lock in today's price without having to immediately front the money.

OTHER WAYS TO USE FUTURES

Futures are relatively straightforward to use. Most contracts tend to trade in liquid markets. Cash requirements are small, other than margin (and margin represents a fraction of the face value). They can be used to hedge or speculate. Some institutional investors treat futures as a separate asset class, whereas others use them to boost short-term returns.

Managed Futures

According to recent studies, treating futures as a separate asset class offers endowments, foundations, and pensions the chance to diversify current holdings. The low correlation between futures and stocks, bonds, and more traditional assets accounts for part of their appeal. For example, the correlation between the S&P 500 Index and managed futures is −0.07. The correlation coefficient between bonds and managed futures is 0.20.[13] The Chicago Board of Trade cites several benefits of managed futures to include liquid markets that ease market entry and exit, lower transaction costs than cash market alternatives, and the "disciplined use of leverage" that permits a large exposure for a small commitment of capital.[14]

EXHIBIT 6.14 Equity Hedge Example

Date	Action	Prices	Comments
Today	Buy eight contracts with a $1,000,000 face value	500 Index level	No cash outlay occurs until later
Ninety days later	Buy S&P 500 Index mutual fund shares	$104 mutual fund share price	Endowment fund pays out $1,040,000 to buy 10,000 units of the mutual fund, an increase of $40,000 because it waited to buy
	Sell eight futures to close out the original long futures position	520 Index level	Selling futures means a gain of $40,000 given the higher futures contract price (i.e., 520 × $250 × eight contracts or $1,040,000 sales price versus $1,000,000 purchase price)
		Net effect	$0 change

Notes:

1. Margin is ignored in this example.

2. To avoid having to settle, the endowment fund closes out the long futures position by selling futures before the delivery date.

3. To determine the size of each S&P 500 Index futures contract, multiply $250 by the S&P 500 Stock Index level as laid out in the "Equity Index Futures & Options 2002 Information Guide," published by the Chicago Mercantile Exchange. In this example, the S&P 500 Stock Index level trades at 500. Multiplying 500 by $250 equals $125,000. Buying eight futures contracts today provides a way to hedge expected contributions of $1,000,000 (i.e., $125,000 × 8).

The creation of several managed futures indices makes this product even more appealing to investors who evaluate performance against benchmarks. One such benchmark mimics returns generated by trend followers using options.[15] A second benchmark is the S&P Managed Futures Index, designed to monitor "systematic managers employing mainly technical trend-following and pattern-recognition trading methodologies."[16] Although managed futures seem poised to remain a mainstay for many institutions, they are not immune from a watchful eye. The risk manager must evaluate risk against the perceived benefits and know if and when to pull the plug.

Enhanced Indexing

Alpha investing is the term often used to indicate that a money manager has added value by generating a return that exceeds the investor's risk-adjusted required rate. Enhanced indexing combines active and passive techniques as a way to generate positive alpha. It takes several forms. One approach is to buy index futures contracts in lieu of investing in the equity index directly. Savings from the cheaper futures strategy are used to purchase "short-duration fixed-income products" with higher returns than leaving funds as idle cash.[17]

An alternative is to buy stocks similar to those in an equity index but with better growth potential. In contrast to traditional active management, the goal is to "ensure that the portfolio's industry weightings, beta, and other volatility measures continue to resemble the index's."[18]

Made popular in the 1990s, published reports name many endowments and foundations that gained from enhanced indexing. Because no investment is free of flaws, the key is to keep track of risk-based performance. Recent studies question the benefits of enhanced indexing given higher transaction fees, relative to active strategies.[19]

SUMMARY

1. Financial futures and forwards are similar in the sense that an agreement is made today to take action later.
2. Unlike forwards, financial futures trading involves margin and daily settlement. Transaction costs may be lower for futures given the fact that they represent standardized terms and are traded on an exchange.
3. Financial futures can be used to hedge the value of an existing or an anticipated investment position for a variety of underlying assets such as

time deposits, major equity indices, commodities, and government bonds, to name a few.

4. Futures hedges can entail buying or selling futures, depending on what is being hedged.

5. Futures can be treated as a separate asset class. Its low correlation with traditional assets offers a chance to improve portfolio diversification with the inclusion of managed futures.

6. Enhanced indexing combines a long position in S&P futures with short-term, fixed-income securities with the goal of improving returns on idle cash or taking advantage of incorrect market valuations.

CHAPTER 7

Financial Options

The oldest, shortest words—"yes"and "no"
—are those which require the most thought.

—Pythagoras

BACKGROUND

Options are another type of derivative instrument. They can be used for a variety of reasons, not the least of which is to hedge interest rate, currency, or equity movements. Some options are exchange traded. Others are bought and sold privately in the over-the-counter (OTC) market. Regardless of the asset class, options come in several forms, as shown in Exhibits 7.1 and 7.2.

Options vernacular is rich in meaning, providing a handy way to describe many of the conditions associated with a trade. Consider the term *long European call. Long* refers to the fact that the owner has the right, but no obligation, to exercise. The word *call* describes the exercise privilege as the right to buy the underlying asset at a prespecified price known as the

EXHIBIT 7.1 Option Types

Option Name	Position Type	Description
Call	Long: Investor buys call option	No obligation to buy underlying asset later
	Short: Investor sells call option	Has obligation to sell underlying asset later if call buyer exercises
Put	Long: Investor buys put option	No obligation to sell underlying asset later
	Short: Investor sells put option	Has obligation to buy underlying asset later if put buyer exercises

EXHIBIT 7.2   Exercise Description

Exercise Type	Explanation
American	Call or put buyer can exercise at any point during a pre-specified time interval
European	Call or put buyer can exercise at one prespecified point in time only

strike price. European specifies that the call can only be exercised at an earlier agreed-upon date and time. The right to exercise is not continuous.

Similar to futures and OTC forwards, options involve a decision made today about action that can occur later. However, there are some major differences, notably whether an institution is obliged to perform or has the right to walk away. Option buyers pay a fee that entitles them to exercise at their discretion. In contrast, an institution with a long futures position must either take delivery or reverse the transaction before expiration by selling a like amount of futures. Other differences relate to whether an option is traded on an exchange or customized and sold in the OTC market. The type of underlying asset is yet another factor, along with the valuation models used to determine the true price.

Option Statistics

Exhibits 7.3 through 7.6 tell an interesting story about the options markets, worth exploring because usage statistics point out which risk factors may cause trouble in bad times. Like futures, exchange-traded options' dollar

EXHIBIT 7.3   Options Contract Turnover in Dollar Terms by Category in 2001

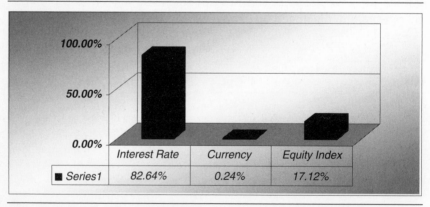

	Interest Rate	Currency	Equity Index
■ Series1	82.64%	0.24%	17.12%

Note: Some percentages are rounded.
Source: BIS Quarterly Review, December 2002. Copyright © 2002, Bank for International Settlements. Reprinted with permission.

EXHIBIT 7.4 Options Contract Turnover in Dollar Terms by Geographic Area in 2001

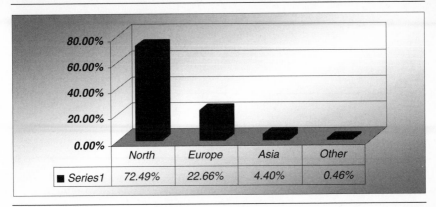

■ Series1	North	Europe	Asia	Other
	72.49%	22.66%	4.40%	0.46%

Note: Some percentages are rounded.
Source: BIS Quarterly Review, December 2002. Copyright © 2002, Bank for International Settlements. Reprinted with permission.

turnover is dominated by interest rate activity, with North American players looming large. Unlike futures, equity trading is a large part of exchange-
traded options activity in terms of number of contracts. Asian traders account
for much of the 2001 reported turnover.[1]

Exhibit 7.7 looks at outstanding amounts for exchanged-traded options versus OTC options, independent of geographic region. Each market

EXHIBIT 7.5 Options Contract Turnover in Contract Number Terms by Category
in 2001

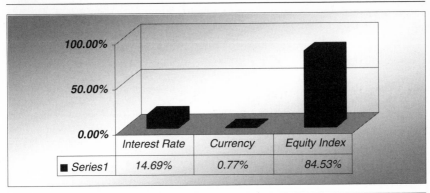

■ Series1	Interest Rate	Currency	Equity Index
	14.69%	0.77%	84.53%

Note: Some percentages are rounded.
Source: BIS Quarterly Review, December 2002. Copyright © 2002, Bank for International Settlements. Reprinted with permission.

EXHIBIT 7.6 Options Contract Turnover in Contract Number Terms by Geographic Area in 2001

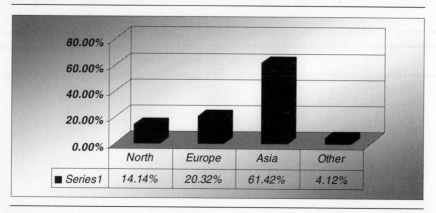

Note: Some percentages are rounded.
Source: BIS Quarterly Review, December 2002. Copyright © 2002, Bank for International Settlements. Reprinted with permission.

is huge and represents a total of about $29 trillion of trades. Their use depends on the underlying asset class. Over-the-counter currency options are nearly 10 times as popular as the standardized alternative. Exchange-traded interest rate outstanding amounts are about 15 percent higher than the OTC equivalent. Equity option trading is about the same for each market.[2]

Published statistics do not break out information by investor type. What information is available about institutional investor use suggests a preference to use OTC derivatives for currency trades and exchange-traded options for equity.[3] What does this mean? Similar to the case of futures versus forwards, exchange-traded options and OTC options are not perfect substitutes for each other.

EXHIBIT 7.7 Exchange-Traded Versus Over-the-Counter Options Volume by Category (Billions of Dollars)

Category	Exchange-Traded Options	Over-the-Counter Options
Currency	27.4	2,470
Equity	1,605.2	1,561
Interest rate	12,492.8	10,879
Total	14,125.5	14,910

Source: BIS Quarterly Review, December 2002. Copyright © 2002, Bank for International Settlement. Reprinted with permission.

Trade-Offs

Exchange-traded options have standardized terms, including rules that govern settlement and trading times. The contract uniformity may appeal to an investor that has to frequently rebalance in order to replicate a particular market index for which options exist. In contrast, the flexibility that customized OTC options offer is a plus for any institution that needs to hedge an investment position for which no matching contract exists. Other trade-offs include margin, upfront fees, and counterparty creditworthiness.[4]

Like futures, standardized options trade in regulated markets. The individual clearinghouse plays a big role. (There is no single clearinghouse for options.) One organization, the New York Clearing Corporation, clears and reconciles futures and options trades for various entities such as the Coffee, Sugar & Cocoa Exchange and the New York Cotton Exchange and its related units, including the New York Futures Exchange.[5] According to their web site, a clearinghouse offers "financial safeguards and transaction guarantees" that defend the "interests of the trading public, members of the Exchanges and the clearing members of the Clearing Corporation."[6]

Another organization, the Options Clearing Corporation (OCC), describes itself as the "world's largest equity options clearing organization." Equally owned by the American Stock Exchange, Chicago Board Options Exchange, International Securities Exchange, Pacific Exchange, and the Philadelphia Stock Exchange, the OCC is "the first clearinghouse to receive Standard & Poor's highest credit rating" of AAA with safeguards that include stringent membership requirements, cautious margin rules, and "a substantial clearing fund."[7]

The existence of an audit trail is cited by the Philadelphia Stock Exchange as a feature of its United Currency Options Market but could also characterize other exchange-traded products.[8] Notwithstanding the benefits of the clearinghouse, some institutions shy away from exchange-traded products for privacy reasons, citing the ease with which others can access information. This might occur if an institution believes that trade transparency moves prices against them, forcing prices up (down) in the case of a block purchase (sale). Exhibit 7.8 provides an overview of the differences.

Some exchanges list options to buy or sell securities or physical goods. Others offer options on futures. Exhibit 7.9 shows a sampling of the different types of options listed by U.S. exchanges. Non-U.S. exchanges likewise trade options. Regarding OTC options, they are traded the world over, subject to the willingness of financial institutions to make a market. Either way, endowments, foundations, and pensions have a wide array of option products from which to choose.

EXHIBIT 7.8 Exchange-Traded Versus Over-the-Counter Option Attributes

Attribute	Exchange-Traded Options	Over-the-Counter Options	Comments
Contract terms	Standardized	Customized	Contract specifications include information such as face value, underlying asset type and quality, strike price increments, expiration date, exercise style, settlement, and margin.
Credit risk	Clearinghouse stands behind every trade	Counterparty with performance obligation could default	Option buyers have no obligation to perform other than paying a fee for a call or put or combination option.
Liquidity	Varies	Varies	There is more than one way to measure liquidity. More liquid markets suggest less risk in being able to exit a market.
Margin	Not uniform across options	Typically none, but subject to requirements of individual broker	Depends on underlying asset and nature of the position (short, long, covered, uncovered)[a]
Price transparency	Exists	Not available	Detailed exchange data are available.
Regulation	Varies	Largely self-regulated	Regulation varies across countries.
Trading venue	Exchange	Private negotiation between two parties	Some financial institutions specialize in a particular type of option.

[a]To illustrate, the product specifications for interest rate options on various U.S. Treasury securities, listed on the Chicago Board Options Exchange, include a section on margin. It states that "Purchases of puts or calls with 9 months or less until expiration must be paid for in full" and that "Writers of uncovered puts or calls must deposit/maintain 100% of the option proceeds* plus 15% of the aggregate contract value (current index level × $100) minus the amount by which the option is out-of-the-money, if any, subject to a minimum for calls of option proceeds* plus 10% of the aggregate contract value and a minimum for puts of option proceeds plus 10% of the aggregate exercise price amount." See http://www.cboe.com.

EXHIBIT 7.9 Exchange-Traded Options

Exchange[a]	Sampling of Option Product Array
American Stock Exchange[1]	Equity options, index options, options on exchange-traded funds
Chicago Board Options Exchange[2]	Equity options, index options, options on exchange-traded funds, interest rate options
Philadelphia Stock Exchange[3]	Currency options, equity options, index options, options on exchange-traded funds

[a]There are numerous exchanges around the world that trade options besides the ones listed here.
Source: [1]American Stock Exchange web site, http://www.amex.com;
[2]Chicago Board Options Exchange web site, http://www.cboe.com;
[3]Philadelphia Stock Exchange web site, http://www.phlx.com.

Option analysis should include an evaluation of exchange-traded versus OTC alternatives. Beyond that, comparing options in general to futures or swaps is advised. A big difference is the asymmetry in expected payoff for options. This is discussed right after a brief review of how standardized options are quoted.

EXCHANGE-TRADED OPTION QUOTATION

Option quotes are easy to obtain. Some sources are more up to date than others. Anyone intending to trade must get a quote that reflects where the market maker is ready to buy or sell. A quote is normally specified by the underlying asset, whether the option is a put or call, the strike price, and month of expiration. Because conventions vary somewhat across options, understanding how to interpret quotes precedes any decision to act.

The following description looks at equity option quotes. Each quote consists of the ticker symbol of the underlying security, a code for expiration month, and a code for strike price. As shown in Exhibit 7.10, the expiration month codes directly indicate whether an option is a call or put. For example, the letter *A* notates a January call, whereas a put that expires in January bears the symbol *M*. Moreover, each code for strike price, shown in Exhibit 7.11, represents multiple dollar prices, making it necessary to know the current price of the underlying stock. Take the letter *M*, which can indicate a strike price of $65, $165, $265, $365, or $465. Its order in the rightmost position informs the reader that it represents a strike price and not that the option is a January put.

EXHIBIT 7.10 Expiration Month Codes

Month	Call	Put
January	A	M
February	B	N
March	C	O
April	D	P
May	E	Q
June	F	R
July	G	S
August	H	T
September	I	U
October	J	V
November	K	W
December	L	X

Source: The Options Industry Council web site, Learning Center. See http://www.888options.com. Copyright © 2003, The Options Clearing Corporation. Reprinted with permission.

EXHIBIT 7.11 Standard Strike U.S. Dollar Price Codes

Price	Price	Price	Price	Price	Code
5	105	205	305	405	A
10	110	210	310	410	B
15	115	215	315	415	C
20	120	220	320	420	D
25	125	225	325	425	E
30	130	230	330	430	F
35	135	235	335	435	G
40	140	240	340	440	H
45	145	245	345	445	I
50	150	250	350	450	J
55	155	255	355	455	K
60	160	260	360	460	L
65	165	265	365	465	M
70	170	270	370	470	N
75	175	275	375	475	O
80	180	280	380	480	P
85	185	285	385	485	Q
90	190	290	390	490	R
95	195	295	395	495	S
100	200	300	400	500	T

Source: The Options Industry Council web site. See http://www.888options.com. Copyright © 2003, The Options Clearing Corporation. Reprinted with permission.

Exhibit 7.12 shows quotes for IBM calls, notated as *IBMCN* and *IBMCO*. The leftmost characters are referred to as the option root. In this case, the root is the same as the ticker symbol for the common stock issued by the International Business Machines Corporation and listed on the New York Stock Exchange.[9] Moving from left to right, the *C* indicates a call that expires in March. The letter *N* reflects a $70 strike price, whereas the *O* for the second quote stands for a $75 strike price. IBM was trading at $79 per share at

EXHIBIT 7.12 Sample Stock Option Quotes for IBM

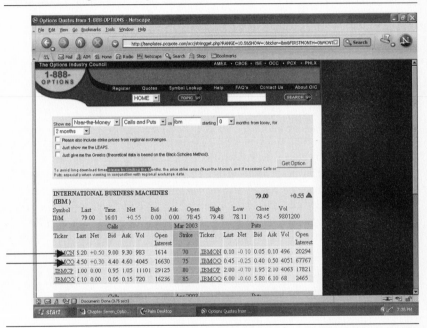

Note: The following disclaimer is shown on the web site for the Options Industry Council: "The trade and quote information is provided by PCQuote.com and NOT BY OCC. OCC makes no representation as to the validity of the information and this information should not be construed as a recommendation to purchase or sell a security, or to provide investment advice. Options involve risks and are not suitable for all investors.

"Prior to buying or selling an option, a person must receive a copy of Characteristics and Risks of Standardized Options. Market data provided by HyperFeed Technologies, Inc. Data is delayed 20 minutes unless otherwise noted, and is believed accurate but is not warranted or guaranteed by PCQuote.com, Inc. All times are Eastern United States."

Source: The Options Industry Council web site. See http://www.888options.com. Copyright © 2003, The Options Clearing Corporation. Reprinted with permission.

the time. Having properly identified the right option from the ticker symbol, the next step is to look at the quoted price. The quote signals the current value of the option, a critical part of assessing any strategy involving options.

MONEYNESS

Option value is broken down into two pieces: the moneyness of an option and its time value. When moneyness of an option is positive, the option is described as being *in the money*. The computation is straightforward, but depends on the option type and whether someone owns the option or has sold it to another party. Exhibit 7.13 provides a rundown of how to calculate and interpret this part of an option's value. Ignoring fees, all it takes is a simple calculation to assess the moneyness of an option. Applying some intuition also helps.

Call Example

Suppose an endowment fund wants to buy stock now but has to wait three months until its fundraising campaign has netted results. The investor can either wait 90 days or, fearing escalating prices, buy a three-month European call option on that stock today with a $100 strike price. Will the long call position be worth something at expiration? One way to tackle this question is to evaluate whether the option would be in the money. This concept is sometimes described as positive moneyness. Said another way, the call has intrinsic value.[10] Computationally, the call's moneyness is the bigger of zero dollars or a positive difference between the terminal stock price and the strike price.[11]

For any price above the $100 strike price, the endowment fund will find it worthwhile to exercise. Given a terminal price of $110 per share, the call

EXHIBIT 7.13 Moneyness by Option Type

Option Type	Position	Moneyness Definition[a]	Description
Call	Long	$\max(0, S_t - X)$	In the money: $S_t > X$
			At the money: $S_t = X$
	Short	$-\max(0, S_t - X)$	Out of the money: $S_t < X$
Put	Long	$\max(0, X - S_t)$	In the money: $S_t < X$
			At the money: $S_t = X$
			Out of the money: $S_t > X$
	Short	$-\max(0, X - S_t)$	

[a]S_t represents the price of the underlying asset at time t; X is the option's exercise price that is agreed upon at the inception of the trade; all transaction costs, including the option premium, are ignored here, moneyness is described from the option buyer's perspective; time value is ignored here, but would ordinarily be considered for European options.

EXHIBIT 7.14   Call Payoff Example

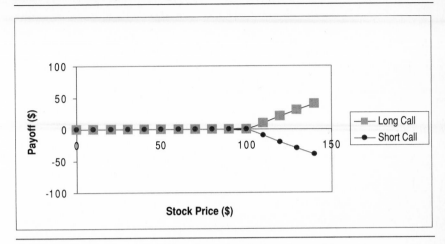

Note: Transaction costs, including the option fee, are ignored here.

buyer would never buy the stock directly. It makes much more sense to exercise the call and buy the stock at $100. In fact, ignoring fees, the call is in the money for any stock price more than $100. Notice that the opposite is true for the option seller.[12] In a zero-sum world, benefits that accrue to the call buyer come at the expense of the option writer. The call writer is obliged to sell stock for $100 in lieu of selling the stock in the market for $10 more. The $10 savings for the call buyer is the opportunity cost to the call writer.

A picture says a thousand words and the graph in Exhibit 7.14 is no exception. At higher prices, the call buyer enjoys unlimited upside potential. The downside is clearly limited to zero dollars. On the flip side, the call writer has a limited chance to gain. When fees are taken into account, the most the call writer can earn is the dollar amount paid by the call buyer to own the option. Rising stock prices spell disaster for the seller by exposing the party to unlimited loss. Of course, no one would write an option without expecting prices to fall because lower prices would invite the call buyer to forego exercise and buy more cheaply in the market.

Put Example

Assuming a strike price of $100, a European put buyer gains if the terminal market price of the underlying stock falls below $100. Suppose the trade price at the time of expiration is $90. The put buyer would exercise the put and sell the stock to the option writer at $100 per share, $10 more than the market affords. Ignoring fees, the put is in the money for

EXHIBIT 7.15   Put Payoff Example

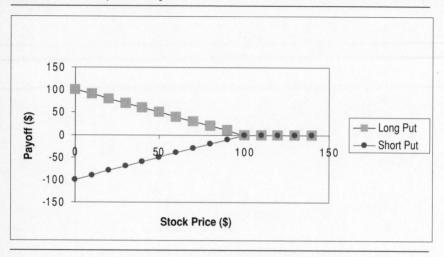

Note: Transaction costs, including the option fee, are ignored here.

any price lower than $100. Similar to calls, the put buyer profits while the put writer incurs a loss in the same amount by being forced to buy the stock at more than the prevailing market price. Exhibit 7.15 demonstrates the potential gain to the put buyer. Where the upside has no bound for a call buyer, a put buyer can never earn more than the strike price because the lowest possible stock price is zero dollars. Negative prices make no sense.

Factoring in Fees: Call Example

The graphs shown in Exhibits 7.14 and 7.15 portray the asymmetry in possible payoffs that is a fundamental characteristic of options. This is easier to understand when fees are considered because any option buyer must pay some amount to purchase a call or put. Suppose that the aforementioned call costs $10 to buy. How does this impact the benefits of owning the call? The call buyer will still be happy when stock prices rise above $100, but the increase should be large enough to offset the $10 fee. Exhibits 7.16 and 7.17 shed some light on the impact of the fee. First, the most the call buyer can ever lose is the $10 fee. Second, the maximum gain to the call seller is the $10 fee. In stark contrast, the call buyer enjoys an unlimited profit potential once the stock price exceeds the sum of the strike price and the fee. This means that the call seller stands to lose considerably in an upward-moving market. The magnitude of the net call (put) payoff depends on variables such as the direction of market moves, fees paid, option valuation approach,

EXHIBIT 7.16   Call Profit and Loss Example

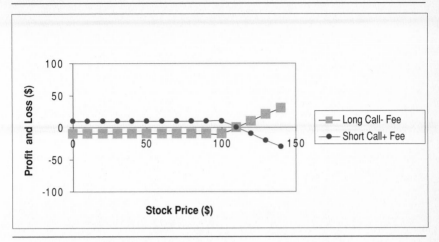

Note: Transaction costs other than the option fee are ignored here.

taxes, and the relationship between the strike price and the price of the underlying asset. The payoff for a call is not expected to mirror the payoff for a put with the same strike price, identical time to maturity, and a common underlying asset.

Factoring in Fees: Put Example

Exhibits 7.18 and 7.19 tell the story for a put. Similar to the case of the call, the risk-reward trade-off for the put buyer and seller is disproportionate across stock prices. The put buyer will never lose more than the fee paid so there is a limited loss. The put seller can never earn more than the fee; therefore, the upside is likewise limited. Slightly different from the case of the call, the most the put buyer can ever receive is the strike price less the fee and this would occur when the stock falls to a price of zero dollars. In the $100 strike example, the put buyer would exercise when the stock is worthless and reap a gain of $100 less the $10 fee, or a net amount equal to $90. In a zero-sum world, this is the seller's maximum loss.

Comparing Position Payoffs

Exhibit 7.20 summarizes the payoffs from the perspective of the four basic positions, assuming a fee is paid by the buyer to the option seller. Only the option position has been discussed so far. Related transactions are ignored. This is unrealistic but simplifies the learning process. Once the decision to

EXHIBIT 7.17 Call Economics

Position	Profit and Loss Computation	Profit and Loss Categories[a]	Example
Long	$\max (0, S_t - X) - \text{fee}$	Profit: $(S_t - X) - \text{fee}$, where $S_t > (X + \text{fee})$ Zero profit: $(S_t - X) - \text{fee} = 0$, where $S_t = X + \text{fee}$ Loss: $\$0 - \text{fee}$, where $(S_t < X)$ and call is out of the money	$\$120\ S_t > (\$100\ \text{strike} + \$10\ \text{fee}) \rightarrow \$10$ profit (Call buyer exercises at \$100 or \$20 less than the market price, but savings is reduced by \$10 fee) $\$110\ S_t = \$100\ \text{strike} + \$10\ \text{fee} \rightarrow \$0$ profit $\$90\ S_t < \$100\ \text{strike} \rightarrow \$10$ loss (Call expires worthless because call buyer is better off buying stock at \$90 in the market, but fee has still been paid)
Short	$-\max (0, S_t - X) + \text{fee}$	Loss: $-(S_t - X) + \text{fee}$, where $S_t > (X + \text{fee})$ Zero profit: $(S_t - X) - \text{fee} = 0$, where $S_t = X + \text{fee}$ Profit: $\$0 + \text{fee}$, where $(S_t < X)$ and call is out of the money	$\$120\ S_t > (\$100\ \text{strike} + \$10\ \text{fee}) \rightarrow \$10$ loss (Call buyer exercises call at \$100, call seller must sell stock to call buyer at \$100 instead of \$120 market price, and difference of \$20 is offset by call seller's fee income of \$10) $\$110\ S_t = \$100\ \text{strike} + \$10\ \text{fee} \rightarrow \$0$ profit $\$90\ S_t < \$100\ \text{strike} \rightarrow \$10$ profit (Call expires worthless because call buyer is better off buying stock at \$90 in the market, call seller is off the hook to sell stock but still pockets the fee of \$10)

[a]S_t represents the price of the underlying asset at time t; X is the option's exercise price that is agreed upon at the inception of the trade; all transaction costs other than the option premium are ignored; and all examples assume a strike price of \$100 and an option fee of \$10.

EXHIBIT 7.18 Put Profit and Loss Example

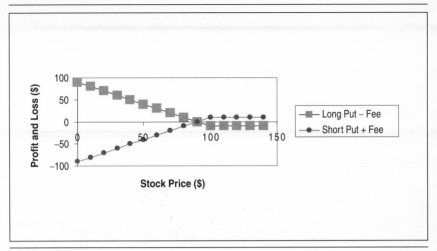

Note: Transaction costs other than the option fee are ignored here.

use options is made, evaluating the option as part of the bigger picture makes sense.

OPTION COMBINATIONS AND EXAMPLES

Options can be used to hedge against adverse changes in market movements, transform an exposure to something more suitable, or act on an expectation about the future. When combined with an investment, the resulting position constitutes a portfolio and is evaluated accordingly. The universe of possibilities is limitless given the many types of asset classes and various subgroups, as well as the numerous ways to use options.

Covered Call Strategy

One popular strategy, the covered call, is used by a variety of institutional investors and combines a short call with a long stock position. In fact, according to the Options Industry Council, the covered call strategy is "perhaps the most common option strategy implemented by option investors."[13] In April 2002, the Chicago Board Options Exchange announced the Buy-Write Monthly Index[SM], a "passive total return index based on selling the near-term, near-the-money S&P 500 Index (SPX) call option against the S&P 500 stock index portfolio each month" and is described as "the first major benchmark for Buy-Write options performance."[14] Exhibit 7.21 provides examples of covered call users.[15]

EXHIBIT 7.19 Put Economics

Position	Profit and Loss Computation	Profit and Loss Categories[a]	Example
Long	$\max(0, X - S_t) - \text{fee}$	Profit: $(X - S_t) - \text{fee}$, where $(S_t + \text{fee}) < X$	$(\$80\ S_t + \$10\ \text{fee}) < \$100$ strike $\rightarrow \$10$ profit (Put buyer sells at \$100 or \$20 more than market price, but profit is reduced by \$10 fee paid)
		Zero profit: $(X - S_t) - \text{fee} = \$0$, where $S_t = (X + \text{fee})$	$\$90\ S_t = (\$100$ strike $- \$10$ fee$) \rightarrow \$0$ profit
		Loss: $\$0 - \text{fee}$, where $(S_t \geq X)$ and put is out of the money	$\$110\ S_t > \$100$ strike $\rightarrow \$10$ loss (Put expires worthless because put buyer is better off selling stock at \$110 in the market, but \$10 fee has already been paid)
Short	$-\max(0, X - S_t) + \text{fee}$	Loss: $-(X - S_t) + \text{fee}$, where $(S_t + \text{fee}) < X$	$(\$80\ S_t + \$10\ \text{fee}) < \$100$ strike $\rightarrow \$10$ loss (Put buyer sells at \$100, put seller must buy stock from put buyer at \$100 instead of \$80 market price, and overpayment of \$20 is reduced by put seller's fee income of \$10)
		Zero profit: $(X - S_t) - \text{fee} = \$0$, where $S_t = (X + \text{fee})$	$\$90\ S_t = (\$100$ strike $- \$10$ fee$) \rightarrow \$0$ profit
		Profit: $\$0 + \text{fee}$, where $(S_t \geq X)$ and put is out of the money	$\$110\ S_t > \$100$ strike $\rightarrow \$10$ profit (Put expires worthless because put buyer is better off selling stock at \$110 in the market, but \$10 fee has already been pocketed)

[a]S_t represents the price of the underlying asset at time t; X is the option's exercise price that is agreed upon at the inception of the trade; all transaction costs other than the option premium are ignored; and all examples assume a strike price of \$100 and an option fee of \$10.

EXHIBIT 7.20 Summary of Profit Potential by Option Type

Position	Loss Potential	Gain Potential
Long call	Limited to fee paid for call	Unlimited
Short call	Unlimited	Limited to fee earned for call
Long put	Limited to fee paid for call	Equal to the strike price less fee paid (because stock prices cannot fall below $0)
Short put	Equal to the strike price less fee earned (because stock prices cannot fall below $0)	Limited to fee earned for put

Consider a private foundation with a long position in stock it bought awhile ago at $50 per share. The investment team is rather sure that stock prices are unlikely to move too far in either direction, but have a bias toward rising prices, if anything. Writing a call on the foundation's long stock position provides one way to make use of this belief.

Assume a $100 strike price and a $10 call premium. To keep things simple, further assume that the underlying asset is identical to the foundation's holdings. If prices rise, three things happen. First, the value of the foundation's stock position increases. Second, the call will be profitable for the buyer for any price greater than $110 per share, the sum of the strike price and the option's cost to the buyer. When "exercise" occurs, the foundation will sell its stock to the call buyer at the strike price. Third, the foundation's net gain is capped at an amount equal to the income earned from having sold the call less the difference between the strike price and the current stock purchase price, plus the difference between the current versus original stock purchase price. In this case, the maximum gain is $60.

Breaking out each component separately, as shown in Exhibit 7.22, helps understand the payoff. At point A, when the stock is worthless, the foundation incurs a loss of $40. Where does this come from? Although the long stock position has decreased in value by $50, the buyer will not exercise the call but instead purchase stock outright for a price of $10. The foundation pockets the $10 from writing the call, with the net effect being a reduced loss in its overall position. Point B is the break-even point, the price at which the call writer has a zero profit. At $40 per share, the stock that was purchased at $50 has decreased in value by $10. This completely offsets the $10 fee that belongs to the foundation for having sold the call to another organization. Moreover, at $40 per share, the call buyer will forfeit its right to exercise and will instead buy stock at $40 versus the $100 strike price. At point C, when the stock trades at $100, the long stock position has increased by $50. If the at-the-money call is exercised, the option

EXHIBIT 7.21 Some Statements about Use of Covered Calls

Institutional Investor	Document Excerpt	Source
The Kresge Foundation	At December 31, 2000, the Foundation held hedge contracts on a portion of its U.S. equity holdings. These contracts created an eighteen month collar, which utilizes S&P 500 Index options, has a put strike price at 1,275, a call strike price at 1,700 and a notional value of $350,000,000.	The Kresge Foundation 2000 Annual Report
The Endowment and Restricted Funds of Christ Church, United Methodist	The investment managers shall have full discretionary authority in the selection and retention of investments, subject to law and the statement of investment policy as it may be amended from time to time and subject to the following restrictions: 1. Securities may not be purchased on margin. 2. Securities may not be sold short. 3. Options (e.g. puts, calls) may not be sold short. Options use is limited to covered call writing, a conservative strategy.	Sample Endowment and Investment Policy, dated April 10, 2000. Copyright © 2000, United Methodist Foundation of New England

EXHIBIT 7.22 Evaluating a Covered Call[a]

Point	Stock Price ($)	Change in Value of Long Stock Position ($)	Value of Short Call Position, Including Fee ($)	Total Value ($)	Comments
A	0	−50	10	−40	The stock is worthless and the call is not exercised. The foundation's loss is offset by the $10 call fee.
	20	−30	10	−20	
B	40	−10	10	0	The $10 stock loss is completely offset by the $10 call fee. The foundation's net portfolio change is $0.
	60	10	10	20	
	80	30	10	40	
C	100	50	10	60	The call has intrinsic value for any price above the $100 strike price. The foundation will never earn more than $60.[b]
	120	70	−10	60	
	140	90	−30	60	
	160	110	−50	60	

[a]Assume a strike price of $100, a call fee of $10, and a stock purchase price of $50.

[b]The break-even price from the call buyer's perspective is $110, that is, the $100 strike price plus the $10 option cost. This breakeven does not reflect any related positions the call buyer may have.

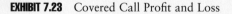

EXHIBIT 7.23   Covered Call Profit and Loss

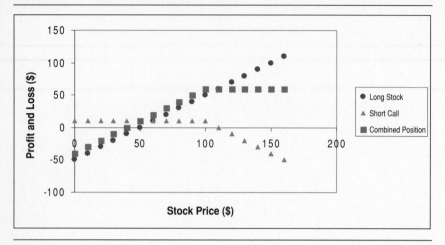

Note: Assume a strike price of $100, a call fee of $10, and a stock purchase price of $50.

writer ends up selling stock at the same price as it would to any other market participant and the call has zero intrinsic value. In any event, the call writer pockets the $10 premium, generating a net gain of $60 for the covered call.

The graph in Exhibit 7.23 illustrates the payoff for the covered call and its two component positions. Owning the stock exposes the investor to more risk, but better upside potential. Writing a call offers some protection as stock prices fall. The precise amount of risk reduction is determined by the initial purchase price of stock, the call's strike price, and the call premium. A covered call makes little sense if an investor anticipates higher stock prices, but could be beneficial if an investor seeks protection against falling prices or believes the strategy can reduce the variability of returns.

Determining Option Combination Payoffs

For every option strategy, there is a set of payoffs whereby each payoff is tied to the prevailing price of the underlying stock.[16] The best way to evaluate the net payoff at a given stock price is simply to evaluate each part of the strategy, one piece at a time. Exhibit 7.24 shows the payoff for a collection of common option strategies. Notice that the payoff for the option component(s) is nothing more than the intrinsic value of the option at a given stock price and point in time. Little has been said about time value so far, other than the fact that it is added to intrinsic value to obtain the total value of an option. An option may have zero intrinsic value but still be worth

EXHIBIT 7.24 Option Strategy Payoffs

Strategy	Components	Generalized Payoff Formula for Strategy
Covered call	Long stock PLUS short call	(stock price at time t − purchase price) PLUS − max [0, (stock price at time t − strike price)] + call fee
Portfolio insurance	Long stock PLUS long put	(stock price at time t − purchase price) PLUS max [0, (strike price − stock price at time t)] − put fee
Long straddle	Long call PLUS long put with same expiration and same strike price	max [0, (stock price at time t − strike price)] − call fee PLUS max [0, (strike price − stock price at time t)] − put fee

something as long as time remains until expiration. Any institution embarking on a plan to use options is best served by first learning about the impact of time, dividends, transaction costs, and taxes on option value and exercise (to the extent that flexibility in exercise exists).

Exhibit 7.25 provides an example of this approach for a strategy known as a long straddle. Combining a long position in both a call and a put, each with the same expiration date and strike price, the net payoff is simply the sum of the payoff of each option position. Assume a stock price of $120, a call (and put) strike price of $100, a call fee of $7 and a put fee of $3. The intrinsic value of the call is $20, but a fee of $7, reduces the payoff to $13. The put has no value because an investor is better off by selling stock at the higher market price rather than exercising at $100. However, the $3 is a sunk cost so the payoff to the put is a loss equal to the fee amount. Taken together, the net profit of the long straddle is $10. This strategy can be highly profitable when stock prices rise or fall by a large amount relative to the strike price.

Some strategies are quite complex because they combine many options with different terms. Some strategies mix options and individual securities (or portfolios of securities), each with its own payoff pattern. As with simpler transactions, the key is to look at each element individually (sound familiar?) before adding together the results.

HEDGING WITH OPTIONS

Options can be used to hedge nearly any type of exposure including stocks, bonds, and foreign currencies. For example, a U.S. pension fund with part of its asset allocation dedicated to sovereign bonds might hedge the currency portion if its goal is exposure to the foreign country issuer alone and not to movements in foreign exchange rates. Alternatively, an expectation of a stronger U.S. dollar drives the need to hedge, something that can be done in one of several ways.

Without a hedge, an appreciating U.S. dollar forces down the value of foreign currency interest payments. It becomes much more expensive to sell foreign currency and buy U.S. dollars. One way to hedge involves the purchase of a put that entitles the pension fund to sell foreign currency later but at today's prices. Whether this makes sense depends on the cost of the option, expectations about foreign currency movements, and the pension fund's required rate of return.

Exhibit 7.26 lists some of the issues associated with hedging with options. Unlike futures, a long position in an option typically entails an upfront fee, payable to the seller. Some organizations find it difficult to justify a large outlay of cash, choosing another derivative instrument instead or an option combination that pays for itself, sometimes referred to as a zero premium

EXHIBIT 7.25 Long Straddle Payoff Example[a]

Payoff of Long Call Component	Payoff of Long Put Component	Total
max [0, (stock price at time t − strike price)] − call fee	max [0, (strike price − stock price at time t)] − put fee	
max [0, ($120 − $100)] − $7 ↓	max[0, ($100 − $120)] − $3 ↓	
↓ $13	↓ −$3	$10

[a]Assume a strike price of $100 for both the call and the put, a call fee of $7, and a put fee of $3.

EXHIBIT 7.26 Hedging with Options Checklist

When to Take Action	What to Do
Before the hedge	1. Determine whether the investment policy permits use of options.
	2. If allowed, identify considerations outlined in the investment policy statement, including the measurement and reporting of risk. Many investment policies specifically outlaw the selling of options.
	3. Write specific procedures for use of options, if not done already.
	4. Identify the exact risk (nature and amount) to be hedged.
	5. Identify the best options contract or OTC instrument to use.
	6. Evaluate the hedge ratio to determine the size of the initial trade, using an appropriate methodology.
	7. Open a brokerage account to transact option trades.
	8. Assign responsibilities to staff, including fee-based money transfers, and train staff.
During the hedge	1. Execute the initial hedge and pay the upfront fee, if applicable.
	2. Evaluate hedge effectiveness on prespecified dates.
	3. Rebalance, if necessary (i.e., option price sensitivities changes or the underlying exposure shrinks or grows).
	4. Evaluate whether early exercise of the option makes sense.
	5. Generate management reports for accounting, tax, and financial analysis use.
After the hedge	1. Determine overall efficacy of the hedge vis-à-vis investment goals.
	2. Identify ways to improve options-related hedging procedures for later transactions.

transaction. Similar to the idea of basis for futures, the relationship between the option and the exposure being hedged is important and requires some knowledge about how options are priced.

OPTION VALUATION

Option values change constantly. Recognizing why and how they change is a necessary part of risk assessment. The Black-Scholes (B-S) option pricing model is probably the most famous of all and merits a brief overview.[17]

B-S Option Pricing Model

The 1997 Nobel Prize in Economics was awarded to Robert C. Merton and Myron S. Scholes for their seminal research on option valuation, acknowledging the vast reach of their work on investors everywhere. Because the Nobel Prize is not awarded posthumously, Fischer Black, a third pioneer in this area, was ineligible although people worldwide continue to recognize his contributions.[18,19] Used to price European calls or puts on a nondividend-paying asset, the B-S model is now a mainstay of finance.

The B-S model makes some simplifying assumptions such as zero transaction costs, restricted short-selling of the underlying asset, constant volatility, and a constant risk-free rate of return. There are times when these restrictions make the B-S model less than ideal. Nevertheless, the model is frequently used. One application is the valuation of stock options for tax purposes. Revenue Procedure 2002-13 allows a taxpayer to "value a compensatory stock option using any valuation method that is consistent with generally accepted accounting principles (such as FAS 123)," adding that "the safe harbor valuation method provided by this revenue procedure is based on the Black-Scholes model."[20]

The B-S model requires five main inputs. Besides stock price, strike price, time to maturity, and risk-free interest rate, the model requires an estimate of historical volatility. Exhibit 7.27 illustrates the relationship between volatility and the value of an at-the-money European call on a stock that currently trades for $50 per share. The volatility inputs represent the midpoint of ranges that are suggested for tax purposes.[21] Notice that the value of the call rises, although not proportionately, with the volatility level. A 15 percent level of volatility translates into a call price of $2.49. In

EXHIBIT 7.27 Call Value and Volatility

Volatility Category	Volatility Range	Volatility Midpoint	Option Value
Low	0% to 30%	15%	$2.49
Medium	30% to 70%	50%	$7.34
High	>70%	85%	$12.10

Notes:
1. Assume a $50 stock price.
2. Assume a $50 strike price.
3. Assume a three percent per annum risk-free rate.
4. Assume a six month time to expiration.
5. Volatility is measured in standard deviation form.
Source: Susan M. Mangiero, "Model Risk and Valuation," *Valuation Strategies,* Vol. 6, No. 4 (March–April 2003), Exhibit 4, Volatility Scenarios, p. 38. Copyright © 2003, Thomson/RIA. Reprinted with permission. All rights reserved.

EXHIBIT 7.28 Option Value Determinants

Increase in Variable	European Call Value	European Put Value
Stock price	Increases	Decreases
Strike price	Decreases	Increases
Risk-free interest rate	Increases	Decreases
Time to maturity	Increases	Increases
Volatility	Increases	Increases

contrast, a volatility of 50 percent nearly triples the price of the call. Although not shown here, European put values likewise rise with higher volatility. Sometimes a market price for a specified option is plugged into the B-S equation to back into volatility as a gauge of investor sentiment about the underlying stock.

Call and put option values do not always respond to changes in inputs in the same way, as shown in Exhibit 7.28. For example, a rise in stock prices, holding everything else constant, increases the value of a call, while doing just the opposite for a put. Intuitively, this makes sense. That is, rising stock prices make it more expensive to buy a stock outright. An investor who owns a put, however, is more inclined to sell stock at a higher market price rather than exercise the option. The impact of higher interest rates is less intuitive. The call is more attractive to an investor when the cost of financing a purchase outright increases. The opposite is true for the owner of a put. The section that follows briefly describes a more formal approach to understanding the impact of changes in model inputs on the price of a call (put).

The discussion on the B-S model so far has been focused on stocks. In practice, however, the B-S option pricing model is sometimes used for warrants, bonds, foreign currencies, or commodities after adjustments are made to reflect the limitations of its original assumptions. Whether its popularity and widespread use continues is far from an academic question. Currently, many people default to the Black-Scholes model because it is relatively well understood and computationally easy to utilize. Regulatory efforts will likely force change by encouraging more suitable models for some instruments such as employee stock options. They do not trade continuously in public markets, thereby violating a key assumption of the Black-Scholes model.

Option Greeks

The term *Greeks* is a fancy way of describing the metrics that show how the value of an option changes as one factor is permitted to increase (or fall) while leaving everything else intact. Familiarity with what each measure represents and expectations about their magnitude are essential parts of the risk management process when options are used. An option's *delta* measures price sensitivity of the option as the price of the underlying asset changes. The rate of change in the delta is referred to as the option's *gamma*. Taken together, they are often used to ensure that an option-based hedge is as effective as possible.

The impact of a change in volatility on the price of an option is referred to as *vega* but also goes by the name of *kappa*. *Theta* looks as the effect of time on the price of an option. Theta is not the same as time value. *Rho* examines the influence of the risk-free interest rate level. More sophisticated risk managers also examine the interplay among the Greeks as a way to better understand what drives the value of an option in a dynamic world where many things change at once.

Entire books are written just about options because there is so much to say. They are an important part of the investment process and are unlikely to lose their appeal any time soon. Yet, this does not let an institutional investor off the hook in terms of understanding how the risk-return trade-off changes with their use. The inherent leverage associated with options makes them a powerful, but potentially dangerous, tool if not used properly.

SUMMARY

1. Options are characterized by their exercise features. A European option is exercised at a single point in time, whereas an American option can be exercised over a specified period.
2. Both OTC and exchange-traded options exist for various asset classes such as stocks, bonds, currencies, indexes, and commodities.
3. An option buyer has no obligation to perform. This is the opposite for option sellers who must perform if the option buyer chooses to exercise.
4. Intrinsic value looks at the relationship between the exercise price and the price of the underlying asset. An in-the-money option has positive intrinsic value.[22]
5. The B-S model is a popular approach to determining the value of a European stock option that pays zero dividends.
6. Options can be used to hedge market risk. Option Greeks are used to evaluate a hedge by quantifying how the value of an option changes as one variable at a time is permitted to increase or decrease.

CHAPTER 8

Swaps

The cautious seldom err.

—Confucius

BACKGROUND

Swaps represent the third major class of derivative instruments. Similar to futures and options, swaps represent terms agreed upon today for later action.[1] Swaps are typically structured as a series of cash flow exchanges. General characteristics of swaps are shown in Exhibit 8.1.

Flexibility, speed of execution, and relatively good liquidity explain their popularity. Swaps can be used to accomplish a variety of things, including (1) hedging to lower currency, equity, interest rate, or default risk; (2) transformation of one exposure into another; (3) yield enhancement; and (4) replication of cash flows not otherwise available or available under less favorable terms. Swaps can be constructed to cover long periods of time. Liquidity in the secondary markets is seldom an issue for the more traditional types of swaps. The transaction size ranges from small to very large although swaps below several million dollars are rare.

EXHIBIT 8.1 General Characteristics of Swaps

Legal contract separate from related investment or financing
Exchange of cash flows
Periodic settlements
No principal exchange with interest rate swaps
Standardized documentation
Maturity typically varies from 2 years to 10 years
Benchmark varies
Can be structured in different currencies
Risk exposure is often a fraction of face value
No margin requirements
Involves counterparty default risk

EXHIBIT 8.2 Swaps Notional Amounts Outstanding (Billions of U.S. dollars)

Category	2000 June	2000 December	2001 June	2001 December	2002 June
Currency	2,605	3,194	3,832	3,942	4,220
Interest rate	47,993	48,768	51,407	58,897	68,274
Total	50,598	51,962	55,239	62,839	72,494

Source: BIS Quarterly Review, December 2002. Copyright © 2002, Bank for International Settlements. Reprinted with permission.

As shown in Exhibit 8.2, market size is considerable with interest rate and currency swaps recently estimated at $72.494 trillion in terms of notional amounts outstanding. (Note that the estimated size of the market varies with respect to how size is measured.) In comparison, seasonally adjusted after-tax corporate profits were recently estimated at $473.3 billion, a number that pales in comparison to the swap market notional outstanding amount.[2]

BASIC SWAP STRUCTURE

Swap structure depends on the type of swap. Probably the most basic form is the fixed-to-floating interest rate swap. It can be denominated in any currency, including the U.S. dollar. The face value is referred to as the notional principal amount, reflecting the fact that principal is not exchanged.[3] The notional principal amount is used to determine the periodic cash flows exchanged on prespecified dates, usually at the end of every quarter or half-year.

At its simplest, the interest rate swap is a separate legal contract between two counterparties, the Fixed Rate Payer and the Floating Rate Payer.[4, 5] However, a swap is often combined with some type of investment or funding vehicle. When this happens, the entire transaction should be analyzed by looking at the economics associated with the swap and the related asset or liability.

As shown in Exhibit 8.3, the "plain vanilla" fixed-to-floating swap involves cash flows moving in both directions, reflecting the concept of interest exchange. Cash flow amounts are easy to compute, as long as information

EXHIBIT 8.3 Basic Swap Structure

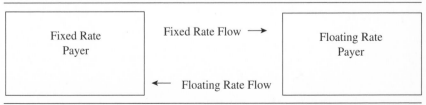

EXHIBIT 8.4 Cash Flow Determination[a]

Period	Fixed Rate Amount	Floating Rate Amount	Difference	Direction of Difference
One	$299,178[b]	$202,222[c]	$96,956	Payment to Floating Rate Payer by Fixed Rate Payer
Two	$300,822[d]	$213,500[e]	$87,321	Payment to Floating Rate Payer by Fixed Rate Payer

[a]Assumptions:
1. Annual swap fixed rate of 6 percent
2. First period LIBOR rate of 4 percent
3. Second period LIBOR rate of 4.2 percent
4. First period day count of 182 days
5. Second period day count of 183 days
6. $10 million notional principal amount
7. Day count of 360 days for LIBOR
8. Day count of 365 days for the fixed rate
[b]$10,000,000 times 0.06 times (182/365).
[c]$10,000,000 times 0.04 times (182/360).
[d]$10,000,000 times 0.06 times (183/365).
[e]$10,000,000 times 0.042 times (183/360).

about notional principal amount, annual swap rate, days between settlement period, and day count convention is available. As shown in Exhibit 8.4, the Fixed Rate Payer is obliged to pay an amount equal to the notional principal amount times the annual fixed swap rate, adjusted for time. In contrast, the Floating Rate Payer makes a payment equal to the notional principal amount times the relevant floating rate, adjusted for settlement period and day count.

Assuming a $10 million notional principal amount and an annual fixed swap rate of 6 percent, the Fixed Rate Payer is obliged to pay $299,178 to the Floating Rate Payer, also known as the Fixed Rate Receiver. This represents a half-year payment when there are 182 days in the first period, assuming a 365-day year. The Floating Rate Payer has a responsibility to pay out $202,222, the half-year interest for a 182-day period and based on a 360-day year. A floating rate of 4 percent is assumed and reflects the prevailing London Interbank Offer Rate (LIBOR) at the beginning of the first half-year period.[6] The floating rate base will be reset for each of the subsequent settlement periods.

Many times, the two payments are netted against each other in accordance with a master agreement. The master agreement is signed before trades begin and lays out general terms. Verification that accompanies an actual swap trade will refer back to the master agreement for many of the terms that would otherwise have to be part of the posttrade confirmation.[7]

In the case of netting, counterparties can reduce costs such as bank wire fees because only one party makes a payment on any given date. Which counterparty pays on each settlement date depends on the relationship between the fixed rate and the new floating rate, something not known at the outset of the trade. Reducing default risk is another benefit of netting, and arguably a more important factor. As noted by Federal Reserve Bank Chairman Alan Greenspan,

> *counterparty risk management has been materially assisted by the widespread use of master agreements for derivatives transactions. In the event of a counterparty default, such agreements permit the termination of all transactions with that counterparty and the netting of resulting gains and losses. Master agreements have been around for years. More recently, big players are seeking legislative support to ensure that an agreement to net is legally enforceable. Data reported by U.S. banks indicate that, on average, netting now reduces counterparty exposures by almost three-fourths.[8]*

Collateralizing estimated default risk is another way to reduce some of the uncertainty associated with a swap. This assumes that high quality collateral is available. Although beneficial, it is difficult—perhaps impossible—to get collateral of any value if a counterparty is already in trouble.

> *The practice of tying the size of thresholds and margin requirements to credit ratings exposes a counterparty to extraordinary demands for collateral if its rating is downgraded. Collateral demands arising from rating downgrades may be especially costly to meet because a downgrade would reduce the availability of funding and increase its costs at the same time.[9]*

Even though far from perfect, both collateralization and netting provide some protection in the event of counterparty nonperformance.

SWAP APPLICATIONS

Enhancing Returns

Interest rate swaps have multiple applications, including yield enhancement. The goal is to earn a higher return than is otherwise available for the given risk. Consider the case of an endowment fund that aims to diversify abroad by investing in sovereign bonds. Any chance to exceed its five and one-half percent annual return goal is attractive as long as incremental risk does not exceed policy levels.

As shown in Exhibit 8.5, the combined transaction has several legs. The endowment fund assumes the risk of default associated with buying the sovereign-issued floating-rate note, something it agrees to do anyhow when it apportions funds to this asset class.[10] Unlike a fixed coupon bond, the purchase of a floating-rate note means that the endowment fund earns interest tied to LIBOR. As market conditions change, LIBOR changes and the endowment fund may or may not meet its annual return target of five and one-half percent. The use of the swap mitigates the variable return risk, but introduces another risk—namely, the risk of counterparty default. In the event that the other swap counterparty cannot fulfill its obligations, the endowment fund is left with a variable rate note and the risk that LIBOR may decline, leading to subpar returns vis-à-vis its target. This swap-related risk must be considered before committing to the combined note–swap trade.

Done properly, the interest from the note should flow straight through to the swap counterparty on the same dates.[11] Exhibit 8.6 breaks down the cash flows for the first several six-month periods into constituent parts.[12] The column labeled "Net Cash Flow to Endowment Fund" reflects the economic effect of combining the note investment with the swap. In this example, the six percent swap fixed rate earned by the endowment fund exceeds its five and one-half percent target by 50 basis points. As long as the likelihood of swap counterparty default is considered low, a 50 basis points pickup is hard to turn down.[13] Transaction costs are ignored here, but should

EXHIBIT 8.5   Investment-Related Interest Swap Structure

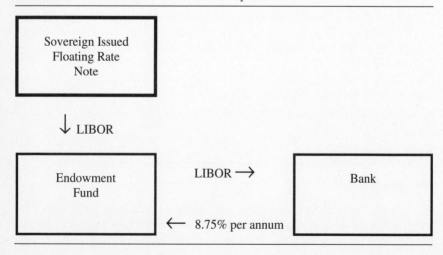

EXHIBIT 8.6 Investment Swap Cash Flows[a]

Period	Swap Fixed Rate Amount Paid to Endowment Fund	Swap Floating Rate Amount Paid by Endowment Fund	Floating Rate Note Proceeds Paid to Endowment Fund	Net Cash Flow to Endowment Fund	Fixed Rate Target (5.5 Percent)	Dollar Bonus to Endowment Fund
One	$299,178[b]	$202,222[c]	$202,222	$299,178	$274,247[d]	$24,931
Two	$300,822[e]	$213,500[f]	$213,500	$300,822	$275,753[g]	$25,069

[a]Assumptions:
1. Annual swap fixed rate of 6.0 percent
2. First period LIBOR rate of 4.0 percent
3. Second period LIBOR rate of 4.20 percent
4. First period day count of 182 days
5. Second period day count of 183 days
6. $10 million swap notional principal amount
7. $10 million face value of floating rate note investment
8. Day count of 360 days for LIBOR
9. Day count of 365 days for the fixed rate

[b]$10,000,000 × 0.06 × (182/365).
[c]$10,000,000 × 0.04 × (182/360).
[d]$10,000,000 × 0.055 × (182/365).
[e]$10,000,000 × 0.06 × (183/365).
[f]$10,000,000 × 0.042 × (183/360).
[g]$10,000,000 × 0.55 × (183/365).

125

always be part of the analysis. Sometimes they are quite low, especially for a swap with a common structure. Frequently, transaction costs are built into the quoted swap price.

Yield enhancement can occur other ways. Suppose instead that a pension fund buys a fixed rate asset. Using an interest rate swap, it converts the bond's income stream into a return tied to LIBOR or some other variable rate benchmark. For the right security, the net effect is a higher return above the floating rate benchmark with the swap than without it. Once again, the swap counterparty risk cannot be ignored.[14]

Asset Transformation

Swaps offer a world of new possibilities to investors. Besides yield enhancement, swaps offer the chance to transform cash flows, synthesize ownership, or transfer credit risk. Capital restrictions, size minimums, market illiquidity, pricing inefficiencies, and limited investment choices are just a few of the reasons that motivate the use of swaps. A popular vehicle is the total return swap that takes potential capital appreciation (or loss) into account. As described in Exhibit 8.7, the swap counterparty known as the Total Return Receiver receives all interim cash flows on a reference security and then pays a reference rate such as LIBOR. When the swap matures, the

EXHIBIT 8.7   Description of a Total Return Swap

During the life of the swap, the *purchaser* (total return receiver) receives all the cash flows on the reference asset from the seller. In exchange the purchaser pays the reference rate (typically LIBOR) plus or minus an agreed spread to the seller. At maturity of the swap, the counterparties revalue the reference asset. If it has appreciated, the *seller* of the TRS pays the appreciation to the purchaser; if it has depreciated, the purchaser pays the depreciation to the seller. Since the purchaser of the TRS receives all of the cash flows and benefits (losses) if the value of the reference asset rises (falls), the purchaser is synthetically 'long' the underlying reference asset during the life of the swap.

A key element of the total return swap is that both market risk and credit risk are transferred. It does not matter whether the asset depreciates in value because the borrower's credit quality declines, credit spreads widen, or underlying interest rates increase. If there is a default on the underlying asset during the life of the TRS, the parties will terminate the swap and make a final payment. Either the TRS will be cash settled, in which case the asset is market to market, or physically settled, in which case the seller delivers the defaulted asset to the purchaser against receipt of the reference asset's price at origination of the swap.

Source: Charles Smithson and Gregory Hayt, "Credit Derivatives: The Basics," *The Journal of Lending & Credit Risk Management,* February 2000 pp. 58–60. Reprinted with permission.

Total Rate Receiver benefits (or loses), depending on whether the asset has appreciated or lost value. The result is similar to owning the reference asset without having to pay for it outright. This might occur if investment funds are limited or in the case of purchase restrictions.

Currency swaps permit transformation from one currency to another. Unlike interest rate swaps, principal is exchanged at the outset of the trade and then again upon maturity. A variation is the combination currency and interest rate swap that includes interim cash flow exchanges in specified currencies.

A relative newcomer, the credit default swap, accounts for about $2 trillion in notional amounts outstanding.[15] As described by the Bank for International Settlements, "in a credit default swap, one counterparty (the 'protection seller') agrees to compensate another counterparty (the 'protection buyer') if a particular company or sovereign (the 'reference entity') experiences one or more defined credit events. The protection seller is paid a premium, usually expressed as an annualized percentage of the notional value of the transaction, over the life of the transaction."[16] A credit event might include bankruptcy, nonpayment, or a change in the reference entity's debt structure.[17]

Not only is there a bounty of different types of swaps, but there is also a large number of ways to put them to use. For example, adjustments can be made by buying or selling assets to correct a duration mismatch or an interest rate swap can be used instead, often reducing transaction costs while achieving the same financial goal.[18]

Hedging

Swaps provide an alternative to using futures or options as a way to hedge against market risk. Suppose a wealthy individual donates a long-term variable rate certificate of deposit to a favorite foundation. Unfortunately, the foundation requires a fixed rate income stream to match its commitments. Instead of selling the variable rate security and buying a fixed rate note, the foundation may choose instead to use a swap to hedge its variable rate stream. This offers several advantages over an outright sale of the floating rate instrument. The foundation avoids realizing any gains or losses on the note and, by extension, avoids having to deal with the related tax consequences. Moreover, the foundation does not have to worry about offending the donor, who may get upset if the note is sold.

As shown in Exhibit 8.8, the swap structure is straightforward and goes a long way to help the foundation with its financial goals. Doing nothing puts the institution at risk if rates fall because the income from the donor certificate of deposit falls accordingly. Remember that getting something for nothing happens rarely and so it is with the swap. Someone has to execute the deal and

EXHIBIT 8.8 Swap Hedge Example

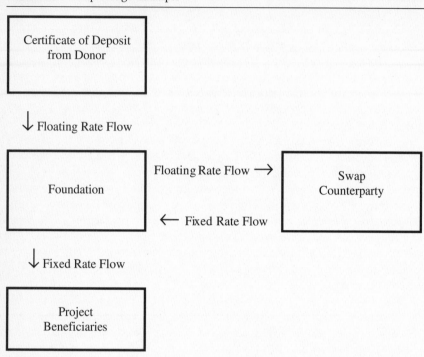

make sure that settlements are made on time. There is incremental risk associated with counterparty default, not to mention a lost opportunity should rates rise, thereby increasing the interest paid out on the certificate of deposit.

Before jumping on the swaps bandwagon, an investor should evaluate what makes sense. Use of a checklist such as the one shown in Exhibit 8.9 for interest rate swaps is a nice start. A similar checklist can be constructed for other types of swaps. Some of the items in a checklist apply to all types of swaps. Other items will be either unique or proportionately more important, depending on the type of swap. For example, defining how to calculate asset return is apropos for total return swaps, but does not apply to interest rate swaps.

INSTITUTIONAL INVESTOR USAGE OF SWAPS

According to one of the few comprehensive surveys about derivative instrument use by institutions, swaps dominate other interest rate choices.[19] How that translates into dollar usage by endowments, foundations, and pensions is hard to measure from publicly available information. Zvi Bodie and

EXHIBIT 8.9   Interest Rate Swaps Hedge Checklist

When to Take Action	What to Do
Before the hedge	1. Determine whether the investment policy permits use of interest rate swaps.
	2. If allowed, identify the expected economic effect of using swaps and performance assessment standards, including how and how often performance will be measured.
	3. Write specific procedures for use of swaps, if not done already, including steps to approve counterparties.
	4. Identify the exact risk (nature and amount) to be hedged.
	5. Identify a list of swaps brokers.
	6. Evaluate the hedge ratio to determine the size of the initial trade, using an appropriate methodology. Often a naïve approach is employed, hedging every dollar of exposure with a dollar of interest rate swap.
	7. Open a brokerage account to transact swap trades.
	8. Execute master swap document with each approved broker or counterparty, if different from the broker.
	9. Assign responsibilities to staff, including fee-based money transfers, and train staff.
During the hedge	1. Execute the initial hedge and pay the upfront fee, if applicable.
	2. Evaluate hedge effectiveness on prespecified dates.
	3. Rebalance, if necessary (i.e., interest rate swap spreads change, underlying exposure changes, or swap counter party creditworthiness changes).
	4. Evaluate whether termination or change in swap terms makes sense.
	5. Generate management reports for accounting, tax, and financial analysis use.
After the hedge	1. Determine overall efficacy of the hedge vis-à-vis investment goals.
	2. Identify ways to improve swaps-related hedging procedures for later transactions.

Robert Merton describe low usage by pension funds as ill advised, asserting that "swap contracts can be used to achieve the goal of improved international risk-sharing without violating restrictions on capital outflows to other countries" and "can mitigate the other barriers to investing abroad—expropriation risk and high transaction costs."[20]

Exhibit 8.10 showcases how swaps are used by some institutional investors. The applications vary across asset class and size.

EXHIBIT 8.10 Some Statements About Use of Swaps

Institution	Statement
Aetna, Inc.	"The Company is using interest rate swap agreements to manage certain exposures related to changes in interest rates on investments supporting experience-rated and discontinued products in the Company's Large Case Pensions business. The use of these derivatives does not impact the Company's results of operations.
	In December 2001, the Company entered into an interest rate swap agreement to convert the fixed rate of 8.5% on $350 million of its senior notes to a variable rate of three-month LIBOR plus 159.5 basis points (approximately 3.5% at swap inception)."[1]
Johns Hopkins University	"The University makes limited use of interest rate swap agreements to manage interest rate risk associated with variable rate debt. Under interest rate swap agreements, the University and the counterparties agree to exchange the difference between fixed rate and variable rate interest amounts calculated by reference to specified notional principal amounts during the agreement period. Notional principal amounts are used to express the volume of these transactions, but the cash requirements and amounts subject to credit risk are substantially less."[2]
Vanderbilt University	"To manage variable interest rate exposure for its debt portfolio, in February 2002 the University entered into two swap arrangements with a major financial institution. Under both agreements, the University receives variable payments based on 70% of LIBOR. The individual notional amounts were $66.5 million for each of these two swap arrangements. The swap notional amounts for each contract will gradually decline, corresponding to the principal amortization of the University's Series 2000A and B bonds. Under one swap arrangement that is scheduled to expire in October 2030, the University pays a fixed rate of 4.175%. Under the second swap arrangement, the University pays a fixed rate of 3.8%. Under this latter agreement, commencing October 2012, the counterparty has the option to terminate the contract without a termination payment.
	These agreements, having an aggregate notional principal amount of $133 million of June 30, 2002, effectively create a synthetic fixed rate of interest on the Series 2000 A and B bond issues, resulting in $1.5 million of additional interest expense for fiscal 2002.
	The fair value of these swap arrangements is the estimated amount that the University would pay or receive to terminate these contracts as of the report date. As of June 30, 2002, the estimated fair value loss of these swap arrangements was $3.4 million, included in accounts payable and accrued expenses."[3]

Source: [1] *Aetna, Inc. 2002 Annual Report.* © Aetna, Inc. 2002.
[2] *Johns Hopkins University Financial Report 2002.* See http://www.jhu.edu/news/info/finance 02/notes.html. Copyright © 2002, The Johns Hopkins University. Reprinted with permission.
[3] *Vanderbilt University 2002 Financial Report: Notes to the Financial Statements,* June 30, 2002 and 2001, p. 18.
See http://www.vanderbilt.edu/divadm/finrpt 2002/notes.html. Copyright © 2002, Vanderbilt University. Reprinted with permission.

SWAP FUTURES

On October 26, 2001, the Chicago Board of Trade (CBOT) launched the 10-year interest rate swap futures contract. According to CBOT Chairman Nicholas J. Neubauer, "these contacts will offer institutional investors a timely and useful new vehicle for hedging credit and interest rate exposure referenced to the long-dated London Interbank Offered Rate ("LIBOR")".[21] As of late August 2003, CBOT reported a record volume, citing liquidity associated with a "designated market maker" and the ability to reach a deal at a single price for large transactions.[22]

Exhibit 8.11 summarizes the contract specifications that are shown on the CBOT web site for the 10-year swap futures contract. Also available on this site is information about the 5-year contract, options on the 10-year futures, and historical data for analysis purposes. In addition, investment portfolio managers will find illustrated examples about the use of swaps-related derivatives, including strategies to adjust rate sensitivity, enhance bond yields, hedge fixed-income holdings, and augment financing alternatives.[23]

SWAPS IN THE NEWS

Municipal Funding

Swaps are gaining more attention for several reasons. For one thing, municipal issuers are seeking authority to enter into interest rate swaps as part of their overall bond issuance activity. The idea is to issue variable rate debt and swap into fixed, taking advantage of a positively sloped yield curve. On January 24, 2003, the Board of the Dormitory Authority approved

> *refunding bonds using interest-rate exchange agreements, or swaps, as part of Governor George E. Pataki's program to restructure the State's bond portfolio to lower debt-service payments and save taxpayers money. For the City University of New York, the Board approved issuances of multiple series of refunding bonds—taxable and tax-exempt, fixed- and variable-rate modes—of no more than $2.7 billion. The Authority plans to use swaps for the variable-rate debt, making fixed-rate payments and receiving floating-rate payments from its counterparties.[24]*

Multiple reasons account for this attraction to swaps. Lowering funding costs is one advantage, especially given tight state, county, and city budgets. Swaps help tax-exempt borrowers avoid "remarketing and liquidity costs associated with variable-rate demand bonds."[25] Like anything else, the benefits must exceed the costs, one of them being the heightened

EXHIBIT 8.11   Contract Specifications for Ten-Year Swaps Futures

Feature	Description
Contract months	The first three consecutive contracts in the March-June-September-December quarterly cycle
Contract size	The notional price of the fixed-rate side of a 10-year interest rate swap that has notional principal equal to $100,000, and that exchanges semiannual interest payments at a fixed rate of 6% per annum for floating interest rate payments, based on 3-month LIBOR.
Delivery method	By cash settlement. The final settlement value will be determined as $100,000 * [6/r + (1 − 6/r)* (1 + 0.01*r/2) − 20] where r represents the ISDA Benchmark Rate for a 10-year U.S. dollar interest rate swap on the last day of trading, expressed in percent terms (For example, if the ISDA Benchmark Rate were five and a quarter percent, then r would be 5.250.) Contract expiration price will be the final settlement value rounded to the nearest one quarter of one thirty-second of one point. It will be reported in points, thirty-seconds of one point, and quarters of one thirty-second of one point.
Price quote	Points ($1,000.00) and thirty-seconds (1/32) of one point of the notional principal of a swap having notional par value of $100,000. Par is on the basis of 100 points.
Settlement	The notional price of the Trading Unit on the last day of trading, based upon the ISDA Benchmark Rate for a 10-year U.S. dollar interest rate swap on the last day of trading, as published at approximately 11:30 am, New York time, on Reuters page ISDAFIX1.
Tick size	One thirty-second of one point ($31.25)
Trading hours	Open Auction: 7:20 am to 2:00 pm, Chicago time, Monday–Friday Electronic: 7:03 pm to 4:00 pm, Chicago time, Sunday–Friday

Source: Chicago Board of Trade.

scrutiny by rating agencies. As Exhibit 8.12 makes clear, rating agencies are likely to look down on a municipality that uses swaps on an ad hoc basis without having a comprehensive program in place, including a sensible and documented policy.

Pension Fund Calculations

Pension fund calculations hinge on what interest rate is used to determine liability amounts and lump sum calculations. Thirty-year U.S. Treasury

EXHIBIT 8.12 Guidelines for Effective Uses of Swaps in Asset-Liability Management

■ Summary

The ongoing decline of interest rates has presented creditworthy borrowers with exceptional financing opportunities. In this low interest rate environment, many borrowers have reduced their debt service costs by refunding outstanding debt and have financed new projects at very low costs. Lower debt service costs have also provided some budget relief. Simultaneously, low interest rates have affected returns on investments. The impact on tax-exempt borrowers with sizeable funds restricted to short-term fixed-income investments has been especially severe, as they repeatedly reinvest maturing principal at ever lower rates.

Responses to the mixed blessings of the low interest rate environment have varied among tax-exempt borrowers and have to some extent depended on their management structure. Those that manage investments and liabilities separately may adjust only their investment policy without changing their debt policy or vice versa. These borrowers may also adjust both their debt and their investment policies—but in isolation.

Alternatively, in recognition of the potentially offsetting impact of interest rate fluctuations on certain assets and liabilities, some tax-exempt borrowers are adopting comprehensive asset and liability management policies. Such policies, which are more prevalent in corporate finance, incorporate coordinated investment and debt structuring decisions. The goal of such coordination is to use each side of the balance sheet to mitigate, or hedge, cash flow risks posed by the other side of the balance sheet.

Either as part of or separate from asset and liability management strategies, increasing numbers of tax-exempt borrowers have used interest rate swaps to hedge their exposure to interest rate fluctuations. They have used swaps to increase exposure to variable-rate debt through fixed-to-floating interest rate swaps and have hedged their exposure to variable interest rates through floating- to fixed-rate swaps. Although the current trend of increased use of interest rate swaps has developed during a period of declining interest rates, the use of interest rate swaps and other interest rate hedging products, such as caps and collars, is expected to continue even if the interest rate environment changes, as these products provide tax-exempt borrowers with financial flexibility not offered by traditional financing methods.

Fitch Ratings recognizes that, when used in the context of comprehensive asset and liability management strategies, variable-rate debt and interest rate hedges can enhance the finances of some tax-exempt borrowers. However, when used without a coherent strategy or by borrowers with finances that are already vulnerable, such financial products can result in adverse credit consequences. Furthermore, because many municipal swap features are both unique and relatively new, borrowers should consider carefully all assumptions underlying risk calculations.

The guidelines in this report are intended to inform municipal market participants of the factors that Fitch considers when analyzing the impact of variable-rate debt and interest rate swaps on debt issuer credit. Fitch finds that, while a number of elements may influence the credit impact of variable-rate debt and interest rate hedging products, the overall management framework is the most relevant indicator

(continued)

EXHIBIT 8.12   *Continued*

of future credit impact. Therefore, Fitch considers borrowers' policies and procedures for managing the benefits and risks of selected debt structures, investments, and any related interest rate hedging products (asset and liability management policies). Fitch also considers the application of asset and liability management policies, including overall debt structure and asset profile, future capital needs, consideration of alternative structures, and reasoning in support of selections, as well as the likelihood of achieving the goals of the adopted policies.

When borrowers use interest rate swaps to create or mitigate exposure to variable interest rates, Fitch focuses on the following aspects of swap transactions: priority of swap payments; basis risk; termination provisions; and counterparty credit risk.

Fitch also considers borrowers' disclosure policies. While Fitch is working with the National Federation of Municipal Analysts to establish uniform disclosure and accounting standards for swaps, the current best disclosure practices for variable-rate debt and the use of interest rate management tools are included in the Disclosure section. This section also discusses policies regarding disclosure of swap transactions by Fitch to the market.

■ Asset and Liability Management Policies

Adoption of comprehensive asset and liability management strategies will increase a borrower's chances to maximize the benefits and minimize the risks of variable-rate debt and interest rate hedging instruments. In Fitch's view, comprehensive policies include the following:

- Identification of investment objectives, including target asset allocations, expected investment returns, and, for fixed-income investments, a breakdown of short- and long-term investments.
- Investment time horizons.
- Identification of debt, investment management products, derivatives, and counterparty ratings acceptable to the debt issuer.
- Forecasts of interest rate volatility over the short and long terms and expected performance of selected financial products under various interest rate scenarios.
- Strategies for responding to changes in short- and long-term interest rates.
- Designation of individuals responsible for negotiating financial products and coordinating investment and debt structuring decisions.
- Designation of individuals responsible for monitoring and reporting on market conditions and their impact on performance of debt, investments, and any interest rate hedging products under consideration or already implemented.
- Frequency and method of marking-to-market and monitoring investments and other financial products.
- Sources and liquidity of funds available for potential swap termination payments.
- Creation of hedge reserve funds.

Although Fitch views adoption of comprehensive asset and liability management policies as a best management practice, Fitch also recognizes that many tax-exempt borrowers have not yet adopted a single comprehensive policy incorporating

EXHIBIT 8.12 *Continued*

all of the elements listed above. Thus, if borrowers do not take such a comprehensive approach, Fitch evaluates the credit impact of variable-rate debt and interest rate hedging products in light of each debt issuer's asset allocation and investment policies, as explained below.

Application of Asset and Liability Management Policies

Adoption of a comprehensive asset and liability management policy is an important first step for tax-exempt borrowers incurring variable-rate debt and/or utilizing interest rate hedging products. In addition to evaluating the contents of such plans, Fitch considers whether the debt structure incorporated into the plan is appropriate for particular borrowers. General bond market conditions, sources and costs of internal or external liquidity, natural and synthetic interest rate hedges, prior experience managing interest rate risk, and margins for tolerating increases in interest rates are factors in making such a determination.

Given that such factors vary for each tax-exempt issuer, Fitch does not recommend universal ratios of net variable-rate debt to total capitalization (total debt plus equity). However, Fitch does recognize common credit characteristics among borrowers for which issuance of higher proportions of variable-rate debt is appropriate. Such borrowers have strong, predictable cash flows and internal liquidity sufficient to absorb fluctuations in interest rates, characteristics which also correlate strongly with high investment-grade credit ratings. These borrowers are generally sophisticated and experienced in debt markets— further indicators of ability to assume percentages of variable-rate debt relatively greater than the percentages manageable for lower rated borrowers.

Furthermore, in evaluating borrowers' exposure to variable interest rates, Fitch focuses on net, rather than gross, variable-rate debt. This calculation subtracts from total (or gross) variable-rate debt amounts that are effectively hedged, either with forms of self-liquidity, including certain short-term investments, or with interest rate swaps meeting the standards outlined in the Interest Rate Swaps section.

Fitch considers short-term investments effective hedges to variable-rate debt because movements in interest rates should have offsetting impacts on both. If interest rates remain low, decreased investment returns should be offset by lower debt service costs. Conversely, if short-term interest rates rise, higher debt service costs should be mitigated by higher investment returns.

Strategy Execution

Fitch's expectation of successfully executed asset and liability management strategies is influenced by the debt issuer's experience in the financial markets and prior successful use of innovative financing tools. Inexperience may, however, be mitigated by longstanding relationships with experienced financial professionals charged with selecting and monitoring the performance of financing and investment products.

In addition, borrowers demonstrating an understanding of the benefits and risks associated with the selected debt structure and related financial products are

(continued)

EXHIBIT 8.12 *Continued*

more likely to realize their benefits. Therefore, Fitch reviews and discusses with borrowers the following:

- Debt structure and financial products selected.
- Alternatives that may have been considered.
- Reasons for selecting or accepting certain provisions of swap documents.
- Suitability of debt structure and selected interest rate hedging products in light of the issuer's policies.

Suitability of debt structure also depends on the nature of a debt issuer's revenues. For example, borrowers with economically sensitive revenue streams, such as tolls, may reasonably expect that their revenues would increase during periods of increased economic activity. Increased revenues would be expected to result from both higher traffic levels and decreased resistance to higher toll rates, which could then offset the higher variable interest rates that are also likely during such periods. In contrast, borrowers with inflexible revenue streams or revenues that are not linked to general economic activity may be unable to offset the consequences of higher interest rates.

■ Interest Rate Swaps

Tax-exempt borrowers have been utilizing interest rate swaps with increasing frequency. Floating- to fixed-rate swaps have been used to hedge interest rate risk on variable-rate demand obligations (VRDOs); lock in fixed interest rates on refunding bonds that will be issued in the future *(for a full discussion of this use of swaps, see Fitch Research on "Trends in Refunding Tax-Exempt Debt," dated Feb. 28, 2002, available on Fitch's web site at www.fitchratings.com)*; or take advantage of opportunities to obtain fixed swap rates that are lower than comparable fixed bond rates.

Other tax-exempt borrowers have created synthetic floating-rate debt with fixed- to floating-rate swaps. Such borrowers may receive the benefits of lower floating interest rates without incurring the remarketing and liquidity costs associated with variable-rate demand bonds. In addition, borrowers, including some hospitals, encountering barriers to obtaining either the liquidity support necessary to market VRDOs or the bond insurance preferred for marketing auction-rate securities, have also utilized fixed- to floating-rate swaps.

Fitch considers the impact of interest rate swaps in light of borrowers' overall asset and liability management policies. Review by Fitch of individual swap documents may be less likely when such policies include detailed parameters for acceptable swap providers and provisions. In those cases, Fitch may rely on the policies and management's commitment to adhere to them. However, when borrowers execute swaps without a comprehensive policy, Fitch may determine that a review of swap documents, including master agreements, schedules, and confirmations, is warranted. In either case, Fitch focuses on the aspects of interest rate swaps described below.

Priority of Swap Payments

Net interest payments on swaps by tax-exempt borrowers often rank on parity with debt service under related bond documents. Fitch believes that such ranking alone generally should not affect bondholder credit adversely. In addition, when

EXHIBIT 8.12 *Continued*

Fitch is informed of swap agreements, the net impact of the issuer's obligations under such agreements is reflected in Fitch's rating. For example, debt service coverage calculations may be based on actual interest payments made after adding or subtracting payments made by or to the debt issuer under related swap agreements.

Borrowers and investors should, however, consider all potential consequences of ranking net interest payments on parity to senior debt. For example, failure by the debt issuer to make net swap payments may cause a default on bonds that are related and/or unrelated to the swap. Also, when swap payments are ranked on parity to senior debt, liquidity facilities supporting VRDOs may be subject to automatic termination following a payment default on the swap. Previously, definitions of senior debt in liquidity facilities included only publicly issued bonds or notes and did not include the debt issuer's contractual obligations, such as interest rate swaps. As long as debt issuer accounting systems treat net interest payments under swaps and debt payments identically, bondholders should incur no additional risk from this expanded definition of parity debt. However, investors should be aware of this development.

In contrast, Fitch supports continued ranking of termination payments below debt service obligations. This industry standard ensures that debt service payments would not be jeopardized by an unexpected or exceptionally large termination payment. Because swap termination events vary with the preferences and policies of borrowers and their counterparties, termination may be unforeseeable (*see Termination Risk*). Furthermore, termination payments are by definition nonrecurring and potentially challenge debt issuer liquidity. Ranking termination payments below debt service should ensure that borrowers have time to adjust their finances, minimizing the risk that a liquidity crunch caused by liability for a termination payment would impair long-term financial health.

Basis Risk
Basis risk arises when floating interest rates on bonds and swaps are based on different indexes. While floating tax-exempt bond rates generally track the Bond Market Association index (BMA), a composite index of weekly variable-rate tax-exempt debt, payments made by tax-exempt borrowers on most floating- to fixed-rate swaps are based on a percentage of the London Interbank Offered Rate (LIBOR), a taxable short-term interest rate. The percentage of LIBOR selected for most swaps is 67%, in recognition of the historical trading relationship between the indexes.

Basis risk is realized when the traditional relationship between the indexes erodes. During periods when BMA exceeds 67% of LIBOR, floating rates received on swaps are inadequate to cover floating rates paid on bonds, and total interest costs increase. For example, during periods of unusually high variable-rate debt issuance, short-term tax-exempt interest rates may rise while LIBOR remains flat. Likewise, if federal tax rates are expected to or actually decline, the BMA rate may rise without any corresponding increase in LIBOR.

If an event with long-term consequence, such as a decrease in federal tax rates, pushes the ratio of BMA to LIBOR above 67%, floating swap payments

(continued)

EXHIBIT 8.12   *Continued*

received on swaps could be inadequate to cover floating rates paid on bonds for the life of the swap. Given the trend toward long-term swaps, borrowers should demonstrate to Fitch that they have considered and planned for this possibility through, for example, establishment of a hedge fund reserve or factoring basis risk into their budget as a cushion. They should also present their reasoning in accepting this risk. Fitch requests projections of additional debt service costs that may accrue under various interest rate scenarios and the debt issuer's means of absorbing and mitigating such additional costs.

Termination Risk

All interest rate swap documents include events of default and events of termination. In addition, if uncured within time periods specified in swap documents, many events of default become events of termination. Termination risk refers to the following two consequences of swap termination: reversion of swapped debt to its original variable- or fixed-rate form, possibly undermining a debt issuer's asset/liability strategy; and liability for potentially large payments if termination occurs during adverse market conditions.

Borrowers may eventually reverse these consequences by executing a new swap or issuing new debt at lower rates. However, in the interim, costs may be incurred and borrowers should have a plan to absorb them. Borrowers should, therefore, prepare or request from potential swap counterparties projections of potential liability for termination payments under a range of interest rate scenarios. Fitch analysts review such projections and evaluate the availability, liquidity, and adequacy of proposed sources of funds.

Limiting events of automatic termination to credit-related events, such as rating downgrades, bankruptcy/insolvency of either party, and nonpayment of debt by either party should further insulate investors. The likelihood of the occurrence of such credit events forms the basis for Fitch's debt ratings, and inclusion of such events of automatic termination should pose no additional risk to bondholders.

In contrast, the likelihood of the occurrence of noncredit-related events of automatic termination, such as default under separate agreements between the parties to the swap, is not necessarily reflected in Fitch's rating. These types of events could pose hidden risks for bondholders. Consequently, swap documents that incorporate noncredit-related events of automatic termination could cause Fitch to disregard such swaps and treat debt as unhedged. Alternatively, if Fitch views management positively, it may determine that there is minimal risk that a noncredit-related event of termination would occur.

Counterparty Risk

Counterparty credit ratings address their ability and willingness to meet their swap obligations. Such ratings should be an important selection factor because counterparty default on a swap and/or consequent termination leads to the results outlined in the Termination Risk section.

Fitch expects borrowers to select counterparties with ratings at least as high as their own ratings. In addition, swaps should include provisions requiring posting of collateral or termination of swaps when counterparty ratings dip below

EXHIBIT 8.12 *Continued*

specified levels. Although termination raises the aforementioned risks, when events of termination relate to counterparty credit, such risks are incorporated into Fitch's counterparty rating.

Disclosure

Fitch now monitors swaps executed by municipal borrowers more closely than in the past and requests that these borrowers disclose to Fitch, on an ongoing basis, the status of their swaps. Particularly, Fitch seeks prompt notification of occurrence of the following significant events, which could affect a debt issuer's financial performance: events of default or termination; triggering of requirements by either party to post collateral; any amendments to swap documents; and annually, the market value of outstanding swaps. Fitch also expects to be kept informed of plans to convert interest rate modes and actual annual interest rates on variable-rate debt. In addition to regular disclosure in financial statements, Fitch expects the occurrence of such events to be disclosed in a timely manner. Fitch believes that better managers take initiative on disclosure of significant events and considers such disclosure a best practice.

In certain cases, Fitch's credit reports and press releases will disclose to investors the existence of swaps and any terms that are unusual or that may pose additional credit risks. In addition, if a legal opinion regarding enforceability of swap agreements is not available, Fitch will also disclose that it has not reviewed such an opinion.

Although many VRDOs are exempted from the continuing disclosure provisions of Securities and Exchange Commission Rule 15c2-12, superior disclosure practices incorporate a commitment to ongoing public disclosure by borrowers of significant events relating to VRDOs. At a minimum, such events should be disclosed to Fitch.

Source: K. McManus, K. Pfeil, & T. Zibit, "Guidelines for Effective Uses of Swaps in Asset-Liability Management," *Government Finance Review,* June 2003, p. 35. Copyright © 2003 Government Finance Review. Reprinted by permission of Fitch, Inc.

bonds were used until the Department of the Treasury stopped issuing them, forcing the choice of a new benchmark. Open to discussion at any time, the subject climbs to the top of the list when private pension funds find themselves with large liabilities that may or may not reflect economic reality, but come across as dangerous to the general public.[26]

Among proposed benchmark choices, the swaps rate is being seriously considered. Liquidity is one factor because secondary markets for swaps with a traditional fixed-to-floating structure are quite broad. Not everyone favors the use of swap rates to determine pension fund liabilities. Some argue for composite corporate bond indices that represent top-quality credits. Be that as it may, swap rates offer real advantages over other types of rates, as shown in Exhibit 8.13.[27] On April 2, 2004, the U.S. House of

Representatives passed H.R. 3108 that temporarily replaces "the 30-year Treasury rate with a rate based on long-term corporate bonds for certain pension plan funding requirements." Senate approval followed and the Pension Funding Equity Act of 2004 was signed into law by President Bush on April 10, 2004.[28]

EXHIBIT 8.13 Swap Rate and Pension Computations

Several pension experts have considered using 30-year interest rate swap rates as the basis for current liability and lump-sum calculations. Interest-rate swaps are generally perceived to contain low credit risk for two reasons. First, the two parties involved in the contract typically have high credit ratings. Second, swap contracts typically use the London Interbank Offer Rate (LIBOR) as the floating rate, and the LIBOR has a low credit risk. The overall credit quality underlying LIBOR-based, interest-rate swap rates is likely comparable to that of high-quality corporate bonds. However, unlike some corporate bonds, swaps are not callable, so their rates would not need to be adjusted for such options and typically would be expected to fall below those on high-quality corporate bonds of similar maturity. The credit rating of insurance companies in the group annuity market is generally Aa or better. Interest rate swaps might give an accurate indication of an insurance company's cost of borrowing funds.

The interest rate swap market has characteristics that likely protect rates from potential manipulation. The swap market is considered to be very active, although the trading volume and amount outstanding for longer maturity interest rate swaps are believed to be low, relative to shorter maturities. The Federal Reserve Board publishes 30-year interest rate swap rates daily based on a private survey of quotes on new contracts offered by 16 large swaps dealers, and quotes on swaps contracts are updated throughout the day and visible via subscription services. A unique advantage of using swaps as an interest rate is that swaps do not require the issuance of debt; rather, swap rates reflect contracts between two parties. Because new contracts are produced every day, it is easier to update 30-year swap rates than other rates involving the issuing of debt, which happens only periodically. The international swaps market represents the largest of the alternatives considered, with an outstanding dollar-denominated value of swaps contracts estimated at approximately $20 trillion, with many new transactions conducted between parties every day. However, some experts have expressed concern about using the 30-year interest rate swaps because the swaps market is relatively new and the outstanding trading volume of 30-year interest rate swaps is believed to be much lower than for shorter maturity contracts.

Source: "Private Pensions: Process Needed to Monitor the Mandated Interest Rate for Pension Calculations (GAO-03-313, February 27, 2003)," *Report to Congressional Requesters,* United States General Accounting Office, pp. 22–23.

SUMMARY

1. A swap is a legal contract that represents an exchange of cash flows between two counterparties.
2. In the case of interest rate swaps, the cash flows represent reference interest rates.
3. A common interest rate swap structure is the fixed-to-floating setup, where one party pays a cash flow based on a fixed swap rate. The remaining counterparty pays interest that increases or decreases, depending on the movement in the variable rate benchmark.
4. An interest rate swap involves no exchange of principal and explains the term *notional principal amount*.
5. Netting is a means by which net interest is paid by the party with the larger obligation on a particular settlement date.
6. Currency swaps involve an exchange of principal amounts in each currency represented in the swap.
7. Swaps can be used for a variety of reasons, including hedging, risk transformation, yield enhancement, investment cash flow replication, or reduction of funding costs.
8. Swap futures are growing in volume and facilitate a number of investment strategies.
9. Swaps are used by many municipalities to reduce funding costs or access a particular liability structure.
10. Swap use is taken into account in the bond rating process.
11. Interest rate swap rates are a proposed alternative discount rate for pension calculations.

CHAPTER 9

Risk Is a Four-Letter Word

*Since we cannot know all that there is to be known about anything,
we ought to know a little about everything.*

—Blaise Pascal

BACKGROUND

Risk is a four-letter word, literally and figuratively. Some disdain it. Others embrace it. Smart investors manage it. Those who ignore it argue that risk is too complex to tackle and that no one can possibly be an expert about the many investment opportunities available to endowments, foundations, or pension funds. Unfortunately, that excuse won't wash when it comes time to explain a big loss or failure to meet a target return.

As stated earlier, a proper evaluation of the trade-off between risk and expected returns goes a long way to avoid mishaps. Better yet, informed and proactive investors have a chance to meet or exceed return targets while minimizing capital exposure, if they do their homework and stay focused on the fact that things can and do change. The problem is that some risks are hard to evaluate because they are hard to identify and therefore difficult to measure. The obvious solution is to ask tough questions about what causes the value of an investment to change, when adversity is likely to occur, and the likely magnitude of loss or gain.

This endeavor is more challenging when derivative instruments are involved. The same questions apply, but must now be considered in the context of what function derivatives will play. This can vary considerably, as shown in Exhibit 9.1. Some of the many applications include return enhancement, risk reduction, security synthesis, or transformation of an existing or anticipated bundle of cash flows. Each application has the potential to alter an investment's risk–return trade-off, sometimes materially.

For example, when derivatives are used for risk minimization purposes, performance centers on the correlation between the hedge instrument and

EXHIBIT 9.1 Derivatives Play Many Roles

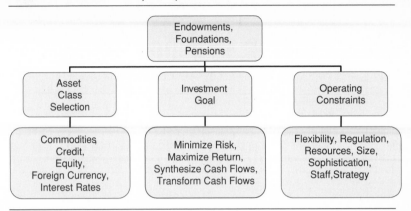

what is being hedged.[1] Recall that a good hedge is defined by a strong positive correlation between the two with a short position in one item and a long position in the other. The net effect, if done properly, is to lock in a specified value. Using derivatives to transform cash flows involves an altogether different approach. Instead of examining the offset potential of a derivative instrument, a future, option, or swap used for transformation purposes may result in the assumption of additional risk. That does not necessarily make the deal unattractive. As long as the investor expects higher returns or can satisfy its stated goal, the incremental risk could make sense.

Without identifying and understanding the risks that attend derivative use, evaluating investment performance is impossible. Predictably, people fear the unknown and derivatives are no exception. Even if some risks can be identified, valuation of derivatives presents another problem because there are risks associated with modeling. This is especially true for complex securities with structures that include an embedded derivative, something that cannot be stripped out and sold separately.

DERIVATIVES-RELATED RISKS

Exhibit 9.2 breaks down the generally accepted categories of derivatives-related risk. The fact that this list is short is deceptive because each risk type encompasses a wide array of situations that reflect risk. However, to simplify things, only the general categories are presented here.

Labeling risks by category is beneficial for two reasons. First, it permits the risk manager to broadly evaluate problem areas. Second, it facilitates resource allocation, something that is particularly compelling for smaller institutions with limited funds to spend on computer systems, trained staff, and data.

EXHIBIT 9.2 Risks Related to Derivatives

Risk Category	Description
Credit	Risk that a counterparty defaults and transaction must be replaced or unwound at a loss
Legal	Risk that a contract is not legally binding
Liquidity	Risk that a transaction cannot be unwound or offset with another transaction quickly, if at all
Market	Risk of adverse price changes that reduce transaction value
Operational	Risk of human or technology error
Settlement	Risk that a counterparty will not settle its obligations on time, if at all

A disadvantage of categorizing risks is that interrelationships are overlooked. This is unrealistic. Postmortems of big derivatives-related losses point out that there is seldom one culprit. Rather, several factors are at play. With no controls to catch any or all of the weaknesses, loss is inevitable. Anecdotally, many of these losses are attributable to a combination of market risk and operational risk factors. For example, a position may lose value if improperly hedged and markets sour. If the investor's computer system fails to pick up big drops in the position value, both market and operational risk manifest themselves in bigger losses than would be the case with good controls.

Market Risk

Market risk is what most people traditionally think of when they think of derivatives. This is the risk that changes in market conditions will reduce the value of an investment. Adversity for one investor is not necessarily the same for a second investor. Political instability abroad that pushes up prices helps a pension fund that owns commodity company stock, but hurts a foundation with a large stake in the food industry because higher input costs reduce profitability.

Hedging provides one way to minimize market risk. Eliminating it completely is more of a theoretical construct, something that is rarely possible in practice. Derivative instruments can be used to hedge a position. Alternatively, an investor can create a natural hedge through portfolio diversification as mentioned earlier in the book. Neither approach is foolproof.

Each method entails different costs. Regulatory or policy constraints may play a role. For example, an institutional investor may be forbidden by law to use derivatives, or may only use them under limited circumstances. The institution's own investment policy statement could preclude the use of short positions, thereby eliminating the possibility of hedging a long position with a short position in derivatives. A derivative instrument may not exist that closely matches the exposure. On the other hand, a natural hedge could be impractical if it violates asset allocation targets set by the trustees.

Even when alternatives are readily available and permitted, warding off market risk requires constant attention. A hedge put in place today will be effective only if economic relationships stay the same, something that hardly ever occurs. Only when someone periodically evaluates the efficacy of the hedge can necessary revisions be made. Otherwise, a "buy and hold" strategy has the potential to worsen the adverse impact on the value of an investment or portfolio of investments due to changes in market conditions. The need to review and revise is more relevant today than in the past. Integration of capital markets and sophisticated technology make it hard to avoid the domino effect associated with a problem that starts miles away, but creeps close to home base at a fast clip.

Operational Risk

Operational risk encompasses a variety of areas, including human error and technology problems. A trading clerk takes a sick day, resulting in failure to exercise a profitable option. A settlement amount is incorrectly calculated due to programming bugs. A system breaks down, leading to the use of outdated ledgers to process transactions. A back office manager retires, passing the reins to someone with much less experience and knowledge to pick up the slack. These are but a few of the operational nightmares that keep risk managers awake, thinking about how to improve things.

Making matters worse, quantifying operational risk is not as straightforward as is the case with market risk. How do you put a price tag on the ability of support staff to identify warning signs? How do you measure the ability of a computer system to track approval limits when information is aggregated from different money managers in an untimely fashion or based on different report formats or both? What is the right metric for determining proper oversight of trades? These are hard questions to answer.

One way to meet the challenges associated with operational risk is to learn from blunders made by others. To this end, Fitch Risk Management offers *OpVantage First*, a case study database targeted to institutional investors with the express purpose of enlightening those investors by providing information. Timelines, related incidents, event description, loss amounts, and lessons learned for over 4,000 cases are provided via a web interface and updated continuously. Exhibit 9.3 provides a sample case study from this database.

EXHIBIT 9.3 Operational Risk Case Study

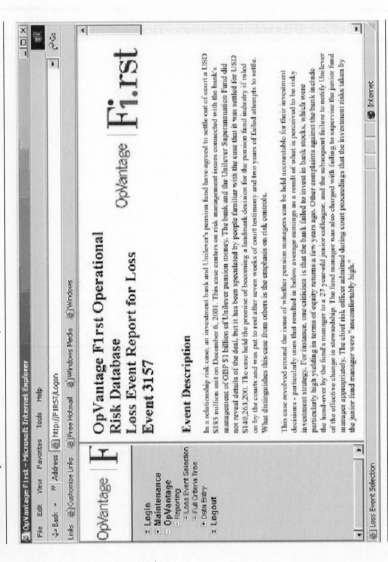

Source: Copyright © 2003, OpVantage, a division of Fitch Risk. Reprinted with permission.

Credit Risk

The surge in credit derivatives, coupled with deteriorating economic conditions and related bankruptcies, has put credit risk at center stage. As seen in Exhibit 9.4, growth in this area can only be described as explosive. As recently as 1997, the global credit derivatives market was estimated at $180 billion and is expected to grow to $4.8 trillion by 2004.[2] More than a few reasons account for this growth. Banks use credit swaps and other types of credit derivatives as a way to manage the risk inherent in their loan portfolios. Others view credit derivatives as a separate asset class and transact accordingly.

Credit risk exists even when other kinds of derivatives are used. In fact, the more traditional view of credit risk looks at counterparty default, defined as the risk the remaining counterparty faces if the other side fails to perform according to the terms of the original agreement. Under certain market conditions, nonperformance can be costly for the counterparty left behind. Creditworthiness of a counterparty, the terms of a particular transaction, and the degree to which value is expected to change as market conditions change are all determinants of current and potential exposure.

Exhibit 9.5 illustrates the notion of credit risk by looking at an interest rate swap between a corporation and a bank. Company ABC is the Fixed Rate Payor, seeking to lock in an annual fixed rate of 5 percent over a five-year period via the swap. One year later, rates have increased, validating their initial decision to enter into the swap. In the event that Bank XYZ defaults at this point in time, several things occur. First, Company ABC has to replace the bank with another counterparty willing to accept a fixed rate interest flow. The problem is that no one will do this for anything less than the now higher fixed rate swap rate, so Company ABC incurs an explicitly higher cost. Second, Company ABC faces an opportunity cost because it loses the chance to pay the lower rate it negotiated in good faith 12 months earlier. In addition, time and money have to be spent on finding a replacement counterparty, evaluating its creditworthiness, and determining whether Company ABC is approved to do business with another organization for the remaining four years.

EXHIBIT 9.4 Global Market Size for Credit Derivatives

2001	2002	2004 Estimate
$1.189 trillion	$1.952 trillion	$4.799 trillion

Source: Copyright © 1996–2003, BBA Enterprises, *BBA Credit Derivatives Report 2001/2002.* Reprinted with permission.

EXHIBIT 9.5　Counterparty Default Example

Date	Event	Comment
September 30, 2003	Company ABC enters into an annual pay five-year interest rate swap with Bank XYZ. Company ABC is designated as the Fixed Rate Payor, agreeing to pay a fixed rate of five percent per annum.	Company ABC anticipates rising rates and seeks to lock in a fixed cost of funding.
September 30, 2004	1. Interest rates have risen and the fixed rate for a similar four-year swap is now seven percent per year.	The value of the original interest rate swap from Company ABC's perspective has increased. The fixed rate on the original swap (with four years left to go) is lower than the market rate for a new swap.
	2. Bank XYZ defaults as Floating Rate Payor (and Fixed Rate Receiver).	Company ABC must replace Bank XYZ with a new counterparty that will only accept the higher market-based fixed rate swap rate of seven percent per year.

Derivatives-related default risk is not the same as the default risk associated with buying a stock or bond nor is it the same across different types of derivative instruments. When an investor buys a security, issuer default—assuming zero recovery later—represents a complete loss. Whatever the investor paid to buy the security is now gone. In contrast, many derivative transactions represent a two-way performance obligation, except for obvious exceptions. For example, option buyers have no obligation to exercise.

Specifically, default analysis for derivatives examines market differentials. Each counterparty looks at its potential loss in terms of the net obligation on each and every remaining settlement date. In the swaps case just discussed, the goal is to quantify how much it will cost Company ABC to replace Bank XYZ if rates rise by some amount such as 10 percent and the bank defaults with four years remaining until the original swap matures. Anyone involved in approving trading lines looks at a host of other possibilities. What is the cost if the bank defaults with only three years left to maturity and rates have risen by 15 percent? What is the value of the swap to Company ABC if rates fall by five percent next year?

Face value does not adequately measure default risk. Ex post, it is the interest rate differential between the old and new fixed rate for the remaining time that determines the actual loss amount, assuming that the floating rate terms on a new swap are identical to the original agreement. Ex ante, an evaluation of the creditworthiness of Bank XYZ and the likelihood of default are critical elements of a complete analysis. There are entire books written on the topic of default risk, a testament to its importance in risk management.

One safeguard is to transact with a well-capitalized counterparty. Large players have taken steps to make themselves more appealing by doing deals in the name of a separately rated subsidiary with its own assets. A typical structure imposes legal restrictions to protect the wronged party in the event of default. This might take the form of segregating certain assets so they are available only to claimants associated with a derivative contract(s). Guarantees and letters of credit are other ways to handle credit risk.

Once deemed creditworthy, lines are made available for transacting purposes. Credit risk can arise if these limits are breached. This can happen when different parts of an institution transact with a counterparty without anyone keeping tabs on outstanding exposures. In a similar sense, credit risk is an issue if multiple money managers are transacting with a counterparty and are not communicating with their client in a timely fashion.

Legal Risk

Legal risk has to do with the enforceability of the contract that sets out the responsibilities of each counterparty to a transaction. A change in or new interpretation of a government regulation may render a derivative contract invalid. Additionally, the question remains as to whether counterparties to derivatives-related deals enjoy the same legal protection afforded creditors. This is more than a passing interest given the large dollar amounts involved in the recent downfall of several corporate monoliths that were active in derivatives markets.

The U.S. Congress recognizes the problem and is considering whether to permit netting across financial contracts, rather than only within categories. The goal is to avoid a spillover effect throughout the global banking system by allowing financial institutions to close out their positions with each other for all outstanding transactions, regardless of transaction type.[3]

Legal risk is a complicated matter. Besides netting, legal risk takes in collateral management issues and the cross-border nature of contracts. London-based law firm, Allen & Overy, recently introduced *Netalytics*, a product designed to provide subscribers with online information about key legal elements regarding the enforceability of the close-out netting provisions of the International Swaps and Derivatives Association, Inc. (ISDA) Master Agreement in more than 35 jurisdictions. According to Mr. Marc-Henry Chamay, head of eBusiness for Allen & Overy, *netalytics* and its sister product designed for collateral management, *CSAnalytics,* help offer firms a chance to "realize a reduction of their capital charges by providing a timely and consistent analysis of the generally long and complex ISDA netting and collateral opinions in major markets."[4]

Suitability is another issue that falls under the rubric of legal risk. As mentioned earlier, whether a transaction makes sense is an absolutely fundamental question that fiduciaries must address before authorizing use of derivatives. (For that matter, an evaluation of suitability applies to any financial instrument, not just derivatives.) A central question is whether an institutional investor is sophisticated and, therefore, fully capable of evaluating the risk and return attributes of any financial deal.[5] When suitability is an issue in litigation, everyone is forced to deal with the issue on a reactive basis. A preemptive strike involves evaluation of suitability before funds are committed. No one should enter into a transaction that is poorly understood, a clear signal that suitability might be an issue.

Interrelationships among Risks

What keeps most managers up at night is the cold harsh reality that risk events do not occur in a vacuum. One problem causes another and so on, or a confluence of bad news hits all at once. To illustrate, suppose a derivatives trade is improperly recorded as $15 million and is later found to have been underreported by $10 million. One result is that trading limits may be breached because $25 million should have been deducted, not the recorded $15 million. A second and not inconsequential result is that asset class allocations are not being followed or that an investor has exceeded permitted asset class limits. Either way, the underreporting leads to problems such as (1) insufficient hedge size if the position was hedged, (2) inadequate collateral or margin amounts, (3) undercapitalization of the position, and (4) incorrect performance reports. Moreover, because managers are typically compensated on the basis of performance reports, an incorrect evaluation number leads to either excess or insufficient remuneration, neither of which is desirable. Underreporting could bring about regulatory noncompliance, in which case the investor might incur penalties, loss of confidence on the part of donors or beneficiaries, and possible restrictions on permitted activities.

Bad price data or use of an incorrect valuation model has the potential to similarly misrepresent credit, market, and/or legal exposure. The integration of risks raises the bar. No mistake should be viewed as too small because of the ripple effect that invariably occurs.

Risk Management Alternatives

Not all risks are created equal. Credit risk is less of an issue for users of exchange-traded derivatives versus over-the-counter alternatives. Liquidity risk is more problematic for a structured derivative as compared with a short-term call on a major world currency. Comparing risks across products is an integral part of effective risk management for a very good reason. That is, there are many ways to accomplish a stated investment goal and its associated risk management objective, and selecting the optimal approach considers risk, return, and related market structure issues.

A good analogy is planning for a trip. Someone who lives in the New Jersey suburbs and needs to travel to New York City has several choices. The train offers a chance to do some work for an hour, but the fixed schedule restricts flexibility. Driving allows for more leeway, but it means being on crowded roads and having to pay for parking. Both alternatives result in getting to the city but differ in several ways, including costs, flexibility, and timing.

Some choices are obvious, whereas others require more thought. Think about a U.S. pension fund with a long position in a foreign currency denominated bond. If the chief investment officer predicts a stronger U.S. dollar, the sensible thing is to look at ways to lock in today's exchange rate. The pension fund is still exposed to potential macroeconomic strength abroad, not reflected in exchange rates. However, a hedge provides some protection against a diminished ability to purchase U.S. dollars (and sell foreign currency) down the road.

One alternative is to buy a series of short foreign currency puts or one long-term put to hedge only bond principal. Selling a strip of foreign currency futures is another possibility. A third choice is to sell foreign currency via forwards with staggered maturities that match the interest receipt dates of the bond. Exotic options, zero-premium derivatives, and long-term currency swaps are other choices.

Despite a plethora of alternatives, a final decision rests on the characteristics of the investor, including objectives and constraints. For example, cash availability to pay upfront fees for the put options can make or break a deal for some institutions. Derivative instrument liquidity is relevant if the bond is likely to be sold before maturity and a hedge must be unwound. Some transaction types are nonstarters if an investor is forbidden from taking short positions. Exhibit 9.6 lays out the kind of analysis that precedes a final decision.

Reality Check

Exhibit 9.7 recaps some of the more publicized losses attributable to derivative instrument use. The numbers are inexact, but provide a general idea of how much money is involved in an absolute sense. Newsmakers are watching.

EXHIBIT 9.6 Foreign Currency Alternatives[a]

Risk Types	Selling Futures Strip	Buying Over-the-Counter Puts	Selling Currency Via Forwards
Credit risk	Lower because of clearinghouse and daily settlement	Higher because of direct contracting with counterparty	Higher because of direct contracting with counterparty
Economic risk	Depends because standardized terms make it harder to hedge exact underlying exposure, but easier to value derivative instrument, assuming futures contracts are available for the entire calendar period associated with life of asset	Depends because customized terms make it easier to hedge exact underlying exposure, but harder to value derivative instrument unless instrument is frequently traded	Depends because customized terms make it easier to hedge exact underlying exposure, but harder to value derivative instrument unless instrument is frequently traded
Legal risk	Lower due to regulation	Higher due to evolving case law and changing regulations	Higher due to evolving case law and changing regulations
Liquidity risk	Lower due to standardization of terms	Higher, especially for longer-term contracts; requires commitment of upfront cash	Higher, but partially reduced because of intervening cash settlements
Operational risk	Depends on quality of staff and technology systems in place to track and make daily settlement cash flow transfers	Depends on availability and knowledge of staff, along with computer system, to monitor and exercise options on time	Depends on quality of staff and technology systems to track and make intervening settlement cash flow transfers

[a]This table generalizes the risk–return trade-off for a handful of possible ways to hedge. In practice, each alternative is individually evaluated, taking the investor's relevant constraints and objectives into account.

EXHIBIT 9.7   Partial List of Losses Related to Use of Derivatives

Counterparty	Estimated Amount[a]	Year	Instrument
Orange County	$1.69 billion[b]	1994	Inverse floater
Barings Bank	$1.36 billion[c]	1995	Equity futures
Long-Term Capital Management	$3.625 billion[d]	1998	Swaps, etc.
Allied Irish Banks	$520 million[e]	2001	Foreign currency options
Enron	Depends on legal treatment of contracts	2001	Energy and credit derivatives, etc.

[a]Estimated amounts shown here do not include any later recoveries by injured parties.
[b]Thomas F. Siems, "Derivatives: In the Wake of Disaster," *Financial Industry Issues,* Dallas Federal Reserve Bank, First Quarter 1995.
[c]Id.
[d]David Shirreff, "Lessons from the Collapse of Hedge Fund, Long-Term Capital Management," IFCI Risk Institute, New York, 1999.
[e]"Case Study: Allied Irish Banks," ERisk Learning, New York, April 2002.

Warren E. Buffet, CEO of Berkshire Hathaway, Inc., talked at length about derivatives, laying out his concerns about their potentially adverse effect on the financial markets.[6] While still recognizing the risks associated with derivative usage, Federal Reserve Chairman Alan Greenspan countered by enumerating the benefits, adding that, "risks are manageable in principle and generally have been managed quite effectively in practice, at least to date."[7]

Whether derivatives are the proverbial "bad boy" of finance remains to be seen. So far, losses in the derivatives market, relative to the overall size, do not appear to be any larger than bond market defaults. As noted by Arthur Levitt, Chairman of the U.S. Securities and Exchange Commission (SEC) at the time, "Derivatives are like electricity—dangerous if mishandled, but also capable of doing enormous good."[8]

EMBEDDED DERIVATIVES

Overview

An embedded derivative is a financial instrument that cannot be stripped from the host security and traded as a separate item. Consider a convertible bond. It can be thought of as a bond plus a call option. The investor has the right but not the obligation to convert the bond into shares of common stock and will do so when it makes sense to exercise the call. (Convertible bond math is not covered here but essentially the investor will exercise when the potential for capital appreciation of the stock offsets the loss of bond interest.) This option is integral to the convertible bond structure. It cannot be bought or sold as a stand-alone instrument. Other examples of embedded derivative securities include structured notes, mortgage-backed securities, and convertible preferred stock, to name a few.

As shown in Exhibit 9.8, embedded derivatives take many forms. They are sometimes part of leases, purchase agreements, or sales contracts. For

EXHIBIT 9.8   Examples of Embedded Derivatives Disclosure

Source	Excerpt
Lucent Technologies[a] Annual Report for 2001, Footnote 15: Financial Instruments	Lucent's foreign currency embedded derivatives consist of sales and purchase contracts with cash flows indexed to changes in or denominated in a currency that neither party to the contract uses as their functional currency. Changes in the fair value of these embedded derivatives were not significant during the year ended September 30, 2001.
	Copyright © 2001 Lucent Technologies. Reprinted with permission. All rights reserved.
Merrill Lynch & Co.,[b] Inc. Annual Report for 2002, Footnote 1: Summary of Significant Accounting Policies	Merrill Lynch issues debt whose coupons or repayment terms are linked to the performance of equity or other indices (e.g., S&P 500) or baskets of securities. The contingent payment components of these debt obligations meet the definition of an "embedded derivative." The debt instruments are assessed to determine if the embedded derivative requires separate reporting and accounting, and if so, the embedded derivative is separated and reported in *Long-term borrowings* on the Consolidated Balance Sheets with the debt obligation; changes in the fair value of the embedded derivative and related hedges are reported in *Interest expense*. The risk exposures in embedded derivatives are economically hedged with cash instruments and/or other non-trading derivatives reported at fair value.
	Merrill Lynch may also purchase financial instruments that contain embedded derivatives. These instruments may be part of either trading inventory or trading marketable investment securities. These instruments are generally accounted for at fair value in their entirety; the embedded derivative is not separately accounted for, and all changes in fair value are reported in earnings.

[a]Copyright © 2001, Lucent Technologies. All rights reserved.
[b]Copyright © 2002, Merrill Lynch & Co., Inc. All rights reserved.

example, a vendor may include a feature in the purchase agreement that permits the buyer to participate in currency appreciation gains above a specified threshold. Embedded derivatives show up in products such as equity-indexed annuity universal life insurance or synthetic guaranteed investment contracts. Whether they realize it or not, many institutional investors own securities with embedded derivatives.[9]

In the last few years, accounting standards have expressly addressed embedded derivatives. Financial Accounting Standards Board (FASB) Statement No. 133, *Accounting for Derivative Instruments and Hedging Activities,* requires separate accounting for the embedded derivative under certain conditions. This includes the situation when "the economic characteristics and risks of the embedded derivative instrument are not clearly and closely related to the economic characteristics and risks of the host contract."[10] The "closely related" argument is likewise an important part of IAS 39, *Financial Instruments: Recognition and Measurement,* promulgated by the International Accounting Standards Committee. In both cases, the rationale is to

> *ensure that contractual provisions that create similar risk exposures are accounted for in the same way whether or not they are "embedded" in a non-derivative contract and to counter the possibility that companies might seek to avoid the requirement to measure derivatives at fair value by "embedding" a derivative in a non-derivative contract.*[11]

Relevance to Endowments, Foundations, and Pension Funds

Identifying what constitutes an embedded derivative is a first step for any organization that must comply with relevant accounting standards and other rules. At this time, private endowments and foundations busy themselves with FASB Statement No. 116, *Accounting for Contributions Received and Contributions Made,* and FASB Statement No. 117, *Financial Statements of Not-for-Profit Organizations.* Public university endowments and pension funds use Governmental Accounting Standards Board rules, including Technical Bulletin 2003-1, *Disclosure Requirements for Derivatives Not Reported at Fair Value on the Statement of Net Assets.*[12]

Private pension plan accounting is complex and looks to ERISA, FASB, and other entities for guidance. Some pundits expect the United States to ultimately adopt something similar to the UK pension accounting standard, FRS 17. Requiring companies to represent pension assets and liabilities on the balance sheet would be a radical departure from the current U.S. protocol that permits smoothing of gains and losses over time.[13]

How endowments, foundations, and pensions account for embedded derivatives is not so much the issue as the fact that these more complicated transactions are harder to value. Because investment valuation drives regulatory compliance and funding ratios, there is a lot at stake. Hence, the topic of valuation of derivative instruments and associated model risk cannot be overlooked.

DERIVATIVE INSTRUMENT VALUATION

Overview

Valuation is a fact of life for anyone involved in investing and, by extension, risk management. Some organizations reassess the value of their investments every day. Others do so periodically. Whatever the frequency, the challenge is the same. How should a security be properly valued so it reflects the price at which a hypothetical buyer and seller would transact?

In the absence of market quotations, value assessment must be reasonable and representative of what others with similar experience and knowledge would conclude. Even then, there is no guarantee of uniformity. Models may vary, but more fundamentally, the definition of value can vary from one investor to the next.

In his testimony before the Senate Committee on Banking, Housing and Urban Affairs, Chairman William H. Donaldson described the valuation process for hedge funds:

> *Registered investment companies must price their portfolio securities at market, or, if there is no market, at their current "fair value"— determined in good faith by the fund's board of directors. Hedge funds are not subject to these requirements. Thus, for example, hedge funds may determine that the appropriate price of a security is its inherent price, a price that looks to the future. Or it may substitute its determination of the value of a security for a market price."*[14]

Although permissible, "it may be impossible for an investor to know the actual value of a hedge fund's portfolio securities."[15]

In an earlier speech, Lori A. Richards, Director of the Office of Compliance Inspections and Examinations of the SEC, stressed the importance of "strong internal controls with respect to valuation," some of which are shown in Exhibit 9.9 and logically apply to all institutional investors, not just the mutual funds about which she spoke.[16]

Derivatives Are Different

Not only is the valuation of cash instruments important, but it also drives the valuation of derivatives. When a risk manager starts off with bad numbers,

EXHIBIT 9.9 Suggestions for Proper Valuation

Guard against a lack of oversight of valuation—make sure that there are good checks and balances in the valuation process.

Because there is a degree of expertise needed to handle valuation and pricing issues, some fund boards have established valuation committees to focus specifically on valuation issues when they arise. The advisor may also have a valuation committee, and many funds have a director on call. These committees should have written policies, regular meetings, and keep minutes.

The more difficult a security is to value, the more the board should be involved in understanding the pricing methodology. The board needs to understand the pricing process—and will want to review the process with the advisor—including the criteria considered and the valuation methods used.

If you use a pricing service, understand exactly what services that pricing service provides. Pricing services vary: they may give you NASDAQ quotes; they may give you their best estimate of value based on communications with the underwriter or issuer; or they may spit back at you exactly the information that your portfolio manager has provided to them.

Some funds use more than one pricing service—this allows the fund to obtain two independent pricing recommendations, and can provide a check for discrepancies.

Ensure that someone who is not involved in the pricing process, such as compliance staff, reviews all overrides to look for individual overrides that aren't supportable, and for patterns of overrides that suggest problems. Also consider providing a periodic report to the board on all overrides and the reasons for them.

Monitor for 'stale' pricing (when the price of a security does not change). Is someone overriding incorrectly or is something wrong with the input?

If you're using fair value, compare any sales in the market to the fair value for accuracy. Also, review any differences that occur over time for any bias that suggests that the fair values being used are either consistently higher or lower than actual sales prices. Also consider providing this data to the board (e.g. quarterly) so that it can ensure it is overseeing the process.

Excerpted from "Speech by SEC Staff: Valuation, Trading, and Disclosure: Three Compliance Imperatives, Remarks by Lori A. Richards, Director, Office of Compliance Inspections and Examinations, U.S. Securities & Exchange Commission," 2001 Mutual Fund Compliance Conference, Investment Company Institute, June 14, 2001.

any subsequent task (e.g., monitoring positions) can easily become an exercise in futility. Even when cash investments are properly valued, the assessment of derivative instruments is far from easy. The article reproduced in Exhibit 9.10 talks about the many challenges. Something as simple as the choice of time period or as advanced as building the right input model—otherwise referred to as a *nested model*—can make a huge difference.

EXHIBIT 9.10 Derivatives Valuation

One Size Does Not Fit All

The derivatives market is huge by any account, with an estimated size of more than one hundred trillion dollars.[1] A market this large invites scrutiny under ordinary circumstances, but times are hardly "business as usual". Today's watchword is information. Financial market participants want better quality information in larger amounts and they want it now. Corporate misdeeds and black box investing has led to unhappy investors seeking redress through the courts as their portfolios have plummeted in value. Policy-makers have been busy too.

New regulations have put derivatives at center stage, all of which entail more information gathering about these products and how they are used to minimize risk, enhance return, raise funds or synthesize securities. Summary of Statement No. 133, Accounting for Derivative Instruments and Hedging Activities, extends earlier accounting standards by requiring publicly traded companies to regularly value any financial instrument that meets the definition of a derivative.[2] This is in addition to the Securities and Exchange Commission's disclosure requirement that companies with a market capitalization larger than $2.5 billion must provide risk information about "market risk sensitive instruments."[3] Corporations are not alone. Banks face challenges in the form of the new Basel Capital Accord, much of which involves the proper estimation of risk as a way to determine statutory capital amounts.[4] Additionally, the Sarbanes-Oxley Act of 2002 sets forth a wide array of rules that affect publicly traded firms that use derivatives.[5] Even closely held companies and non-profit organizations are evaluating whether they should comply with this new legislation even though they are not obliged to do so.

Clearly, understanding how to value instruments that "derive" their value from some underlying asset is an important topic for investors, regulators, attorneys and managers alike. Climbing the learning curve, however, is easier said than done. Derivative instrument valuation is a complicated business that requires a solid understanding of the many factors that determine fair value. An important first step is the selection of an appropriate model.

Model Selection

Derivatives come in all shapes and sizes and no one model can possibly work all of the time. The partial list shown in the following table hints at the problems associated with the "one size fits all" concept. The variety of derivative instruments mandates the use of different models for different situations. The model used to value a commodity forward is completely different from that used to value an equity swap. Even when derivatives can be classified similarly, valuation model selection is still not a straightforward task.

Derivative Instrument Categories

Forwards	Futures	Options	Swaps
Commodity	Commodity	Commodity	Commodity
Currency	Currency	Currency	Currency
Credit	Equity	Credit	Credit
Equity	Fixed Income	Embedded	Equity
Fixed Income	Index	Equity	Fixed Income
	Swaps Futures	Fixed Income	
		Options on Futures	

EXHIBIT 9.10 *Continued*

Consider two options: a warrant issued by a closely-held company and the option embedded within a callable bond that gives the issuer the right to buy the bond back before its original maturity date.[6] The Black-Scholes option-pricing model provides one way to value the warrants as long as adjustments are made to reflect the fact that the warrant does not trade in an established market. Unfortunately, the assumption of a constant interest rate makes the Black-Scholes model a poor choice for valuing the callable bond option.

An alternative is to use a model that recognizes the possibility that interest rates can move around over time. With something known as the lattice approach, an analyst starts by forecasting interest rate scenarios for each time period during which the bond is outstanding. The future expected interest rates are then used to value the callable bond on each coupon payment date. The process is repeated to generate a value for the option-free bond. The final step requires finding the value of the embedded option as the difference between the option-free bond and the callable bond.[7]

Importantly, both situations involve options but the valuation is completely different because the options are themselves different. The warrant is a call on equity and assumes stable interest rates. The callable bond option is quite sensitive to interest rate movements and must be priced accordingly.

Model Implementation

Identification of an appropriate method is just the beginning. Implementing the model requires care in evaluating inputs. What frequency of data should be used? Will valuation estimates be consistent across different data vendors? Will the input form affect the outcome and, if so, what is the likely result? Is the data stable over time? For more complicated valuations, the objective will guide the tradeoff between precision and computational costs. An average or range may suffice for purposes of regulatory compliance or assessing legal damages.[8]

Other situations call for a point estimate. This might occur if the derivative position will be sold or, if used to hedge something else, it must be adjusted for size.

Sometimes the inputs themselves must be modeled. When this happens, valuation of the derivative instrument will be based on what is referred to as a nested model. Consider the example of a path dependent bond such as a mortgage-backed security. The first task is to simulate a sufficient number of interest rate paths for all time periods until the bond matures. The output from this first model is used as an input for a second model. The goal is to project future cash flows that reflect prepayment of principal when rates decline. Complicating things, the prepayment rate depends on multiple factors such as changes in interest rates, population mobility, household disposable income, economic expectations and overall financial market health.

The process does not end after running the second model. The present value of the expected cash flow outputs are then calculated using the interest rate paths from the first model. The result is a set of discounted cash flow totals that are typically averaged in order to estimate today's value of a particular mortgage-backed

(continued)

EXHIBIT 9.10 *Continued*

security. Inaccuracies can arise from a flawed interest rate model, a poor prepayment model or both. Either way, trouble looms.

Even within a given asset class, the valuation analysis depends on the characteristics of the underlying security. For example, the option that gives homeowners the right to prepay their mortgage when interest rates fall does not affect all mortgage-backed security values in the same way. A Collateralized Mortgage Obligation that consists of principal and interest payments will be less price-sensitive to early payments of principal than is the case with an Interest Only ("IO") strip. When the outstanding principal on underlying mortgages falls, interest on that debt will likewise fall and thereby reduce the dollar cash flows associated with the IO strip.

Model Risk

Derivative instrument valuation is a time consuming process that requires care in selection and implementation of a model. The risks associated with a bad or ill-fitted model can be costly, sometimes in the millions of dollars. Low valuations can result in additional tax liabilities and penalties. High valuations might cause a potential buyer to walk away. When a model is being used in court, the consequences are just as dire.[9,10] Model results that fail to meet rules of evidence can be devastating for the attorney who hired the expert witness. The solution is to carefully consider alternative models, the objective at hand and the risk-return tradeoff inherent in what is being valued.

Conclusion

The spotlight shines brightly on derivatives and all signs point to more of the same going forward. Their vast market size makes them a force to be reckoned with. Regulatory action and investor lawsuits share the need to know more about how derivative instruments are being used and the extent to which changes in their value affect the bottom line. This is no time for senior management to stick their heads in the sand. Understanding the economics of derivative instruments and knowing when to call in outside help is de rigueur.

Disclaimer: The information provided by this article should not be construed as financial or legal advice. The reader should consult his or her own advisors.

1. According to the International Swaps and Derivatives Association, interest rate and currency notional amounts outstanding approximated $98.8 trillion at year-end 2002 with another $4.59 trillion in default swap and equity derivative outstanding amounts.
2. Summary of Statement No. 133, *Accounting for Derivative Instruments and Hedging Activities,* issued in June 1998, "requires that an entity recognize all derivatives as either assets or liabilities in the statement of financial position and measure those instruments at fair value." Go to www.fasb.org for more information. On April 30, 2003, the Financial Accounting Standards Board issued Statement No. 149, *Amendment of Statement 133 on Derivative Instruments and Hedging Activities.*
3. See http://www.sec.gov/divisions/corpfin/guidance/derivfaq.htm#risk.

EXHIBIT 9.10 *Continued*

4. See http://www.bis.org/publ/bcbsca.htm.
5. Securities and Exchange Commission, "Disclosure in Management's Discussion and Analysis about Off-Balance Sheet Arrangements and Aggregate Contractual Obligations," 17 CFR Parts 228, 229, and 249. See http://www.sec.gov/rules/final/33-8182.htm.
6. An embedded option cannot be sold separately from the host security.
7. A callable bond represents a portfolio consisting of a long position in an option-free bond and a short position in a call. This reflects the sale of a call by the investors to the bond issuer.
8. Even compliance-related valuations will vary since not all regulations require the same thing.
9. Mangiero, Susan M. "Financial Model Risk Looms Large," *The Investment Lawyer,* Volume 9, Number 11, November 2003, pages 16–21.
10. Mangiero, Susan M. "Model Risk and Valuation," *Valuation Strategies,* Volume 6, Number 4, March/April 2003, pages 34–39.

Source: Copyright © 2003. The Michel-Shaked Group. Reprinted with permission.

Model Risk

A discussion of valuation is incomplete without mention of model risk. Simply put, any time a model is inappropriately or incorrectly used, the output could be imprecise at best and possibly outright wrong. Going back to the domino theme, bad output is seldom self-contained, can be a direct result of bad data, and is sometimes left unchecked. No one wants to deal with mistakes, but they are particularly ugly when problems at one level lead to problems elsewhere.

Suppose the equity investment manager for an endowment of a large university employs futures to hedge the fund's U.S. equity position. Heretofore, the manager based hedge size on historical price relationships, but is contemplating the use of returns instead. Exhibits 9.11 and 9.12 demonstrate that a seemingly simple decision like this can have a big impact on the ultimate outcome.

To simplify things, assume that the face value of the derivative instrument is identical to the amount of stock being hedged. Furthermore, assume that fractional contracts can be bought or sold. Looking at the first case shown in Exhibit 9.11, the endowment fund should sell 9.3 contracts to hedge against possible declining equity values. In this case, the hedge ratio is the same whether prices or returns are used. In contrast, the second case shown in Exhibit 9.12 tells a different story altogether. Using returns data, the hedge size is 6.5 contracts, instead of the 8-contract hedge ratio that results with price data. Investment performance that considers the hedge type and size is affected accordingly.

EXHIBIT 9.11   Data Form, Case One

Month	Derivative	Exposure
Prices ($)		
1	10	9.9
2	10.3	10.4
3	10.4	10.7
4	10.7	11.4
5	9.8	10
6	10.2	10.1
7	10.3	10.45
8	10.2	10.3
9	9.9	9.9
10	9.95	9.8
11	10.4	10.6
12	10.3	10.3
	Correlation:	0.93
	Hedge ratio:	9.3 contracts
Returns (%)		
1		
2	3.00	5.05
3	0.97	2.88
4	2.88	6.54
5	−8.41	−12.28
6	4.08	1.00
7	0.98	3.47
8	−0.97	−1.44
9	−2.94	−3.88
10	0.51	−1.01
11	4.52	8.16
12	−0.96	−2.83
	Correlation:	0.93
	Hedge ratio:	9.3 contracts

Notice that time interval is another source of model risk. In the cases just discussed, the impact of data form depends on time in several ways. The hedge ratio is significantly different for returns data in the second 12-month period, demonstrating that the selection of the exact calendar period can affect results. Frequency of data—daily, weekly, monthly—is yet another matter, not to mention the troubles that ensue when data are not readily available or are reported differently over time.

On the face of it, data decisions may seem unimportant, but their impact is far from academic. The quality of a hedge depends on proper size, and this in turn depends on the choice of time period and data form. On the

EXHIBIT 9.12 Data Form, Case Two

Month	Derivative	Exposure
Prices ($)		
13	15	11
14	14	11.9
15	9	9.6
16	13	11.4
17	10	10
18	10.4	9.3
19	9.7	10
20	10	9.1
21	9	10.2
22	10	9.8
23	11	10.45
24	12	10.45
	Correlation:	0.80
	Hedge ratio:	8.0 contracts
Returns (%)		
13	1	
14	2	−6.67
15	3	−35.71
16	4	44.44
17	5	−23.08
18	6	4.00
19	7	−6.73
20	8	3.09
21	9	−10.00
22	10	11.11
23	11	10.00
24	12	9.09
	Correlation:	0.65
	Hedge ratio:	6.5 contracts

regulatory front, data choice can influence whether a hedge passes the requisite effectiveness tests that support favorable accounting treatment, and in due course, determine the constancy of reported earnings. In its June 25, 2003, press release, the Federal Home Loan Mortgage Corporation (Freddie Mac) wrote that "the reported fair values of certain option-related derivatives did not incorporate all applicable market pricing data."[17]

Model risk extends far beyond issues of data and includes questions about appropriateness of a model. Stock option valuation comes to mind given its recent prominence in the financial news. Many executive stock options come with strings as to when they can be exercised. Moreover, they do not trade in open markets and the volatility of the underlying stock is seldom constant. This is especially true for fast-growing industries that favor option-based compensation because it preserves cash by reducing current wage-related expenses. Taken together, these features limit the usefulness of the familiar Black-Scholes option pricing model.[18] When an incorrect valuation affects expenses and therefore impacts earnings or investment return, making a model-related mistake is far from trivial.[19]

Bad Valuations Are Expensive

Mistakes are costly. When they result in financial restatements, money and time go out the door, along with investor confidence. Add in the public relations nightmare that often ensues and life can get pretty nasty for those whose names are tethered to the problem. Probably the worst situation is an organization that ends up in court, on the wrong end of the adjudication. A quick look at the headlines shown in Exhibit 9.13 suggests that valuation issues are here to stay, at least for now.

Valuation was at the very heart of a U.S. Tax Court case involving interest rate swaps. The final ruling cites nine flaws in the methodology used to determine swaps income, including the fact that the method "used a static rather than dynamic procedure to ascertain the applicable credit adjustments."[20] Clearly, valuation and related issues of model risk should be at the top of the agenda for anyone who has responsibility for the integrity of reports that are produced from model outputs.

EXHIBIT 9.13   Valuation Headlines

Headline	Publication (Date)
"Investment Adviser Defrauded Hedge Funds, SEC Suit Alleges"	*Derivatives Litigation Reporter* (January 15, 2001)
"First Eagle SoGen Sues Int'l Bank, Alleges Unfair Stock Valuation"	*Derivatives Litigation Reporter* (January 29, 2001)
"Private Pitfalls of Public Funds"	*Financial Times* (January 30, 2002)
"Ambiguity Clouds Valuation Methods"	*Financial Times* (February 25, 2002)
"Mutual Funds Turn on Valuations as SEC Moves to Steady the Spin"	*Financial Times* (March 27, 2002)
"Enron Inquiry Now Focusing on Valuations"	*The New York Times* (May 13, 2002)

Source: Adapted from "Financial Model Risk Looms Large" by Susan M. Mangiero, *The Investment Lawyer,* Vol. 9, No. 11, November 2002.

SUMMARY

1. There are several types of risks related to derivative instruments. These include market risk, credit risk, liquidity risk, settlement risk, operational risk, and legal risk, respectively.
2. Risks associated with use of derivatives are interrelated.
3. Risks inherent to derivative instruments are not the same across product types. Selecting the best product depends on what trade-offs an investor is willing to make.
4. Embedded derivatives cannot be stripped and traded separately from the host security.
5. The valuation of derivative instruments is complicated by the fact that some inputs to the model must themselves be modeled.
6. Model risk can arise from an inappropriate use of a model or poor choice of data or time period.

Three

Putting It All Together

CHAPTER 10

Getting Started

A journey of a thousand miles begins with a single step.

—Confucius

RISK MANAGEMENT SETTING

The Myth of Uniformity

The risk management process is hard to generalize. As shown in Exhibit 10.1, there are many types of organizational structures, each one tied to a particular regulatory mandate and operating environment. These differences across industries have a profound influence on the risk management function, starting with the primary objective. The risk manager for a manufacturing company is likely to hedge as a way to stabilize reported earnings. An insurance company executive may need to bring together accounting and financial teams to evaluate an annuity product because its structure involves embedded derivatives. A hedge fund professional, worried about liquidity risk, could choose derivatives over securities that seldom trade.

Even within a seemingly homogenous group such as banks, differences in clientele will drive the product offerings and the related risk management function. A bank that caters to retail customers will tailor its products accordingly, offering smaller-size mortgage loans, life insurance, and college tuition savings plans. A bank that focuses on institutional investors and corporations may aggressively market its securities safe-keeping services, the capability to trade a variety of currencies, and the ability to manage large pools of money. Where settlement and foreign exchange volatility issues grab the attention of the wholesale bank risk team, the retail bank risk manager might spend more time on the kind of mortgage loans it needs to hedge.

Setting up a risk management program starts with the fundamentals about why an organization exists and what it is charged to do. This point

EXHIBIT 10.1 Different Types of Organizational Structures

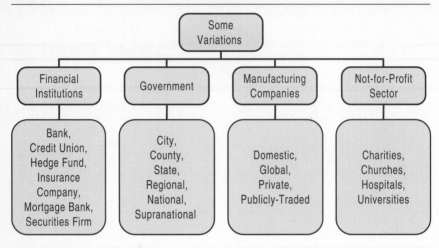

bears repeating. Without a clear statement of purpose, no risk management program can survive. Everything follows from the risk management objectives, which themselves are determined by organizational type, operating environment, and in-house policies.

Common Threads

Endowments, foundations, and pension plans are similar in several respects. They enjoy certain tax advantages, are regulated in some fashion, serve a large number of beneficiaries, and, as shown in Exhibits 10.2 through 10.4, represent huge pools of money. Beyond that, each type of organization has to consider investment characteristics in achieving its financial goals. That includes earning a sufficient rate of return, driven by distribution requirements.

Private Foundations

U.S. law currently requires private foundations to give away at least 5 percent of their assets each year or risk pecuniary penalties. Unless they are willing to see their asset base diminish over time, they need to earn at least 5 percent each year, assuming zero growth in annual contributions and no inflation. Relaxing these assumptions changes things. Exhibit 10.5 lays out a general approach for determining the net growth in foundation assets. Using a little algebra and plugging in a few numbers makes it easy to impute the break-even nominal investment return. This is the rate that results in a

EXHIBIT 10.2 Top 25 University Endowments for 2002 and 2003, Ranked by Market Value of Assets

Institution (Rank)	State	2003 Endowment Funds ($000)	2002 Endowment Funds ($000)	Percent Change in Endowment
Harvard University (1)	MA	18,849,491	17,169,757	9.8
Yale University (2)	CT	11,034,600	10,523,600	4.9
Princeton University (3)	NJ	8,730,100	8,319,600	4.9
University of Texas System (4)	TX	8,708,818	8,630,679	0.9
Stanford University (5)	CA	8,614,000	7,613,000	13.1
Massachusetts Institute of Technology (6)	MA	5,133,613	5,359,423	−4.2
University of California (7)	CA	4,368,911	4,199,067	4.0
Columbia University (8)	NY	4,350,000	4,238,162	2.6
Emory University (9)	GA	4,019,766	4,551,873	−11.7
The Texas A&M University System and Foundations (10)	TX	3,802,712	3,743,442	1.6
University of Pennsylvania (11)	PA	3,547,473	3,393,297	4.5
University of Michigan (12)	MI	3,464,515	3,375,689	2.6
Washington University (13)	MO	3,454,704	3,517,104	−1.8
University of Chicago (14)	IL	3,221,883	3,255,368	−1.0
Northwestern University (15)	IL	3,051,167	3,022,733	0.9
Duke University (16)	NC	3,017,261	2,927,478	3.1
Rice University (17)	TX	2,937,649	2,939,804	−0.1
Cornell University (18)	NY	2,854,771	2,853,742	0.0
University of Notre Dame (19)	IN	2,573,346	2,554,004	0.8
Dartmouth College (20)	NH	2,121,183	2,186,610	−3.0
University of Southern California (21)	CA	2,113,666	2,130,977	−0.8
Vanderbilt University (22)	TN	2,019,139	2,019,612	0.0
University of Virginia (23)	VA	1,800,882	1,686,625	6.8
Johns Hopkins University (24)	MD	1,714,541	1,695,150	1.1
Brown University (25)	RI	1,461,327	1,412,364	3.5
Total Assets		116,965,518	113,319,160	

According to NACUBO, the percent change represents the change in market value "between fiscal year-end 2002 and fiscal year-end 2003," and not the investment rate of return for each endowment. Factors that determine the fiscal year-end market value include growth in donations, expenditures, withdrawals and invested asset returns.
Source: Reprinted with permission from the *2003 NACUBO Endowment Study.* Copyright © 2004 National Association of College and University Business Officers.

EXHIBIT 10.3 Top 50 Foundations by Assets, 2001[a]

Foundation	State	Foundation Type[b]	Assets
Bill & Melinda Gates Foundation[c]	WA	IN	$32,751,466,000
Lilly Endowment	IN	IN	12,814,397,581
Ford Foundation	NY	IN	10,814,696,000
Robert Wood Johnson Foundation	NJ	IN	9,044,511,000
J. Paul Getty Trust[d]	CA	OP	8,793,485,757
David and Lucile Packard Foundation	CA	IN	6,196,520,868
William and Flora Hewlett Foundation	CA	IN	6,080,721,309
W. K. Kellogg Foundation	MI	IN	5,530,494,099
Starr Foundation	NY	IN	4,781,056,809
Pew Charitable Trusts	PA	IN	4,338,580,605
John D. and Catherine T. MacArthur Foundation	IL	IN	4,215,930,831
Andrew W. Mellon Foundation	NY	IN	4,135,567,000
California Endowment	CA	IN	3,366,256,100
Rockefeller Foundation	NY	IN	3,211,126,000
Annie E. Casey Foundation	MD	IN	2,592,378,126
Duke Endowment	NC	IN	2,489,158,509
Charles Stewart Mott Foundation	MI	IN	2,460,169,524
Robert W. Woodruff Foundation	GA	IN	2,422,622,552
Kresge Foundation	MI	IN	2,415,971,841
Annenberg Foundation	PA	IN	2,354,837,085
Casey Family Programs[d]	WA	OP	2,349,848,837
Harry and Jeanette Weinberg Foundation	MD	IN	1,936,263,883
John S. and James L. Knight Foundation	FL	IN	1,900,829,942
McKnight Foundation	MN	IN	1,877,703,000
New York Community Trust	NY	CM	1,785,215,504
Carnegie Corporation of New York	NY	IN	1,711,510,640
Ewing Marion Kauffman Foundation	MO	IN	1,681,000,000
Richard King Mellon Foundation	PA	IN	1,661,919,000
Freeman Foundation	NY	IN	1,619,093,718
Robert R. McCormick Tribune Foundation	IL	IN	1,599,796,701
Cleveland Foundation	OH	CM	1,499,767,419

EXHIBIT 10.3 *Continued*

Foundation	State	Foundation Type[b]	Assets
Doris Duke Charitable Foundation	NY	IN	1,444,832,885
James Irvine Foundation	CA	IN	1,378,433,649
Houston Endowment	TX	IN	1,367,954,880
Alfred P. Sloan Foundation	NY	IN	1,314,367,357
Wallace-Reader's Digest Funds	NY	IN	1,303,278,360
W. M. Keck Foundation	CA	IN	1,263,938,000
Brown Foundation	TX	IN	1,183,622,138
Donald W. Reynolds Foundation	NV	IN	1,177,625,153
Chicago Community Trust and Affiliates	IL	CM	1,157,517,684
William Penn Foundation	PA	IN	1,047,720,982
Marin Community Foundation	CA	CM	1,035,000,000
Lumina Foundation for Education	IN	IN	991,267,826
California Wellness Foundation	CA	IN	985,910,600
Walton Family Foundation	AR	IN	948,658,074
Kimbell Art Foundation[d]	TX	OP	933,077,515
Moody Foundation	TX	IN	926,916,215
Howard Heinz Endowment	PA	IN	907,657,792
Henry Luce Foundation	NY	IN	905,305,357
Joyce Foundation	IL	IN	868,298,527
Total Assets			171,574,279,234

[a]The foundation fiscal information is based on data provided to the Foundation Center as of January 24, 2003.
[b]IN, independent; CM, community; OP, operating.
Source: Excerpted from *Foundation Yearbook,* Table: "Top 50 Foundations by Assets," page 25. Copyright © 2003, The Foundation Center.

net zero change in assets. Here, the break-even rate is 7.0 percent, assuming a 3.2 percent inflation rate, a 1.8 percent increase in gifts, and a 5.6 percent spending rate.

Pending regulation has the potential to increase per annum distribution, along with the way the spending rate is determined.[1] If this happens, investment return goals will likewise be affected. School is still out with respect to whether and how legislative changes will occur. Some private foundations are already distributing more than is required. According to the Foundation Center, "the premier source of information"[2] about the approximately 65,000 active grant-making foundations in the United States, independent foundations gave away about 5.8 percent of their assets in 2002.

EXHIBIT 10.4 Top Pension Funds by Category

Fund Sponsor	Assets (Millions of Dollars)
Corporate	
General Motors	82,500
General Electric	68,769
Verizon	65,936
Boeing	57,940
IBM	56,500
Lucent Technologies	52,995
Ford Motor	50,000
SBC Communications	46,405
Lockheed Martin	32,289
AT&T	27,601
Total assets	540,935
Public	
California Public Empl.	143,887
New York State Common	106,091
California State Teachers	95,553
Florida State Board	88,514
Texas Teachers	75,109
New York State Teachers	74,915
New Jersey	66,691
Wisconsin Investment	55,473
New York City Retirement	54,512
North Carolina	52,575
Total assets	813,320

Source: Reprinted with permission, *Pensions & Investments*, January 21, 2002. Copyright ©, Crain Communications, Inc. All rights reserved.

As with many institutions, foundations feel the pinch when market conditions worsen. In its April 5, 2004, press release, the Foundation Center attributed a 2.5 percent decline in foundation giving to "three consecutive years of stock market losses and a sluggish and uneven economic recovery.[3,4]

University Endowments

University endowments also have been hit hard. The National Association of College and University Business Officers (NACUBO) reports that "for the second consecutive year, the average college and university endowment lost value amidst investment market declines and a poor economy" at the same time that survey participants were reported to have spent 5.3 percent

EXHIBIT 10.5   Net Rate of Return Example

General formula	Nominal return on investments
	Less inflation rate
	Plus or minus changes in contributions
	Less spending
	Equals net growth in assets
Example	7.0% Nominal investment rate of return
	Less 3.2% inflation rate
	Plus 1.8% change in contributions
	Less 5.6% spending
	Equals zero net growth in assets

Notes:
1. Administrative expenses are ignored.
2. Nominal annual rates are assumed.
3. Spending rates are assumed to meet or exceed statutory requirements, permitting the exclusion of financial penalties.

of "the market value of their endowments."[5] Exhibit 10.6 demonstrates the flexibility of university spending rate policies.

Diversification goes a long way to dampen the ill effects of underperforming investments. Unfortunately, as shown in Exhibits 10.7 and 10.8, an asset allocation mix that favors equities when they are getting hit hard is less than ideal. Making matters worse, some investors have responded to bear markets by reallocating funds to higher-risk securities, thereby changing the risk profile of the fund.

Endowment size is a factor. According to the NACUBO 2002 study, endowments with more than $1 billion in assets outperformed their smaller peers and recorded better numbers than most market benchmarks. At the same time, these larger institutional investors reported lower equity holdings—44.8 percent versus the dollar weighted survey average of 49.4 percent—along with higher allotments for alternative investments such as hedge funds and venture capital.

Pension Plans

Current headlines are replete with news of pension plan woes. In more halcyon days, little heed might be given, the idea being that any problems would likely work themselves out and affect only a small group of people. However, times have changed. Many experts predict a bumpy ride ahead with issues that are destined to plague more than a handful of companies and municipalities and that have the potential to cost beneficiaries and taxpayers a lot of money. *Pensions & Investments* describes pension plan cash

EXHIBIT 10.6   Endowment Spending Rates

Institution	Stated Spending Policy
Carleton University	The spending rate on the Carleton University Endowment Fund has been changed from six percent to five percent. The new rate will be applied to the April 30, 2002 distribution. A lower spending rate will protect the endowment against fluctuations in market returns, given the relatively high equity content of the endowment fund and the fact that the high rates of return experienced in the last few years in the capital markets may not continue in the future.[1]
Embry-Riddle Aeronautical University	Our spending policy establishes an initial spending rate of 5% (a rate used by many institutions). When the actual return (averaged over three years and adjusted for inflation) is higher than expected, the spending rate is increased 0.5%. If the actual return is lower, the spending rate is reduced by 0.5%. This adjustment method moderators the annual volatility of the returns.[2]
Princeton University	While Princeton's policy does not establish an explicit spending rate—it results from the application of the spending rule and fluctuations over time in the value of the endowment—the University has long thought that a spending rate between 4% and 5% of the market value of the endowment was desirable and appropriate.[3]

Sources:
[1] "Endowment Spending Rate Modified," *This Is Carleton,* Vol. 4, No. 5, March 11, 2002.
[2] *Embry-Riddle Aeronautical University Endowment Investment/Spending Strategy.* Copyright © 2003, Embry-Riddle Aeronautical University. Reprinted with permission.
[3] "Endowment Spending Policy Fact Sheet," *News from Princeton University,* January 2001. Copyright © 2001, Princeton University. Reprinted with permission.

infusions by major corporations as the "tip of the iceberg."[6] They are not alone with predictions of gloom, especially with respect to defined benefit (DB) plans.[7] After years of excess earnings, many pension funds face the harsh possibility that large cash infusions are inevitable, diverting funds from capital expenditures that could put a damper on corporate earnings.[8]

Public pension funds are not immune to the ill effects of a down market. One solution, reduction of benefits, is problematic because legislation is almost always required. Unless faced with unavoidable shortfalls, rating downgrades, or taxpayer complaints, politicians may be shy about cutting pension benefits. States with excess debt capacity may opt to issue Pension

EXHIBIT 10.7 Asset Allocation Mix for University Endowments by Investment Pool Asset Size (Percent of Total)

Asset Class	Greater Than $1 Billion	$501 Million to $1 Billion	$101 Million to $500 Million	$51 Million to $100 Million	$26 Million to $50 Million	Less than $25 Million	Public	Independent
Equity	44.8	54.4	56.5	58.7	60.2	57.0	58.1	56.7
Fixed Income	18.6	18.2	23.5	27.2	27.7	29.8	27.9	24.9
Real Estate	4.2	4.2	2.9	2.8	2.6	2.2	2.1	3.1
Cash	1.8	1.4	2.7	4.9	3.5	6.6	4.0	4.0
Hedge Funds	19.9	13.4	8.3	4.3	4.2	1.6	4.3	6.9
Private Equity	5.2	4.2	2.2	0.6	0.2	0.2	0.9	1.5
Venture Capital	3.0	2.7	1.3	0.3	0.2	0.1	0.5	0.9
Natural Resources	1.9	1.1	0.8	0.1	0.1	0.0	0.4	0.4
Other	0.7	0.4	1.8	1.1	1.4	2.5	1.6	1.6

Source: Reprinted with permission from the 2003 *NACUBO Endowment Study.* Copyright © 2004 National Association of College & University Business Officers.

EXHIBIT 10.8 Investment Rates of Return for University Endowments by Asset Size (%)

Time Horizon	More Than $1 Billion	$501 Million to $1 Billion	$100 Million to $500 Million	Less Than $100 Million	Public	Private	Median
1-year	−1.6	−5.2	−3.4	−3.7	−3.8	−3.4	−3.7
3-year	11.9	7.5	6.4	5.1	5.6	6.7	5.8
5-year	15.1	12.2	11.4	10.2	10.7	11.6	11.0
10-year	14.6	12.8	12.0	10.8	11.4	12.1	11.8

Source: Reprinted with permission from the *2002 NACUBO Endowment Study*. Copyright © 2003, National Association of College and University Business Officers.

Obligation Bonds, using the proceeds to reduce a pension plan's liability. A panacea for the short run, additional leverage could lead to further problems down the road.[9] Everyone is watching with so much at stake.

Time to Act

All in all, trustees are forced to rethink old paradigms concerning asset allocation and long-held traditions about spending, program structure, actuarial assumptions, and accounting rules. Pension plan sponsors are mulling over design issues. Should they move to a defined contribution (DC) plan or cash balance approach? Should permitted investments in DC plans be modified? Endowment managers are contemplating what reserves they need to cushion against a sustained period of weak investment performance. Should payouts be reduced if permitted by law and are acceptable to donors? Foundations may find themselves having to reduce administrative expenses if proposed legislation passes. This is no time for the faint of heart. More than ever, those in charge have to rise to new challenges, deciding whether to take preemptive action or fight fires after the fact.

INVESTING AND RISK MANAGEMENT: TWO SIDES OF THE SAME COIN

Investment Policies

Whether an investor is large or small, the process is pretty much the same. It starts off with goal setting that expressly takes constraints and particular needs into account. Exhibits 10.9 through 10.11 provide examples of stated investment goals, reflecting some of the unique characteristics of endowments, foundations, and pension plans.

Typically the goal investment statements vary in detail, length, and scope, emphasizing what is relevant to the particular organization. To the extent that generalizations can be made, the investment goal for an endowment will depend on why it was established in the first place, how soon funds are needed and the amount and form of anticipated gifts. The investment goal for a foundation is partly influenced by whether the organization is a private, community, or operating foundation. Statutory distribution rules and funding sources are other factors. The investment goal for a DB plan will emphasize the long-term nature of what is owed to existing and future retirees. A company with a relatively young workforce can be somewhat more flexible than is the case when employees are disproportionately older and therefore closer to collecting benefits. Laying out proper investment choices is one of many priorities for DC plan trustees.

The goal statement is just the start. In its "Investment Policy Checklist for Pension Fund Assets," the Government Finance Officers Association

EXHIBIT 10.9   Example of Investment Goal Statements for Endowments

Institution	Statement
Smith College	The overall financial goal of the endowment is to maintain its real (i.e. inflation-adjusted) market value while providing the College's operating budget with a relatively predictable and growing (in nominal terms) stream of revenue targeted at approximately 5% of the endowment. Therefore, the financial objective is to earn a total return (net of all fees and expenses) equal to or exceeding the foregoing spending rate plus the inflation rate—as measured by the Consumer Price Index.
	Investment objectives for the overall endowment include the following:
	Attain a total return matching or exceeding the portfolio's composite benchmark.
	Incur only a reasonable and prudent level of risk, which is codified in the target asset allocation and portfolio benchmark.

Source: "Investment Policy Statement Approved by the Smith College Board of Trustees at its May 2002 Meeting." Copyright © 2002, Smith College. Reprinted with permission.

recommends that an investment policy include the eight elements shown in Exhibit 10.12. Furthermore, it should be prepared with input from "investment advisors and other professionals who regularly provide input on the plan's investment policy."[10] Note that many of the publicly available investment policies for endowments and foundations include a section about the projected spending rate and rules for adjusting this rate from time to time.[11]

Under the Employee Retirement Income Security Act (ERISA), a covered pension plan must have a funding policy, something that is not necessarily the same as an investment policy. According to Bruce Ashton, president of the American Society of Pension Actuaries and then co-chair of its Government Committee when he testified before the ERISA Advisory Council in 2002, a plan should have both. Without a cogent investment policy in place, plan sponsor fiduciaries are ill equipped to make the vital decisions for which they are held responsible. Exhibit 10.13 showcases some of the best practices he urges regulators to consider.

Risk Management Does Not Exist in a Vacuum

Entire books and articles are written about how to establish effective investment policy guidelines, including the determination of a proper asset

EXHIBIT 10.10 Examples of Investment Goal Statements for Foundations

Institution	Statement
Minneapolis Medical Research Foundation	The Operating Fund provides funding for daily operations. Operating Fund investments are intended to generate revenue to support the general and administrative activities of MMRF. Investment Objectives and Constraints:
	1. Time Horizon: The Time Horizon for investments in the Operating Fund is generally one to 30 days, but may extend up to twelve months depending upon the projected need for liquidity.
	2. Liquidity Needs: Investments in the Operating Funds must satisfy the need for daily liquidity.
	3. Return Objective: The return objective for the Operating Fund is to maximize current income within the parameters of principal preservation.
	4. Risk Tolerance: The Operating Fund should be invested to avoid principal loss.[1]
The San Diego Foundation	. . . in accordance with the Foundation's goal of improving the surrounding San Diego Community.
	The investment objectives for the Foundation will be for the asset value, exclusive of contributions or withdrawals, to grow over the long run and earn, through a combination of investment income and capital appreciation, a rate of return (time-weighted total return) in excess of the benchmarks established for the medium term (3 years) and long term (5 years).
	Example of Medium Term Performance Objective: The fixed income segment of the Fund shall exceed (net of fees) the Lehman Brothers Government Corporate Index as well as the median fixed income return in a representative performance universe.
	Example of Long Term Performance Objective: The Total Fund is to produce, after investment expenses, a minimum annual compound total rate of return of 5% in excess of the rate of inflation.[2]

Sources:
[1]*Investment Policy—Operating Fund (unrestricted), Investment Policy Statement, Minneapolis Medical Research Foundation, Adopted May 13, 2002.*
[2]*Investment Policy Statement: The San Diego Foundation Investment Objectives and Policy Guidelines, Effective May 16, 2002.* Copyright © 2003, The San Diego Foundation. Reprinted with permission.

EXHIBIT 10.11   Examples of Investment Goal Statements for Pensions

Institution	Statement
Colorado Public Employees' Retirement Association	The function of the Colorado Public Employees' Retirement Association is to provide present and future retirement or survivor benefits for its members. In keeping with that function, the preservation of capital is of paramount importance. The investment performance of the fund directly affects its future financial strength. Earnings on portfolio assets in excess of the assumed actuarial rate of return of 8.75 percent reduce unfunded actuarial liabilities. The fund is long-term in nature and the selection of investments is regulated by: statutory limitation, investment time horizon, the limits of acceptable risk, and the objective of optimizing the total rate of return. The targeted strategic asset allocation is designed to provide an optimal diversification to reduce risk and maximize total rate of return relative to risk.[1]
NY State Teachers' Retirement System	The Board's objective is to establish a long-term asset allocation plan that maximizes expected returns with an appropriate level of risk. To accomplish this, the asset allocation process takes into consideration capital market expectations, risk or expected volatility, how asset classes perform in comparison to other asset classes, investment goals and cash flow needs. Asset allocation is a long-term, strategic process and is not meant to be a reaction to short-term market fluctuations. The program is structured to generate a long-term return that equals or exceeds the actuarial assumption of 8% per annum.[2]

Sources:

[1]*PERA Investments Overview: Investments Policy Goal,* December 31, 2002, Colorado Public Employee's Retirement Association. Copyright © 2002, Colorado Public Employees' Retirement Association. Reprinted with permission.

[2]*Chief Investment Officer's Overview: Overall Objective and Performance,* Annual Report for the Fiscal Year Ended June 30, 2003, New York State Teachers' Retirement System, p. 40. Copyright © 2003, New York State Teachers' Retirement System. Reprinted with permission.

EXHIBIT 10.12 Suggested Elements of an Investment Policy

Element Number	Description
1	Statement of purpose
2	Identification of roles and responsibilities
3	Standard of care definition
4	Asset allocation statement
5	Rebalancing to confirm with the asset allocation
6	Investment guidelines
7	Reporting and monitoring
8	Corporate governance

Source: "Investment Policy Checklist for Pension Fund Assets," Government Finance Officers Association, May 2003.

EXHIBIT 10.13 Best Practice Recommendations for Fiduciary Education

Item Number	Description
1	The requirement of a written investment policy statement
2	Issues covered by the written investment policy statement to include:
	a. Investment objective of the plan
	b. Investment time horizon, risk profiles and expected return for the plan
	c. Investment structure of the plan—that is, identification of core investment categories and the criteria used to select them
	d. Identification of the lifestyle or lifecycle funds or asset allocation models to be offered by the plan, nondesignated investment options, whether the plan offers mutual funds windows or brokerage accounts
	e. Monitoring benchmarks for each investment alternative
	f. Frequency of monitoring and how the plan will deal with underperforming funds
3	Types of due diligence the fiduciaries should conduct in selecting and monitoring investment options and providers, including investment managers or advisors
4	How frequently monitoring activities should be undertaken
5	Types of due diligence records the fiduciaries should retain and for how long

Source: "Bruce Ashton's Testimony before the ERISA Advisory Council on Behalf of the American Society of Pension Actuaries, Working Group on Fiduciary Education," September 19, 2002. Copyright © 2002, Bruce Ashton. Reprinted with permission.

allocation mix and the nature of subsequent reviews. The purpose in introducing the topic here is not to restate what so many others have already laid out, but rather to emphasize the point that the processes of investing and risk management go hand in hand. As stated before, risk management cannot occur in a vacuum.

In its simplest form, risk management can be thought of as controlling uncertainty to the extent possible. Even when an institutional investor fails to explicitly address the management of risk, it is nevertheless making a statement about attitudes toward risk. In other words, "no policy" is in fact a policy, albeit a passive one. Whether an institution could have done better by actively managing its risk is the central question, and that depends on many things, including the relevant time perspective.

Analyzing historical performance is an altogether different exercise than having to make strategic and tactical decisions based on expectations. Consider a pension fund with a long position in U.S. bonds. If yields subsequently rise, the value of bonds falls. In hindsight, one can easily cite the merits of having hedged by taking an offsetting bond position or using an interest rate derivative instrument. The challenge is to decide, before the fact, whether active risk management is appropriate for the fund, given its objectives and constraints. The same applies for endowments and foundations. What makes sense today, given projections about the future and the organization's stated investment goals?

Exhibits 10.14, 10.15, and 10.16 excerpt statements about derivative use, one aspect of the risk management process. In the best of worlds, the link between investing and risk management is crystal clear. Anecdotally, history has shown otherwise. Sometimes honest mistakes in judgment regarding economic relationships are to blame. Fraud or weak or nonexistent controls account for the mayhem in other situations. If lessons can be learned from the past, everyone is ahead of the game. That's why a postaudit that examines what went wrong and why can be invaluable. The problem is that they are not done as often as they should be and even when they are, they are not always made available for public consumption.

Some posit that institutional investors are warming to the idea that active risk management can play a role in enhancing value. If true, many people stand to benefit. However, this can only happen when the right people are in place and resources are happily committed to training and systems.

THE FIVE "Cs" OF ESTABLISHING A RISK MANAGEMENT PROGRAM

As stated earlier in the book, establishing a risk management process is a multistep activity, starting with identification of risk and followed by various stages of implementation. Some tasks can take place contemporaneously.

EXHIBIT 10.14 Example of Derivative Use Statement: The University of Texas
System General Endowment Fund

- The Fund may utilize Derivative Securities with the approval of the UTIMCO
  Board to a) simulate the purchase or sale of an underlying market index while
  retaining a cash balance for fund management purposes; b) facilitate trading; c)
  reduce transaction costs; d) seek higher investment returns when a Derivative
  Security is priced more attractively than the underlying security; e) index or to
  hedge risks associated with Fund investments; or f) adjust the market exposure
  of the asset allocation, including long and short strategies; provided that leverage is not employed in the implementation of such Derivative purchases or
  sales. Leverage occurs when the notional value of the futures contracts exceeds
  the value of cash assets allocated to those contracts by more than 2%. The cash
  assets allocated to futures contracts is the sum of the value of the initial margin
  deposit, the daily variation margin and dedicated cash balances. This prohibition against leverage shall not apply where cash is received within 1 business
  day following the day the leverage occurs. UTIMCO's Derivatives Guidelines
  shall be used to monitor compliance with this policy. Notwithstanding the
  above, leverage strategies are permissible within the alternative equities investment class with the approval of the UTIMCO Board, if the investment strategy
  is uncorrelated to the Fund as a whole, the manager has demonstrated skill in
  the strategy, and the strategy implements systematic risk control techniques,
  value at risk measures, and pre-defined risk parameters.
- Such Derivative Securities shall be defined to be those instruments whose
  value is derived, in whole or part, from the value of any one or more underlying assets, or index of assets (such as stocks, bonds, commodities, interest
  rates, and currencies) and evidenced by forward, futures, swap, option, and
  other applicable contracts.

  UTIMCO shall attempt to minimize the risk of an imperfect correlation
  between the change in market value of the securities held by the Fund and the
  prices of Derivative Security investments by investing in only those contracts
  whose behavior is expected to resemble that of the Fund's underlying securities. UTIMCO also shall attempt to minimize the risk of an illiquid secondary
  market for a Derivative Security contract and the resulting inability to close a
  position prior to its maturity date by entering into such transactions on an
  exchange with an active and liquid secondary market. The net market value
  of exposure of Derivative Securities purchased or sold over the counter may
  not represent more than 15% of the net assets of the Fund.

  In the event that there are no Derivative Securities traded on a particular
  market index such as MSCI EAFE, the Fund may utilize a composite of other
  Derivative Security contracts to simulate the performance of such index.
  UTIMCO shall attempt to reduce any tracking error from the low correlation
  of the selected Derivative Securities with its index by investing in contracts
  whose behavior is expected to resemble that of the underlying securities.

  UTIMCO shall minimize the risk that a party will default on its payment
  obligation under a Derivative Security agreement by entering into agreements

(continued)

EXHIBIT 10.14 *Continued*

that mark to market no less frequently than monthly and where the counter-party is an investment grade credit. UTIMCO also shall attempt to mitigate the risk that the Fund will not be able to meet its obligation to the counter-party by investing the Fund in the specific asset for which it is obligated to pay a return or by holding adequate short-term investments.

The Fund may be invested in foreign currency forward and foreign currency futures contracts in order to maintain the same currency exposure as its respective index or to protect against anticipated adverse changes in exchange rates among foreign currencies and between foreign currencies and the U. S. dollar.

Source: "The University of Texas System General Endowment Fund Investment Policy Statement."

Others must be done sequentially. The timing depends on the infrastructure already in place, including the quality and quantity of human capital. People are a key resource and drive the process from start to finish. Even the use of technology relies on a person's comfort level, which in turn depends on educational background, training, and problem-solving skills. That said, nothing happens without a pledge from the top. Everyone has to understand that risk management is a top priority of the organization, something that is easier said than done. Communicating the message and putting policies in place to support this leadership resolve are paramount. Executive

EXHIBIT 10.15 Example of Derivative Use Statement: Community Foundation of Madison and Jefferson County, Inc.

The investment managers shall not utilize derivative securities to increase the actual or potential risk posture of the portfolio. Subject to other provisions in this Investment Policy Statement, the use of primary derivatives, including, but not limited to, structured notes* lower class tranches of collateralized mortgage obligations (CMOs)**, principal only (PO) or interest only (IO) strips, inverse floating securities, futures contracts, options, short sales, margin trading and such other specialized investment activity is prohibited."

Moreover, the investment managers are precluded from using derivatives to effect a leveraged portfolio structure (if options and futures are specifically approved by the Finance and Investment Committee, such positions must be offset in their entirety by corresponding cash or securities.

*Permit investments in 'conservative' structured notes which are principal guaranteed, unleveraged, and of short to intermediate maturity.
**Lower class defined by Federal Financial Institutional Examination Council (FFIEC).
Source: "Investment Policy Statement," Community Foundation of Madison and Jefferson County, Inc.

EXHIBIT 10.16 Example of Derivative Use Statement: State of Connecticut Retirement Plans & Trust Funds (CRPTF)

Derivative instruments may be used for any of the purposes listed below. Derivative instruments are defined as any contract or investment vehicle whose performance, risk characteristics, or value is based on a specific asset, interest rate, or index value.

- Market Exposure: To gain broad stock or bond market exposure in a manner that does not create the effect of leverage in the overall portfolio.
- To convert financial exposure in a given currency to that of another currency (e.g., to hedge Japanese Yen exposure back to the U.S. dollar). Any and all international managers may enter into foreign exchange contracts on currency provided that: a) such contracts are one year or less, and b) use of such contracts is limited solely and exclusively to hedging currency exposure existing within the manager's portfolio. There shall be no foreign currency speculation or any related investment activity.
- To adjust the duration of a bond portfolio in a manner that is consistent with the accepted approach of the manager and other policies and guidelines provided to the manager.
- To make portfolio adjustments that are consistent with other elements of the CRPTF's investment policies and guidelines and that do not systematically increase risk or expected volatility of the rate-of-return of the total Fund.
- For trading purposes which are intended to enhance investment returns. This purpose is subject to the requirement that it be consistent with other elements of the CRPTF's investment policies and guidelines and that it does not systematically increase the risk or expected volatility of the rate of return of the total Fund.

All other uses of derivatives are prohibited unless specifically by the Treasurer, and reviewed by the IAC. Investment managers are expected to have internal risk management programs in place to ensure that derivatives-based strategies do not result in inappropriate risks to the portfolio.

Source: "Investment Policy Statement for the State of Connecticut Retirement Plans & Trust Funds," Article VI, March 13, 2002, page 14.

commitment is only the beginning. Comprehension through training, controls, computing, and communications comprise the remaining four "Cs" of setting up a risk management initiative.

COMMITMENT

Motivation: Carrot or the Stick?

Acknowledging the importance of risk management occurs in one of several ways. An organization can sit idly by until moved into action. State or federal regulation can force organizations to establish better controls, increase the quantity—and hopefully, quality—of financial disclosure, and accept responsibility for mistakes. This has and will continue to occur as any combination of poor oversight, fraud, and imprudent risk taking leads to the next big debacle. An alternative is industry self-regulation that seeks to both preempt new legislation and reinforce the pillars that define the operating environment. A primary motivation is preservation of trust in free markets. After all, lost confidence in an industry or sector hurts all participants, even those who do everything by the book all along. The less obvious posture is to do nothing. Ignore the clamor for better corporate governance and wait out the storm.

Like everything else, there are advantages and disadvantages to each approach. Doing nothing is illusory. The point was made earlier that sitting idly by does in fact imply a decision to passively accept whatever the future holds. Regulation is certainly the answer that many policy makers favor. The problem is what inevitably follows. Some organizations spend huge amounts of money to game the system or figure out the loopholes. Others comply, but in a way that runs counter to the original purpose of the rule.

The aftermath of FAS 133 illustrates this notion, often described as the law of unintended consequences.[12] Survey results indicate a reduced use of derivative instruments for hedging and a tendency to use simpler products. If true that this behavior is in direct response to the promulgation of regulation and end users are made worse off by not hedging or using less customized products, the accounting rule will have increased financial transparency at the expense of economic benefits.

Industry self-regulation is gaining momentum, but not evenly, across market sectors. Some associations have actively sought a voice in the way the industry works, motivated by the belief that being proactive is the best course of action. Others are more reticent and moved to act due to pressure from various constituencies to do a better job of putting controls in place. Even when industry momentum is a factor, investment committee members, boards of directors, or savvy executives of individual committees are taking action because they view risk management as an integral part of effective governance.

Whatever the motivation, senior management buy-in is a critical element. More often than not, it means the difference between success and failure. For one thing, establishing the infrastructure to support the risk management function costs money and someone has to approve the expenditures. Benefits may not accrue right away and executives have to justify the lag time involved before a program starts to reap rewards. This includes the monetary costs of setting up a comprehensive training program and the time it takes for people to attend training classes away from the office. Compensation is a huge factor in substituting risk management for risk taking. Those in charge must justify things like hiring an outside consultant to set up an optimal compensation program.

Risk Management Leadership

The article shown in Exhibit 10.17 spells out some of the difficulties and challenges inherent in finding the right person for the top risk management job. (To see the article reproduced in its entirety, please see the Appendix.) For endowments, foundations, and pensions, the task is even more daunting. At a minimum, the person who leads the risk management function needs to have a solid command of investment fundamentals, along with a knowledge of relevant state and federal regulations. Other requirements include a working knowledge of how futures, options, and swaps work and an understanding of their impact on investment performance in both an economic and accounting sense. Worth emphasizing is the need to plainly communicate the institution's policies and procedures to persons who are affected by investment decisions, but who lack the technical knowledge to question them in depth. More is said about this later in the chapter.

COMPREHENSION

Training

Training is in the news a lot lately, notably as it relates to pension fund fiduciaries. Besides questions about fiduciary education—what it represents and how it can be improved on—the U.S. Department of Labor Working Group on Fiduciary Education and Training observed that

> *there are two universes of ERISA fiduciaries: professional fiduciaries, who generally are responsible for the administration and asset management of large plans; and "part-time" fiduciaries, who tend to come in two varieties: the fiduciary of a plan of a small employer and the relatively inexperienced employee or union member suddenly thrust into a fiduciary role by being named to a company benefits committee or to a trustee position in a Taft-Hartley Trust.*[13]

Experts describe the problem that arises when people are unaware that they even have a fiduciary responsibility, adding that "small plan fiduciaries are not likely to have to deal with sophisticated investment issues or the voting of proxies on stock."[14] More than several professionals who represent various endowments and foundations make similar claims about the need for training that provides knowledge without intimidation. One solution is to offer tiered training that is targeted to specific subgroups. For example, financial analysts might be asked to attend a seminar that includes more than a few number-crunching exercises. Benefit administrators would attend a more intuitive seminar that emphasizes how the absence of risk controls can affect the clients they speak with on a regular basis. The message

EXHIBIT 10.17   Life in Financial Risk Management

Instead of looking at risk management as a roadblock, it should be promoted as part of your culture and viewed as the best way to ensure the firm's longevity.

Life in Financial Risk Management
Shrinking Violets Need Not Apply

When you think of risk management, what comes to mind? Some people think of liability and casualty insurance, some conjure up visions of protecting against computer hackers, while others link the term to the process of ensuring a safe workplace. But this article focuses on financial risk management, sometimes referred to as financial engineering and often involving the use of derivative instruments.

Financial risk management is a global industry that represents a wide array of employment opportunities. As seen in "Various Risk Management Job Categories" on the next page, someone who works in this field may end up dealing with a distinct type of risk, a specific asset class, a particular type of organization, a given function or any combination thereof.

The typical day for an equity hedge fund risk manager is not at all the same as for a corporate treasury professional whose job is to prepare regulatory reports or stress test the exposures of a foreign business unit. Risk classifications aren't universal (e.g., model risk is sometimes categorized as a type of pricing risk while others may attribute it to operational risk).

This makes it virtually impossible to create one boilerplate job description. But the unifying theme is the employment of technology, quantitative analysis and a lot of common sense to balance risk against expected returns. In that sense, it's no different than any other financial decision-making activity.

Susan M. Mangiero, CFA, FRM, Ph.D.
GSM Associates, LLC

that risk management is important does not vary by audience type. Rather, it is the way the message is conveyed that varies.

Like any other type of training, risk management education ought to be cost effective. An advanced seminar about derivative instrument pricing can be invaluable to members of the audit team or traders who have to verify values. In contrast, it is money ill spent for advisors or support staff for whom valuation falls outside the scope of their job responsibilities.

Rotations

On-the-job rotations can enhance the effectiveness of outside training, even if only for a short period of time. Practical cross-training offers several advantages otherwise not available. For one thing, it is much easier to appreciate how different functions contribute to the investment—and related risk management—process by either observing someone or assisting them as they carry out their everyday duties. In addition, rotations facilitate improved communications among employees. Arguably, some organizations might counter that their small size makes this impractical because many activities are outsourced. An alternative is to have an employee rotate outside the organization, perhaps spending time with the money manager, investment consulting firm, or plan administrator.

Broadly defined, an external rotation provides benefits for everyone who is part of the supply chain.[15] The money manager and consultant have an opportunity to learn more about their client's needs and constraints, beyond the information exchange that takes place during periodic meetings. However, the institutional investor has a chance to see what goes on behind the scenes. At a minimum, everyone enjoys a better understanding of each other's operations. The best-case situation is that all parties have a chance to make things better. This might mean better or more frequent reporting, improved analytics, lower costs if things can be done more efficiently, or a combination thereof.

Rotations may be difficult to arrange, especially if a money manager or investment consultant does a lot of business with other institutional investors and information cannot be shared due to its highly confidential nature. Even within an endowment, foundation, or pension, it may be hard to let someone rotate for more than a few days due to staffing constraints. Nevertheless, it can augment formal training and merits serious consideration.

CONTROLS

Weakest Link

Policies and procedures define any process, and risk management is no exception. Training may precede this activity given the technical nature of what has to be done, including goal setting, constructing limits by asset class and instrument, authorizing traders, putting credit lines in place, and developing report formats. Even with proper preliminaries, no process is fail-proof. This is especially true in the absence of controls or when controls exist but they are not monitored on a regular basis.

If history is a good teacher, no or little oversight inevitably leads to disaster. Even a small financial loss can be an embarrassment because it begs the question as to whether those in charge are up to the job. Because both internal and external controls play a role in safeguarding assets, they should work together to provide an early warning that something is awry. Thus, any problems can be fixed immediately. If internal controls fail, external controls should pick up the slack. The goal is to ensure that somewhere, someone intervenes.

Controls take many forms, not the least of which is constant monitoring. This includes, but is not limited to, independent verification of trade details, matched against approved limits, credit availability, and the list of who is permitted to transact. Having an operational person rotate through the trading department or the converse can go a long way in helping both sides do their job well. Report frequency depends on available resources but should represent short enough periods that corrective action can take place and thwart any problems before they get out of hand. Daily reports are not uncommon. Relying exclusively on audit reports to uncover honest mistakes or outright fraud is ill advised because of the relatively long time period between statements.

An endowment, foundation, or pension fund that contracts out the investment function must identify and communicate controls to money managers, consultants, and technology vendors. Controls should be uniformly applied by all interested parties to avoid damage from an undetected weak link. For example, trade verification against available and authorized limits should be awarded the same care whether it is done in-house or by an outside manager. Data confidentiality and computer security should be given equal priority across the spectrum and so on.

Build on Existing Protocol

Exhibit 10.18 lists some of the publicly available documents that address controls. Auditors are asked to consider not only the controls in place, but also the "direction from management or those charged with governance."[16] Management's unwillingness to establish and monitor controls, including the proper identification and valuation of derivative instruments, would likely be viewed as a red flag, as well it should. Suitability is yet another yardstick. If the auditor sees big swings in reported—and verified—values of derivative instruments with little offset from assets, the question naturally arises. Has management invited excessive leverage by using derivatives in a speculative

EXHIBIT 10.18   Some Guidelines about Controls

Document Title	Source	Date
Derivatives: Practices & Principles	Group of 30	1993
Guidelines for Pension Fund Governance	Organization for Economic Co-operation and Development (OECD) Secretariat	July 2002
Internal Control Issues in Derivatives Usage: Executive Summary	Committee of Sponsoring Organizations of the Treadway Commission (COSO)[a]	1996
Public Pension Systems: Statements of Key Investment Risks and Common Practices to Address Those Risks	Association of Public Pension Fund Auditors[b]	July 2000
Risk Management Guidelines for Derivatives: Internal Controls and Audits	Committee of the Bank of International Settlements	1994
Risk Standards for Institutional Investment Managers and Institutional Investors	Risk Standards Working Group	1996

[a]COSO plans to release its *Enterprise Risk Management Framework* in the ummer of 2004.
[b]Several groups have endorsed this document.

fashion or was a hedge poorly designed? A good hedge should exhibit little net change in a position's value and suits an organization that is charged with the task of preserving assets or cash flow to pay beneficiaries.

As the world changes, so too should controls. For example, trading line amounts and counterparties set up long ago are likely stale and must be revisited. Computer systems put in place to monitor exposure amounts by instrument should be modified as new products are developed. Controls that authorize erstwhile employees make no sense.

COMPUTERS

Beauty or Beast?

Selecting a good risk management system is impossible without taking into account information needs. Trade verification, financial instrument valuation, limit availability checks, and much more can only be done when accurate information is reported on a timely basis in an easy-to-use format. Vendor sales and service support staff must be knowledgeable about systems as well as the financial dimensions of risk management, a combination that is sometimes hard to find. Buying any system follows the decision to automate. A good system can help rather than hinder. A system that integrates investing with risk management has the potential to streamline repetitive tasks, reduce errors, simplify regulatory compliance, control exposures, and enhance strategic decision making through analysis. An unreliable setup may cause more problems than it solves.

Despite its promise, the technology factor is often overlooked or under-emphasized. Computing resources may represent a small part of the operating budget with a short-term view that favors economy over utility. This is almost always a mistake. Although an endowment, foundation, or pension fund may not be able to afford the fanciest of systems, technology expenditures should reflect a long-term commitment to getting the job done well.

Systems Functionality

Institutional investors may get software from their external money managers, in which case the issue of compatibility becomes especially important. Trying to piece together information from different sources may be annoying at best and costly at worst, especially if performance results from an outside firm must be manually entered into an institutional investor's internal database. Even seemingly minute issues can become huge stumbling blocks to financial analysis. For example, a large pension fund may have 30 different money managers, each using different codes for the same security. Without some way to aggregate trades with different codes, either by hand or with a change in software design, tracking limit availability is difficult. What happens if no one even recognizes the problem? Then there is the issue of valuation. Models can vary by money manager, making it nearly impossible to compare reported security values across money managers or system vendors. This invites trouble when valuation numbers are then used to adjust hedge size or report assets to regulators.[17]

Aside from compatibility, a good system has to satisfy the investor's risk management needs. Exhibit 10.19 provides a partial list of broad functions a system should be able to handle for both investment and risk management purposes. It is far from complete and requires breaking down each function into more specific subfunctions. Exhibit 10.20 demonstrates this idea, using risk management as the primary category.

Each institution will have its own requirements that sometimes entail some customization. Although higher in cost, customization is a good choice if it makes it easier for the investment team—portfolio managers, investment committee members, trustees, and auditors—to do their job effectively.

EXHIBIT 10.19 Suggested System Functionality Requirements

Function	Comments
Benchmarking	Variety of choices with flexibility to change or modify is critical to evaluation of money managers as well as for performance attribution studies
Compatibility	Broad compatibility with other systems such as those used by external managers
Controls	Checks and balances in the system to catch errors or limit overages immediately
Data retrieval	Ability to retrieve current and historical prices for trade verification, valuation, and analysis
Documentation	Easy to read documentation minimizes need for systems support
Flexibility	System that allows for new products, new counterparties, changed limits, etc.
Manual override	Ability to intervene makes sense if restricted to persons with supervisory responsibilities
Regulatory compliance	Fields that comport with accounting and/or regulatory reporting requirements simplify compliance
Report generation	Ability to drill down by asset class, counterparty, security issuer, and sector (country, industry) to facilitate detailed analysis of exposures and period-to-period changes
Risk management analytics	Value at risk, stress testing, and simulation tools that interface directly with investment management components of the system and support their economic integration
Security	Different levels of access to protect against unauthorized trading
Trade repository with archiving capabilities	Password-protected database to permit analysis of trading patterns
Training	In-person training, online manual, and access to vendor support staff
Valuation	Explanation of models should be documented with flexibility to modify inputs

Technology Venue

The complexity of dealing with multiple money managers and numerous investment mandates requires a certain amount of flexibility, not to mention compatibility. It may be as simple as making sure that files prepared by a money manager can be opened by the client with ease and used in various formats. Ideally, systems work together seamlessly. For example, a state's pension fund would be able to aggregate data from the U.S. equity manager

EXHIBIT 10.20 Risk Management Functionality

Exposure/settlement risk
  Ability to define credit and delivery risk groups
Limit monitoring
  Credit risk limits
  Currencies
  Earnings at risk limits
  Gap and balance sheet limits
  Market risk limits
  Maturities
  Notional amounts
  Other amounts
  P&L limits
  Positions limits
Limit management
  By counterparty
  By currency
  By portfolio
  By product
  By trader
Limit utilization
  Limit updating
  Potential maximum loss calculation
  Trading portfolios limit

Source: Reprinted with permission from "Product Functionality Charts: Risk Management," *Wall Street & Technology Online,* June 18, 2003, http://www.wstonline.com/systemsChart/pfc. Copyright © 2003, CMP Media, LLC. All rights reserved.

with information sent by the global bond manager and perform various risk assessments on the combined information. A foundation with an office in Asia would be able to retrieve grant disbursement numbers, while taking time zone differences into account.

An application service provider that is used by various money managers and the institutional investor provides one alternative, enabling the distribution of data and generation of reports via the Internet, using the same server and pre-designed matching format. One advantage is the ability to convey (or input) information quickly to (by) multiple parties, regardless of physical location. Moreover, it avoids the often laborious process of upgrading software on a large number of computers.

However, as Chris Lewis, Managing Director, Fitch Risk Management, points out, "security is an important concern with electronic transmission and may render this approach unattractive for certain participants" adding that "desk-top or server-based applications are still quite popular for specific risk management applications, especially when customization can be done at an affordable price."[18] Furthermore, it may not appeal to a money manager if all their other clients use something else.

A thorough comparison of alternatives is outside the scope of this book, but is nevertheless integral to the purchase decision. This is especially true for expensive systems, ones that require a lot of customization upfront. Even if better systems become available later, replacement can be costly, perhaps overwhelmingly so. An institutional investor's operations may be too closely aligned with the system already in place. People then have to be trained on the new system, old report formats and data inputting methods may differ, and errors due to lost data could occur during transition.

Going Shopping

Purchases should be made by an individual—or committee—who knows something about both investing and technology. The objective is to explicitly communicate what the organization needs and match that against available systems, hopefully avoiding buyer's remorse. Sometimes this requires an interpreter, someone who can translate "techno speak" into plain English. At the same time, a systems sales representative has to be able to recommend what will or won't work, something that is hard to do without an appreciation of what investing is all about. An endowment that buys foreign stocks may grapple with a variety of settlement procedures that reflect local market rules. A foundation that buys futures as part of its enhanced indexing program could require a regular data feed in order to adjust position size. Duration metrics will be invaluable for a pension fund that invests in corporate bonds.[19] Both buyer and seller should be able to have an intelligent conversation about these applications and many others.

Once both the sales representative and the institutional buyer have arrived at an understanding of a suitable system, the system should be tested for awhile. "Kicking the tires" is the best way to identify kinks and work them out beforehand, if feasible. Large or complicated systems will be hard to implement for a trial period. In some cases, the vendor may have substantial documentation that addresses common problems. In other situations, the problem may be unique to a particular buyer and stem from systems already in place. If support is part of the package, now is the time to discover whether on-site assistance means getting help today or waiting a long time.

Ask for a client list. Are other endowments, foundations, and pension funds using the system and, if so, how and why? What do they like about it? What can be improved upon? Does the vendor have a user group with a view to upgrading the product in the future? Does the seller emphasize one particular function or offer a variety of analytical tools? Finally, take ample time to make an intelligent decision. Technology can go a long way in making the integration of investment and risk management a smooth ride if judicious decisions are made at the outset.

The relatively recent push for improved corporate governance and tighter regulatory controls has increased interest in better managing operations and credit risk. Investors on the buy side cannot afford to wait for information given a "renewed focus on tactics versus strategy."[20] They must seek out solutions. The good news is that vendor response increasingly includes real-time data access and report generation at a reasonable cost.

COMMUNICATION

Last but not least, the fifth "C" is frequent and understandable communication, without which an institution is unable to grow and prosper. Top-down communication is necessary but not sufficient to minimize risk and/or enhance value. Operational employees often have a tremendous reservoir of knowledge about the little details that can make or break an organization. Ignoring their feedback about process is ill advised. In fact, implementing a suggestion program with rewards is a terrific way to encourage awareness (and appreciation) of the close link between the front and back office.

Educating the trustees goes a long way to convey the organization's commitment to duty and care. After all, investment professionals who are in the markets every day have a much better grasp of how assets change in value and why. Reaching out to trustees enables each group to work together in a more productive manner. When an individual policy or procedure no longer make sense, the investment team can explain why, giving trustees a solid basis for the changes they must approve. A periodic newsletter is one approach.

According to Gary Findlay, Executive Director of the Missouri State Employees' Retirement System (MOSERS),

> *I think you'll find that most systems have a communications program of some sort, we've just chosen to establish it for the board in a little more formal and long lasting fashion. While somewhat time-consuming to prepare, the newsletters serve a number of purposes. For one thing, there is probably no better way to understand a subject than to have to explain it to someone else in writing. When we get to the board meeting stage, the presenter is well prepared regarding the subject, having participated in the writing of the newsletter that goes to board members. Second, the newsletters build a great track record of the subjects we have discussed with the board in detail, much better than would probably be available in board minutes. Finally, the regular newsletters are a great resource for bringing new trustees up to speed on various subjects.[21]*

EXHIBIT 10.21   Communicating with the Board of Trustees: MOSERS newsletter

"Where Do Returns Come From?"   June 2003
Volume 5 Issue 6

Value Added
A Product of the MOSERS Investment Staff

Answering Tough Questions

If you are a parent, you can probably recall the first time your child asked you with the most naïve and angelic face, "Where do babies come from?" We polled some of MOSERS' staff to see how they answered this difficult question, and got some pretty interesting answers. They ranged anywhere from "Ask your Dad," to "My wife handled that," to "Heaven," to "The stork brings them," and some were even brave enough to engage in a lengthy discussion of the birds and the bees. Regardless of their response, one thing everyone seemed to have in common was that it made them very uncomfortable. We in the Investment Department are faced with an equally challenging and discomforting question. Specifically, "Where do we expect investment returns to come from?" Unlike the child's question, there is no set of stock answers from which to choose. The difference between babies and investing is that investing is a very dynamic process with rules that change over time. Luckily for the stork, baby making is a pretty static process. As the investment landscape changes, we believe that a good investment program must adapt to the opportunities that the markets are offering. Historically, the MOSERS investment program was driven by a long-term adherence to rigid allocations. While this type of process is more easily understood and certainly provided excellent results through the decade of 1990s, it appears that the investment landscape and the economic uncertainty that we currently face is not the same animal we were dealing with just a few short years ago.

We believe that to be successful in today's markets, investors must focus more on diversification, the separation of asset class returns from skill-based strategies, flexibility in portfolio implementation, and last but not least, risk management. In this edition of Value Added, we will explore where

returns came from in the past and the philosophies that worked in that environment. We will attempt to contrast that with where we believe returns will come from in the future and why we believe the tenets starting at the bottom of page 3 will be the successful drivers of our investment program going forward.

Sources of Return: Understanding the Basics

We begin by establishing the foundation for where returns come from. This is the "conception" portion of the equation. In other words, these components of return will never change. What will change is the amount of the total that each component is expected to generate. We will address this in more detail later, but for now we'll just focus on the equation below.

$$TOTAL\ RETURN = RISK\text{-}FREE + \underbrace{RISK\ PREMIUM}_{BETA} + ALPHA$$

Beta Defined: Another name for beta is "asset class return." Essentially, this is the portion of the total return that we attribute to being invested in a particular asset class. As referenced in the formula, there are two components of beta. They are (i) the risk-free rate and (ii) the risk premium. The risk-free rate is the return that theoretically would be

1

Exhibit 10.21 shows the June 2003 issue of *Value Added,* one of several newsletters that is regularly distributed to the MOSERS Board of Trustees and available online for other interested readers (To see the newsletter in its entirety, please see the Appendix.) The communication style is straightforward and augmented with statements that apply specifically to MOSERS, thereby avoiding the claim that information is not made relevant to trustees. In this particular newsletter, the close relationship between risk and return is emphasized several times.

SUMMARY

1. Risk management does not occur in isolation and must be viewed as an integral part of investment activity.
2. The temptation to take on more risk with the potential for higher return is inevitable in a bear market, but should be avoided if it introduces excess leverage that is unsuitable for the endowment, foundation, or pension.
3. An investment goal(s) is the cornerstone of the investment policy statement.
4. The investment policy statement lays out the organization's asset allocation mix, permitted investments, and any restrictions, including if and how derivative instruments can be used.
5. Establishing a risk management program involves the five "Cs": commitment, comprehension, controls, computers, and communication.
6. Buy-in from senior management is a precursor to implementing any meaningful risk management program.
7. Training must be practical and cost-effective and should make clear the relevance of risk management to those who will carry out related duties.
8. Viable controls must provide early warning signs for things such as error, fraud, unauthorized trading, and limit violations.
9. Technology should support an integrated investment and risk management process and be flexible enough to accommodate changes.
10. Communication should flow in both directions of the organizational hierarchy. Back-office staff can often suggest ways to streamline things, while educating trustees enables them to approve appropriate policies and procedures.

CHAPTER 11

Risk Management: Fine-Tuning

We are what we repeatedly do. Excellence, then, is not an act, but a habit.

—Aristotle

RISK MANAGEMENT CYCLE

What to Do Next

As shown earlier in Exhibit 1.8, the risk management process is an ongoing process. Once risks are identified, the process of controlling them begins. Appropriate product selection and determination of transaction size follow and are two of the key issues. Once derivative instruments are in use—whether to hedge or otherwise transform risk—a periodic review lets the risk manager know how things are proceeding, providing support for any subsequent policy revisions.

Fortunately, the risk manager has many ways of checking under the hood to get a feel for where things stand. Some jobs require sophisticated quantitative skills. Computer programmers, valuation professionals, and modelers have backgrounds in areas such as math, physics, engineering, or statistics. However, not everyone is a math star, nor do they need to be. Risk budgeting, Value at Risk (VaR), stress testing, and other popular techniques are possible to use with an intuitive grasp of risk measurement and control. This includes knowing what each concept represents, the primary advantages and disadvantages, and why and how the concepts can be applied.

Cautionary Warnings

Ask a roomful of people to name the best-looking or smartest person there. Not surprisingly, the answers will convey a variety of opinions because there is no one "best" selection. Context is everything, and so it is with risk management tools.[1] There are advantages and disadvantages to each method, and the use of each method depends on what is right for an individual endowment, foundation, or pension fund. Even within a category, there can be competing approaches. Ranking them according to what makes sense for the purpose at hand is a logical precursor to committing funds to a particular trade.

As discussed in an earlier chapter, arbitrarily assuming that history repeats itself is a common mistake. A model that relies on historical data may doom an analysis before anyone puts it to use if new market developments, structural change or excess volatility characterize the present and expected landscape. Simulation and other forecasting techniques are possible solutions. Either way, competing methodologies must account for the relationship between past and future.

RISK ASSESSMENT: VALUE AT RISK

Performance Counts

Regular performance evaluation is the mainstay of institutional investing regardless of investor type. Although absolute return is important, comparative return is arguably even more so. Managers are frequently measured by how well they perform relative to a benchmark. In some cases, benchmarking is used for regulatory compliance purposes and an improper choice can lead to violations. This focus on performance attribution is often cited as a major point of distinction between institutions and corporations with respect to financial risk management.

A good benchmark should behave like the investment portfolio. An investor exposed to stocks issued by small companies unwisely benchmarks against an index of larger capitalized firms.[2] Sometimes the best index choice is not immediately obvious or available.[3] When the two diverge, large tracking errors result and signal a need for revision. Left alone, a poor benchmark choice has both short-run and longer-term consequences. When derivatives are used in conjunction with an investment position, benchmark choice necessarily affects the analysis of whether they are being used effectively.

Consider a pension fund that employs large cap index futures to synthesize an equity position in mid cap stocks. This may occur if a mid-size company index derivative is unavailable. Far from ideal, things get worse if the investor tracks performance against a mid cap index. On top of absolute return issues, the investor now confronts relative return problems. In the risk management world, relative performance measures like some forms of Value at Risk are gaining in popularity.

VaR

Value at Risk (VaR) is a broad topic with several dozen books and hundreds of articles committed to it. What is it, and why all the fuss? According to Investorwords.com, VaR is a technique that employs statistical information to approximate the "likelihood that a given portfolio's losses will exceed a certain amount." [4] Advocates cite the flexibility of this risk measure, permitting a comparison of potential losses across disparate asset classes. The article reproduced in Exhibit 11.1 provides some alternative definitions, along with a discussion of the concept itself. Note the statistical nature of VaR, specifically the use of a confidence level that defines the number of times the investor hopes to avoid a big drop in the value of its investment portfolio. By extension, it also defines the number of times an investor is willing to be wrong in predicting loss.

EXHIBIT 11.1 Value at Risk Definitions and Discussion: "An Irreverent Guide to Value at Risk" by Barry Schachter

INTRODUCTION

Value at Risk ("VaR") is much on the minds of risk managers and regulators these days, because of the promise it holds for improving risk management. It is common to hear the question asked, could VaR have prevented Barings, or Orange County, or Sumitomo. No answer to questions of that sort will be attempted here. Instead, this essay will take a normative approach. My purpose is more modest, namely, to provide the reader with some background by describing VaR and its evolving role in risk management.

Because of its technical nature, it is customary to begin any discussion of Value at Risk VaR with a definition. I offer three equivalent definitions.

(1) A forecast of a given percentile, usually in the lower tail, of the distribution of returns on a portfolio over some period; similar in principle to an estimate of the expected return on a portfolio, which is a forecast of the 50th percentile.
(2) An estimate of the level of loss on a portfolio which is expected to be equaled or exceeded with a given, small probability.
(3) A number invented by purveyors of panaceas for pecuniary peril intended to mislead senior management and regulators into false confidence that market risk is adequately understood and controlled.

THE QUEST FOR THE "HOLY SCALE"

Folklore (if it is fair to attribute as folklore that which only dates back five years) tells us that VaR was developed to provide a single number which could encapsulate information about the risk in a portfolio, could be calculated rapidly (by 4:15), and could communicate that information to nontechncial senior managers. Tall order, and not one that could be delivered upon without compromises.

(continued)

EXHIBIT 11.1 *Continued*

Modern Portfolio Theory ("MPT"), as taught in business schools, tells us that the risk in a portfolio can be proxied by the portfolio standard deviation, a measure of spread in a distribution. That is, standard deviation is all you need to know in order to (1) encapsulate all the information about risk that is relevant, and (2) construct risk-based rules for optimal risk "management" decisions. [The more technically proficient will please forgive my playing somewhat fast and loose with the theory in the interests of clarity.] Strangely, when applied to the quest for the Holy Scale, standard deviation loses its appeal found in MPT. First, managers think of risk in terms of dollars of loss, whereas standard deviation defines risk in terms of deviations (!), either above or below, expected return and is therefore not intuitive. Second, in trading portfolios deviations of a given amount below expected return do not occur with the same likelihood as deviations above, as a result of positions in options and option-like instruments, whereas the use of standard deviation for risk management assumes symmetry.

An alternative measure of risk was therefore required. Why not measure the spread of returns, then, by estimating the loss associated with a given, small probability of occurrence. Higher spread, or risk should mean a higher loss at the given probability. Then senior management can be told that there is [a] 1 in 100, say, chance of losing X dollars over the holding period. Not only is this intuitively appealing, but it's easy to show that when returns are normally distributed (symmetric), the information conveyed is exactly the same as were standard deviation employed, it's just that the scale is different. This approach can be consistent with MPT. It seems, then that perhaps the Holy Scale has been found in VaR.

> "VaR was developed to provide a single number which could encapsulate information about the risk in a portfolio."

THE SLIP 'TWIXT CUP AND LIP

It's perhaps too easy to criticise efforts to implement the VaR concept. It takes some courage to venture into unfamilar terrain and missteps are inevitable. The VaR paradigm is still evolving (as is that of financial risk management in general) and experimentation should be encouraged. To speak of "best practices" is surely premature.

The general approaches to VaR computation have fallen into three classes called parametric, historical simulation, and Monte Carlo. Parametric VaR is most closely tied to MPT, as the VaR is expressed as a multiple of the standard deviation of the portfolio's return. Historical simulation expresses the distribution of portfolio returns as a bar chart or histogram of hypothetical returns. Each hypothetical return is calculated as that which would be earned on today's portfolio if a day in the history of market rates and prices were to repeat itself. The VaR then is read from this histogram. Monte Carlo also expresses returns as a histogram of hypothetical returns. In this case the hypothetical returns are obtained by choosing at random from a given distribution of price and rate changes estimated with historical data. Each of these approaches have strengths and weaknesses.

> "To speak of 'best practices' is surely premature."

EXHIBIT 11.1 *Continued*

The parametric approach has as its principal virtue speed in computation. The quality of the VaR estimate degrades with portfolios of nonlinear instruments. Departures from normality in the portfolio return distribution also represent a problem for the parametric approach. Historical simulation (my personal favorite) is free from distributional assumptions, but requires the portfolio be revalued once for every day in the historical sample period. Because the histogram from which the VaR is estimated is calculated using actual historical market price changes, the range of portfolio value changes possible is limited. Monte Carlo VaR is not limited by price. Monte Carlo usually involves many more repricings of the portfolio than historical simulation and is therefore the most expensive and time consuming approach.

RULE OR TOOL?

It seems that VaR is being used for just about every need; risk reporting, risk limits, regulatory capital, internal capital allocation and performance measurement. Yet, VaR is not the answer for all risk management challenges.

No theory exists to show that VaR is the appropriate measure upon which to build optimal decision rules. VaR does not measure "event" (e.g., market crash) risk. That is why portfolio stress tests are recommended to supplement VaR. VaR does not readily capture liquidity differences among instruments. That is why limits on both tenors and option greeks are still useful. VaR doesn't readily capture model risks, which is why model reserves are also necessary.

> "No theory exists to show that VaR is the appropriate measure upon which to build optimal decision rules"

Because VaR does not capture all relevant information about market risk, its best use is as a tool in the hands of a good risk manager. Nevertheless, VaR is a very promising tool; one that will continue to evolve rapidly because of the intense interest in it by practitioners, regulators and academics.

Source: Barry Schachter, "An Irreverent Guide to Value at Risk," *Financial Engineering News*, Vol. 1, No. 1, August 1997, reprinted in *Risks and Rewards*, March 1998, pp. 17–18. Copyright ©1997, Barry Schachter. Reprinted with permission.

To illustrate, a VaR of $10 million, calculated daily for a one-month time period at the 95 percent confidence level, suggests that there is a 95 percent chance that the investor will avoid a loss of more than $10 million on any given trading day during a typical month. Said another way, this VaR number implies that there is a 5 percent chance that over the course of a typical month, the portfolio will experience a loss in value of at least $10 million.

The choice of confidence level is uncomplicated and follows the same decision-making process used for any other statistical analysis. It reflects a trade-off between precision and economic reality. Setting the bar too high

---

EXHIBIT 11.2   How to Choose a Confidence Level

There is nothing magical about confidence levels. In choosing confidence levels for market risk, companies should consider worst-case loss amounts that are large enough to be material, but that occur frequently enough to be observable. For example, with a 95% confidence level, losses should exceed VaR about once a month (or once in 20 trading days), giving this risk statistic a visceral meaning. Risk takers are thus encouraged to compare their daily P&L's against their VaR and consider return on risk.

Some maintain that using a higher level of confidence, such as 99.9%, would be more conservative. One might also reason, however, that a higher confidence level can lead to a false sense of security. A 99.9% VaR will not be understood as well or taken as seriously by risk takers and managers because losses will rarely exceed that level (we expect a loss of that magnitude to occur about once in four years). Furthermore, due to fat-tailed market returns, a high confidence level VaR is difficult to model and verify statistically. VaR models tend to lose accuracy after the 95% mark and certainly beyond 99%. Note, however, that when using VaR for measuring credit risk and capital, we should apply a 99% or higher confidence level VaR because we are concerned with low probability, event-driven risks (i.e. *tail risk*).

We can't rely on models to do all the "thinking" for us. Beyond a certain confidence level, rigorous stress testing becomes more important than statistical analysis. The choice of 95% confidence level at J.P. Morgan goes back to former CEO Dennis Weatherstone, who reputedly said, "VaR gets me to 95% confidence. I pay my risk managers good salaries to look after the remaining 5%."

Source: "VaRBaR: How to Choose a Confidence Level," *Risk Management: A Practical Guide,* RiskMetrics Group, 1999, p. 10. Copyright ©2003, RiskMetrics Group. Reprinted with permission.

---

may result in missing an adverse market event until it is too late to try to fix the problem. Setting the bar too low may lead to frequent intervention, costly trading fees, and lost opportunities. Exhibit 11.2 explains more about how to choose a confidence level.

Simplicity accounts in part for the growing attraction to VaR. A single number, it is routinely expressed in dollars and easy to interpret. Many commercially available risk management programs have a built-in VaR functionality so computations can be done by analysts without a heavy-duty technical background. It is often used as an early warning sign to take corrective action before things get out of hand. For example, a corporate pension plan sponsor might respond to a large VaR number by revising its investment strategy before a drop in asset value forces an infusion of cash to maintain its required funding ratio. A college endowment fund might use the VaR information to realign its asset allocation mix so that adequate funds are available to carry out the wishes of donors.

Value at Risk has been around for awhile. According to the U.S. Securities and Exchange Commission (SEC),

> *companies may choose one of three alternatives for market risk sensitive instruments entered into for trading purposes and another alternative for all other market risk sensitive instruments. Also, a company may choose any of the three disclosure alternatives for each risk exposure category within the trading and other than trading portfolios. For example, a company may use value-at-risk (VaR) to present information about the trading portfolio and a sensitivity analysis to present information about the end-user portfolio. It may also use VaR to present information about interest rate exposures, but use a sensitivity analysis to present information about risk of loss for derivative commodity instruments.[5]*

Value at Risk was likewise mentioned as one of several areas that should be part of internal controls examinations conducted by the SEC, as shown in Exhibit 11.3. Even though an organization does not fall under the

EXHIBIT 11.3 Internal Controls Examination Areas

Review Areas

Senior management, to look for establishment of overall policies and active involvement in the process of risk management and the oversight of risk parameters and controls

Adequacy of resources and systems used for risk management, and compensation incentives that may adversely impact independence

Internal audit, to ensure that comprehensive and independent assessments get to management and that deficiencies are addressed in a timely manner

Market risk in trading activities and firm inventory, including VaR (value at risk), economic models, scenario analyses, stress testing and back testing; we follow trades from the trading desk through the entire risk management system

Funding, liquidity and credit risks, including counterparty credit risk across all products and businesses, credit limits, pricing models, guarantees, collateral, margin, and settlement and legal risks

Operational risks, including segregation of duties, checks and balances, protection of customer funds and securities, operating systems, management information systems, management and reporting, front and back office operations, security, contingency planning and disaster recovery

And finally, we look to see that new products and activities are assimilated into the risk management system in a timely and appropriate manner

Source: "Speech by SEC Staff: SEC Risk Management and Compliance Examinations" by Mary Ann Gadziala, 2003 Fiduciary and Investment Risk Management Association, Fiduciary and Risk Management Seminar, February 26, 2003.

auspices of this regulatory body, it is worth noting that their rules often influence the standard-setting process for other types of entities and are therefore worth more than a fleeting glance.[6]

The traditional VaR measure can be computed in one of several ways. The Variance/Covariance Method involves several steps, beginning with the use of historical data to calculate the mean and variance of each component security held as part of a specific portfolio. The next step requires computing correlation coefficients for each unique pair of securities. Once done, the standard deviation of portfolio returns is relatively easy to find and can then be compared with a standard normal table.[7] This comparison reflects an interpretation of VaR as the number of standard deviations associated with a stated probability level for the tail of the distribution that represents loss.[8]

The remaining two methods estimate VaR by simulating portfolio values either on a historical or projected basis. The Historical Simulation Approach entails the collection of data such as the changes in long-term bond yields. A portfolio value is generated at each yield level scenario and then ranked. Imposing a confidence interval on the resulting probability distribution is the final step in determining the VaR. The Monte Carlo Simulation Approach looks to the future by randomly generating a multitude of scenarios and computing asset (or portfolio) values for each one. Although some consider it a more flexible approach, it does require making assumptions about expected parameters, something that is not always easy to do. Exhibit 11.4 compares the three methodologies, taking complexity into account.[9]

In its 2002 annual report, J.P. Morgan Chase & Co. states a preference for historical simulation

> because it involves fewer assumptions about the distribution of portfolio losses than parameter-based methodologies. In addition, the firm regularly assesses the quality of the market data because their accuracy is critical to computing VaR. Nevertheless, to the extent that VaR is largely based on historical market data, it may not accurately reflect future risk during environments in which market volatility is changing. In addition, the VaR measure on any particular day is not indicative of future risk levels because positions and market conditions may both change over time.[10] Importantly, this method assumes that "historical changes in market values are representative of future changes."[11]

Not coincidentally, risk management activity at J.P. Morgan is of continued interest given its relationship with the RiskMetrics Group in earlier days.[12]

An investor may start with one method but switch to another method later. As earlier discussed, there is always a risk that a selected methodology is ill suited for a given purpose. It may be inappropriate, hard to understand, computationally expensive, or unstable over time.[13] Backtesting

EXHIBIT 11.4 A Comparison of Value-at-Risk Methodologies

Methodology	Strengths	Weaknesses	Portfolio Suitability	Resources Needed
Variance-Covariance Methodology	*Ease of calculation *Readily available market data *Analytical framework by J.P. Morgan Risk Measurement Based upon modern portfolio theory	*Historic correlations and volatilities may break down under certain market conditions *Non-normal distributions will need to be accounted for using advanced statistical techniques *Requires cash flow mapping which alters risk characteristics	While non-linear risk can be approximated using the option delta and gamma, portfolios best suited to this methodology have no optionality	Requires a "VaR calculator." Most companies choosing this methodology are looking for a calculator which is Risk Metrics compatible
Historical Simulation	*Straightforward and understandable *Makes no assumptions about linearity or normality *Makes no assumptions about volatility or relationships among positions (correlations)	*Requires extensive amount of market data to value positions over the time horizon *Requires the use of valuation models, which may or may not be complex, depending upon the nature of positions *Historical path of market values may not be representative of future events	Suitable for portfolios with optionality	*Valuation capability *Access to historic market data (prices, rates, etc.)
Monte Carlo Simulation	*More comprehensive *Generates a large number of simulated paths (vs. historical simulation which generates one historical path) *Makes no set assumptions about linearity, normality or position relationships *Assumptions are defined by user	*The greater the number of risk characteristics in the portfolio, the greater the number of scenarios required (this can be somewhat mitigated by deterministic sampling), the greater the computational horsepower required *Requires sophisticated mathematical modeling	Suitable for portfolios with optionality	*Extensive computer horsepower *Historical market data (as a reference for setting simulation parameters) *Mathematical modeling capability

Source: Reprinted with permission of *The Journal of Performance Measurement* ®, Summer 1997, Table 1, p. 41. Copyright © The Spaulding Group, Somerset, NJ. All rights reserved.

provides one way to evaluate whether a selected methodology comports with economic reality. Plugging historical data into a model and comparing what it would have predicted with what really happened is good practice. It imposes some discipline on what models are used, how they are used, and the integrity of the input–output relationship. In some cases, it is required by law. Banking regulations permit the use of internal models but require evidence of "kicking the tires." This includes backtesting.[14] Although written for banks in the context of capital adequacy standards, Exhibit 11.5 explains why backtesting is important for everyone.[15]

According to one of the few published surveys about risk management and institutional investors, "about 10% use VaR for externally managed assets, under 6% use VaR for internally managed assets, and only 8% use VaR for their derivatives positions."[16] If true that institutional investors are late to the party, they may have good reasons for their delay, as spelled out by Katerina Simons. Value at Risk techniques developed by trading-oriented banks reflect short time horizons, liquid markets, and positions that reflect market neutrality. "In contrast, investment managers generally stay invested in the market, can have illiquid securities in their portfolios, and hold positions for a long time."[17]

In the plus column, VaR "provides a common framework of language to aggregate risk regardless of the asset, portfolio, or product being evaluated."[18] According to Mary Ellen Stocks and Christopher Ito, other benefits include the ability to (1) isolate risk factors from the VaR analysis as a way to better understand where a portfolio is vulnerable to loss, (2) set trading limits, and (3) reconstruct portfolios by examining the impact on VaR as volatility or correlation numbers change.[19]

Variations of VaR

Value at Risk is a measure of total risk. It is of little help to those who are seeking information about the variation in relative return, notably whether and to what extent an investment underperforms its benchmark. Relative VaR is an attempt to fill this void. Defined as a "percentile of the distribution of excess returns," Jorge Mina and Gavin Watson add that "in the case that the excess returns are normally distributed, the tracking error is equivalent to the Relative VaR with an 84% confidence level."[20]

One limitation of tracking error, the variance of portfolio performance relative to a specified benchmark, is its inability to accommodate anything other than a symmetric distribution of excess returns. This hampers its use for securities with option features because option payoffs are not linear. Moreover, tracking error looks backward in time. Unless past performance is an accurate predictor of future outcomes, tracking error does little to help a risk manager prepare for a market meltdown, however unlikely.

EXHIBIT 11.5 Reasons to Backtest

Many banks that have adopted an internal model-based approach to market risk measurement routinely compare daily profits and losses with model-generated risk measures to gauge the quality and accuracy of their risk measurement systems. This process, known as "backtesting", has been found useful by many institutions as they have developed and introduced their risk measurement models.

As a technique for evaluating the quality of a firm's risk measurement model, backtesting continues to evolve. New approaches to backtesting are still being developed and discussed within the broader risk management community. At present, different banks perform different types of backtesting comparisons, and the standards of interpretation also differ somewhat across banks. Active efforts to improve and refine the methods currently in use are underway, with the goal of distinguishing more sharply between accurate and inaccurate risk models.

The essence of all backtesting efforts is the comparison of actual trading results with model-generated risk measures. If this comparison is close enough, the backtest raises no issues regarding the quality of the risk measurement model. In some cases, however, the comparison uncovers sufficient differences that problems almost certainly must exist, either with the model or with the assumptions of the backtest. In between these two cases is a grey area where the test results are, on their own, inconclusive.

The Basle Committee believes that backtesting offers the best opportunity for incorporating suitable incentives into the internal models approach in a manner that is consistent and that will cover a variety of circumstances. Indeed, many of the public comments on the April 1995 internal models proposal stressed the need to maintain strong incentives for the continual improvement of banks' internal risk measurement models. In considering how to incorporate backtesting more closely into the internal models approach to market risk capital requirements, the Committee has sought to reflect both the fact that the industry has not yet settled on a single backtesting methodology and concerns over the imperfect nature of the signal generated by backtesting.

The Committee believes that the framework outlined in this document strikes an appropriate balance between recognition of the potential limitations of backtesting and the need to put in place appropriate incentives. At the same time, the Committee recognises that the techniques for risk measurement and backtesting are still evolving, and the Committee is committed to incorporating important new developments in these areas into its framework.

Source: "Supervisory Framework for the Use of 'Backtesting' in Conjunction with the Internal Models Approach to Market Risk Capital Requirements," Bank for International Settlements, Basel Committee on Banking Supervision, January 1996.

Advantages offered by Relative VaR over tracking error are several. First, relative VaR is a forward-looking measure that forecasts benchmark deviations. Second, it reflects more current information than does tracking error since VaR can be computed every day and tracking error is measured on a less frequent basis. This goes a long way to prevent investors from revising strategy on the basis of stale information. Third, investors are able to decompose Relative VaR as a way to better understand the relationship between price and risk.

Marginal VaR, another risk assessment measure, looks at the effect of adding one more dollar of a particular exposure on the portfolio VaR. It is a sensitivity measure and can be used to guide changes in total VaR by knowing what risk exposure is likely to result in the biggest value drop. Other risk control measurements include Minimum VaR, Maximum VaR, Conditional VaR, Earnings at Risk, and Cash Flow at Risk, to name a few.

"WHAT IF" ANALYSIS

Forward-Looking Tools

Sensitivity analysis, scenario analysis, and stress testing look at possible market outcomes and the likely impact on asset value. They are routinely used by all sorts of organizations. A corporation could use "what if" tools to analyze a change in sales revenue and its influence on earnings. A bank might perform these tests to assess its capital reserve sensitivity to interest rate fluctuations. An institutional investor could examine any number of variables with one or all of these tests to better determine its optimal asset-allocation mix. The applications are far reaching and provide invaluable results about what might occur.

With similar-sounding names, these tests are frequently performed in conjunction with each other. The mechanics differ by the number of variables used and the type of investigations to be performed. A sensitivity analysis tweaks one single variable and shows what happens to the object of scrutiny such as portfolio return. The effects are seldom contained at one level. To see this, consider a foundation that anticipates an increase in systematic risk for stocks in the retail sector. Interested in knowing how this affects hedge size, the analyst increases retail stock betas by 2 percent and even integer increments thereafter up to 20 percent. Not only will the portfolio beta change to reflect greater risk of component retail stocks, but the hedge ratio also will change, along with the size and cost of the hedge.

To conduct a scenario analysis, the institutional user defines scenarios and steps back to see how the portfolio performs in each case. A pension fund with a long stock option position might vary both volatility and underlying asset price to evaluate how its mark-to-market value responds.[21] Exhibit 11.6 illustrates 12 possible scenarios, but the combinations are endless because the user is free

EXHIBIT 11.6   Scenario Matrix Illustration

	Stock Price		
Volatility	$5.00	$10.00	$15.00
10%	$0.31	$5.20	$10.20
30%	$0.69	$5.20	$10.20
50%	$1.07	$5.30	$10.21

Notes:
1. Assume a $5 per share strike price.
2. Assume that the European call option expires in 365 days.
3. Assume an annual interest risk-free rate of 4 percent.
4. Note that the option has value even when its moneyness is $0, i.e., time value.

to define whatever scenarios make sense. Knowing what assumptions have been made in generating scenario results is critical to their evaluation. In the case of the stock option, a departure from the constant volatility assumption or permitting disruptions in stock trading will each alter scenario analysis results.

Generating a table of possible outcomes seems fairly straightforward. The problem arises when big market moves lead to unexpected outcomes that are not accurately represented by a tightly incremented scenario matrix. These regime shifts or structural changes are hard to predict, but cannot be ignored. Moreover, a model may not work the same way under extreme conditions, thereby introducing risk not already accounted for.

Stress testing attempts to reconcile these issues by considering what happens to asset values in the event of a calamitous event such as a big spike in interest rates or a devaluation of a foreign currency. One use is to identify outliers and analyze them statistically. Others may use stress testing to examine the parameters of a model or evaluate whether the model should hold up in dire circumstances.

Overall, sensitivity, scenario, and stress analyses, when done properly, are rich in possibilities. Some of the characteristics that valid tests should exhibit are presented in Exhibit 11.7, excerpted from a lengthy discussion of these three assessment tools by the Committee of Chief Risk Officers, a group that represents "companies that account for approximately half of the power and natural gas transactions in the U.S."[22] However, "what if" method attributes such as plausibility and applicability also extend to other industries.

Risk Management Applications

Looking at possibilities is a way of life for anyone involved in financial activities, investing, or otherwise. Stress testing is a particular favorite of

EXHIBIT 11.7 What Constitutes a Good Test

Attributes
Stressful enough
Plausible
Key assumptions, drivers and vulnerabilities to the portfolio and earnings identified
Risks (and results) transparent
Not compartmentalized (i.e. universal) with linkages among markets identified
Updated systematically and refreshed periodically
Appropriate for the portfolio and its risks

Source: "Sensitivity Analysis, Scenario Analysis, and Stress Testing," *Volume 3 of 6: Valuation and Risk Metrics White Paper,* Committee of Chief Risk Officers Valuation and Risk Metrics Working Group, November 19, 2002. Copyright © 2002, CCRO.

risk managers who recognize the incomplete nature of VaR. Although it conveys loss information in probabilistic terms, VaR gives no hint as to what scenario could trigger a loss. This makes it difficult, if not impossible, to foretell when the worst case might occur and to take preventative action accordingly. The statistical nature of VaR is another issue. "By definition, exceptional circumstances occur rarely, and statistical inference is imprecise without a sufficient number of observations. Stress tests partially fill this gap, and thus complement VaR analyses. Stress tests offer a quantitative picture of the exposure associated with a possible extreme event."[23] Although some organizations stress test on a voluntary basis, "banks that use the internal models approach for meeting market risk capital requirements must have in place a rigorous and comprehensive stress testing program."[24]

Potentially helpful, stress tests, like other analytical tools, are not failproof. Recognizing their limitations goes a long way in ensuring that they are used effectively. What spells trouble is a false belief that they provide a panacea against adverse market events that precede loss in asset value. For one thing, aggregating results for stress tests done on individual securities is not the same as stress testing the entire portfolio. Moreover, mismatch of time intervals is a problem. Daily VaR figures are hard to use in conjunction with "what if" tests that reflect longer time intervals. Stress tests must be done repeatedly and on a regular basis, especially when volatilities and correlations that characterize a portfolio change over time.

A good risk manager looks behind the numbers, using judgment and experience to forestall calamity. Still, success is not guaranteed. "Once in a lifetime" events can create a domino effect that is impossible to reverse. Nevertheless, stress testing and related analytics are powerful tools, despite some degree of subjectivity in their use. Specifically, decision makers must identify what constitutes an unacceptable loss amount and work toward avoiding any situation that makes the loss a real possibility.

Last but definitely not least, results must be communicated in a meaningful and concise manner to senior management. Otherwise, they are of little use in taking corrective action before things get bad. J.P. Morgan Chase & Co. reports that it "stress tests at least once a month, at both the corporate and business segment levels, using multiple scenarios" with "results, trends and explanations . . . provided each month to the Firm's senior management to help them better measure and manage risks to understand event risk-sensitive positions."[25]

RISK BUDGETING

Rising Star

Risk budgeting has taken the investment world by storm with several books devoted entirely to this measure of ranking investments on a risk-adjusted basis and allocating capital accordingly. As laid out in Exhibit 11.8, several reasons account for the attention being paid to this risk management tool, notably an increased interest in better information overall and a desire to look forward rather than dwell on the past. As Martin Veasey and Mark Benfold point out, risk budgeting is a multistep process whereby a portfolio is first decomposed into separate risk groups. Following this, "portions of the overall target risk appetite are allocated to each grouping depending on the degree of conviction of potential positive returns, as well as relative risk and correlation contributions."[26]

Supporters offer that risk budgeting imposes discipline on the investment management process by forcing decision makers to concurrently consider risk and return from the outset. The goal is to balance the obligations of the institutional investor against its return requirements without ignoring

EXHIBIT 11.8 Factors That Encourage Interest in Risk Budgeting

Increased acceptance of more sophisticated models of asset–liability management at the strategic level, going so far as to explicitly form a core internal benchmark against which total assets are managed.

More internal and external pressure for institutional investors to be seen to take a proactive stance in their selection of managers and their participation in the asset management process.

Better availability and take-up of forward looking risk estimation models such as value-at-risk (VaR) and tracking error as opposed to the exclusive use of retrospective, performance related measures.

Source: Martin Veasey and Mark Benfold, "New Take on Risk," *GARP Risk Review,* October/November 2001. Copyright © 2002, Global Association of Risk Professionals. Reprinted with permission.

the higher risk that accompanies higher return. It can be applied to both passive and active strategies.

There are many ways to employ risk budgeting. For example, an active investor with a favorable expectation about certain currencies has several choices that span the gamut from buying forwards or options, or simply investing in those securities for which return is dominated by the foreign currency factor. Risk budgeting empowers the investor by providing a fuller set of information about which choice makes sense. For a passive investor, risk budgeting can guide the process of allocating funds across money managers, taking style, expected performance, and internal ranking into account.

New Paradigm

Allocation of risk more fully considers the mandates of an endowment, foundation, or pension. This is a departure from traditional asset allocation and its often heavy emphasis on equity, frequently resulting in an asset–liability mismatch.[27] Importantly, risk budgeting does not replace asset allocation, but instead enhances it. As shown in Exhibit 11.9, the asset planning

EXHIBIT 11.9   Risk Budgeting and Asset Planning

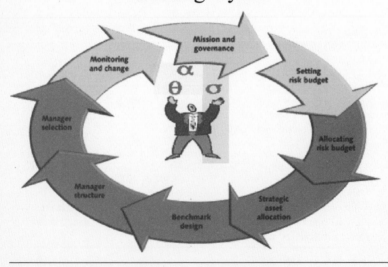

Source: Reprinted with permission from Strategy@ Work © Watson Wyatt Worldwide 2003. For more information, visit www.watsonwyatt.com.

cycle is ongoing, exhibiting a precise sequence that starts with the creation of a risk budget. Only after risk "spending" has occurred will the investor commence with mapping out its proper asset allocation mix.

Exhibits 11.10 through 11.12 illustrate the role of risk budgeting for several institutional investors. Worth noting is the focus on strategy. Risk budgeting occurs at the top of the hierarchal process that defines how the investor carries out its responsibilities on behalf of beneficiaries.

None of these statements categorically rejects the acceptance of higher risk. Rather, the point is made that higher returns should accompany higher risk as long as risk tolerance levels are not breached. Analytics that support risk budgeting break out contributions to risk and return by asset class or manager, or both.

In essence, risk budgeting looks at the cost of risk. It enables institutional investors to know whether taking on more risk is worthwhile or unacceptable, given its primary commitment to beneficiaries.

EXHIBIT 11.10   Risk Budgeting and the Ohio Public Employees Retirement System

RISK CONTROL

The Board ensures adequate risk control through the following means:

Diversification

Investments shall be diversified to minimize the impact of the loss from individual investments. In addition to achieving diversification by asset class, careful attention shall be paid to diversification within each asset category (e.g., real estate) and subcategory (e.g., direct investments, mortgages and REITs).

Portfolio Guidelines

Every portfolio that is a part of the OPERS overall investment portfolio shall operate under written guidelines, approved by the Board, and which are designed to ensure the portfolio meets its objective and operates within acceptable risk parameters.

Risk Budgeting

A formal process shall be established whereby the total active risk (risk of achieving performance different than the total fund benchmark) shall be within a margin approved by the Board. The Board shall also approve the risk budget by which active risk is apportioned among the various asset classes. Estimates of active risk shall be performed regularly and reported to the Board to ensure compliance with the risk budget established.

Source: Excerpted from *OPERS Investment Department: Statement of Investment Objectives and Policies*, Ohio Public Employees Retirement System (OPERS), May 16, 2001.

EXHIBIT 11.11 Risk Budgeting and the California State Teachers' Retirement System

One of the cutting edge processes to manage strategic risk is the concept of "risk budgeting". In a broad sense, this assumes a Fund/Board has a maximum given risk tolerance. That limit is the risk budget. From there, the Board allocates that budget among the asset classes.

Some asset classes provide a better pay off for a given level of risk. This is best illustrated by the expected out performance or alpha above a benchmark from fixed income vs. private equity. The more efficiently and rapidly information is disseminated within a given market, the less chance to add value. For a given increment of risk, CalSTRS expects to get a small gain in fixed income (currently 25 basis points over the index) versus a larger gain in private equity (where the target is 500 basis points over the public market).

As a result, the concept of risk budgeting is indirectly incorporated in the CalSTRS asset allocation process by the choice of management styles. In the current policy, we choose to emphasize passive or enhanced index strategies in the highly efficient asset classes such as U.S. equity and fixed income. While in inefficient asset classes, such as private equity and real estate, CalSTRS deploys a pure active management strategy and assumes a high level of risk.

Source: Excerpted from *Teachers' Retirement Board Investment Committee, Risk Management Study,* May 1, 2002, p. 3

EXHIBIT 11.12 Risk Budgeting and the University of Texas

We use several very sophisticated risk measurement services to keep a close eye on where we are taking risk in the endowment portfolios. The general process is very similar to budgeting capital in a business. We monitor risk being assumed in each asset category so that we can be sure that we are taking risk in the areas with the best return for that risk. This process is called risk budgeting.

Source: Excerpted from *Update and Commentary,* The University of Texas Investment Management Company, December 2002. Copyright © 2002–2003, by the University of Texas System.

SUMMARY

1. The risk management cycle is ongoing as performance is reviewed against objectives.
2. Many tools enable an institutional investor to control risk by first measuring it. VaR, sensitivity analysis, scenario analysis, and stress testing are commonly used risk measurement tools.
3. Value at Risk estimates loss in probabilistic terms. Typically expressed in dollar terms, it is intuitively appealing and used by many organizations, even when not required to do so by law.

4. There are three primary ways to compute VaR. These are the Variance/Covariance Approach, the Historical Simulation Approach, and the Monte Carlo Simulation Approach.

5. Some methods are more suitable than others. Selecting the wrong VaR model is a problem.

6. Relative VaR is a good way to examine loss potential, relative to a benchmark, and has several advantages over the more traditional tracking error metric.

7. Other forward-looking risk control tools, besides relative VaR, include sensitivity analysis, scenario analysis, and stress testing.

8. A sensitivity analysis perturbs one variable to understand its effect on a variable of interest such as earnings or portfolio return.

9. A scenario analysis examines the impact of two or more variables on a specified variable such as portfolio returns. Results for each scenario are typically presented in matrix form.

10. Stress testing looks at extreme scenarios. It is done by many organizations even when not required by law and complements VaR by providing additional information about market conditions that could lead to loss.

11. Risk budgeting apportions capital on the basis of risk-adjusted returns.

12. Risk budgeting offers several advantages over traditional management tools.

13. The asset planning cycle includes both risk budgeting and strategic asset allocation.

14. Risk budgeting can be used to select assets, investment managers, or both.

The Future

CHAPTER 12

Looking Ahead

Let not future things disturb thee, for thou wilt come to them, if
it shall be necessary, having with thee the same reason which
now thou usest for present things.

—Marcus Aurelius Antoninus

ROCKY TIMES

Who knew things would be so good for so long? After awhile, surplus funds and healthy rates of return seemed like the natural order with no end in sight. Then overnight, the bull market of the 1990s came to an abrupt end, forcing countless numbers of trustees, plan administrators, policy makers, and other interested parties to reevaluate decisions involving asset allocation mix, rebalancing, and risk control.

Things are so bad that the U.S. General Accounting Office now describes the Pension Benefit Guaranty Corporation as high risk. This is a major concern for the 34 million participants in the more than 30,000 private defined benefit (DB) single-employer plans who count on this insurance program to kick in if the plan sponsor is unable to fulfill its obligations.[1] "The program has moved from a $9.7 billion accumulated surplus in 2000 to a $3.6 billion accumulated deficit in fiscal year 2002."[2] As shown in Exhibit 12.1, participant demographics, economic weakness in certain industries, and limitations in funding rules account for the current state of affairs.

How quickly things change is hard to say. Even as this book goes to press, standard-setters, industry specialists, and regulators continue their efforts to enhance transparency, refine measurement rules, and tighten oversight. More than economics, there seems to be a dramatic shift in attitude and a desire for more accountability. Trustees are going to find it tough to hide from the public spotlight and will increasingly be asked to explain their actions.

EXHIBIT 12.1 Pension Benefit Guaranty Corporation Assessment of
Private Pension Risks

The degree of underfunding in the private pension system has increased dramatically
and additional severe losses may be on the horizon. PBGC estimates that financially
weak firms sponsor plans with over $35 billion in unfunded benefits, which ultimately
might become program losses. The termination of large underfunded pension plans
of bankrupt firms in troubled industries like steel or airlines was the major cause of
the deficit. Declines in the stock market and interest rates and certain weaknesses in
the current funding rules contributed to the severity of the plan's underfunded
condition. However, these factors mask broader trends that pose serious program
risks. For example, the program's insured participant base continues to shift away
from active workers, falling from 78 percent of all participants in 1980 to 53 percent in 2000. In addition, the program's risk pool has become concentrated in industries affected by global competition and the movement from an industrial to a
knowledge based economy. In 2001, almost half of all program insured participants
were in plans sponsored by firms in manufacturing industries.

Source: "Pension Benefit Guaranty Corporation Single-Employer Insurance Program:
Long-Term Vulnerabilities Warrant 'High Risk' Designation," U.S. General Accounting Office, July 23, 2003.

MAKING CHOICES

As unfair as it may be, it only takes a handful of bad players to create a
chain of events that inevitably results in more legislation. Economists have
argued for ages about the merits of mandatory versus voluntary action, so
only a few brief points are made here. When institutional investors fail to
govern themselves, they invite tighter statutory rules and everything that
accompanies them.[3]

As discussed in Chapter 10 and summarized in Exhibit 12.2, regulatory
mandates cost money and result in lost opportunities. They dilute management's attention and force a reallocation of resources. Free market advocates
measure the toll in terms of fewer innovations in a higher-risk, lower-return
environment. Information theorists posit the disruption of a free flow of information among buyers and sellers that impairs the pricing mechanism
and efficient delivery of service.

Perhaps the most pernicious harm is the failure to consider all possible
effects of any new law.[4] A prime example is the suggestion by some experts
that more complicated laws and regulations will discourage entities from
offering generous charitable grants or retirement benefits, if they offer anything at all. To illustrate, consider the results of a survey conducted by the
National Association of Pension Funds. This organization found that a
large majority of its U.K. members were less likely to offer pension plans

EXHIBIT 12.2   Costs Associated with Mandatory Regulation

Description
Direct compliance costs
Reduced product innovation
Imperfect information flow
Unintended consequences
Redirecting staff away from profitable activities
Market inefficiencies
Lost opportunities
Reduced flexibility
Changed incentives

following the implementation of FRS 17, a relatively new and many would say onerous standard for pension fund accounting.[5]

On the plus side, trustees can start improving things any time they want. Funds that have done the hard work already play a role by providing leadership and hands-on advice, to the extent legally possible. Preventing malfeasance and improving governance is a win–win situation for all institutional investors, especially the ones that already recognize the benefits of good reputation and fiduciary prudence. After all, good players do not want to bear the costs of others' misdeeds.

As shown in Exhibit 12.3, being a pioneer means being proactive. This occurs when tax-exempt organizations set up a disciplined risk management process as part of their everyday business practices. Ideally, pioneer organizations would dominate the corporate governance landscape. Knowing how many fiduciaries take precautionary action before it is necessary requires public disclosure of their risk management philosophy. As already discussed, some organizations maintain a private profile and do not divulge much information on a voluntary basis. Then there is the question of human behavior when it comes to the carrot versus stick approach. Are fiduciaries likely to respond to coercion or to incentives that induce them to practice better management on a voluntary basis, either to catch up with peers or to lead the way?

EXHIBIT 12.3   Trustee Choices

Motivation	Reactive	Proactive
Regulatory compliance	Status quo	Anticipatory
Best practices implementation	Catch up with peers	Pioneer

EXHIBIT 12.4 Some Risk Management Guidelines

Title	Source	Year
Derivatives: Practices and Principles	Group of 30	1993
Guidelines for Pension Fund Governance	OECD Secretariat	2002
Internal Control—Integrated Framework	The Committee of Sponsoring Organizations of the Treadway Commission	2004[1]
Principles for the Management and Supervision of Interest Rate Risk	Basel Committee on Banking Supervision	2003
Public Pension Systems: Statement of Key Investment Risks and Common Practices to Address Those Risks	Association of Public Pension Fund Auditors and Other Groups	2000
Risk Management of Financial Derivatives: Comptroller's Handbook	Comptroller of the Currency Administrator of National Banks	1997
Sound Practices for Hedge Fund Managers	Managed Funds Association	2003
Valuation and Risk Metrics Best Practices	Committee of Chief Risk Officers	2002

[1]According to its web site, the COSO Enterprise Risk Management Framework should be published in 2004. See http://www.coso.org.

RISK MANAGEMENT GUIDANCE

As shown in Exhibit 12.4, a lot of work has been done to outline risk management procedures and policies, much of which is freely available to the public. Even guidelines written with specific constituencies in mind—banks, energy companies, and insurance firms—are worth reviewing because the fundamentals are often the same. Endowments, foundations, and pensions may prefer to adapt some of the guidelines already available that apply specifically to them, whether about derivatives, risk management, transparency, or overall governance. Either way, reviewing guidelines that have been accepted by other organizations saves time and represents a resource when small staff size or limited experience is an issue.

Even when derivative instruments are not used, internal policies should reflect the fact that risk management can and should occur. Techniques such as risk budgeting can be powerful tools in putting capital to work in the best way possible. Going one step further, communicating a commitment to good risk management sends a clear message that fiduciaries and related persons are properly entrusted with the responsibility of keeping financial promises.

CONCLUSION

When risk management is fully integrated with the investment management process, everyone benefits. No one can completely eliminate risk nor should they try, especially if an institution has a particular hurdle rate to meet in discharging its obligations. However, ignoring risk is a mistake no one should make.

The goal here was to provide a gentle introduction to this vast topic area, recognizing that it is impossible to cover all aspects of risk management. More investment choices, a huge and global derivatives market, and heightened focus on leadership actions make it almost certain that fiduciaries will have to shoulder more responsibilities regarding investments made on behalf of beneficiaries. Like starting an exercise program, comprehensive corporate governance can be viewed with dread or looked upon as a wonderful way to age gracefully.

SUMMARY

1. Trustees have several choices—waiting for inevitable regulation, taking self-policing action to prevent stricter rules, or adopting best practices that recognize the value enhancement of effective risk management.
2. Only a handful of losses are needed to invite stricter statutes regarding financial management, as unfair as it may be to the many organizations

that are diligent about making risk controls an everyday part of their business.

3. Mandatory regulations cost money, time, and lost opportunities, some of which are hard to evaluate before the fact. Nevertheless, policy makers must evaluate proposed regulations in the context of unintended consequences. Compliance often results in behavior that is counter to original goals.

4. Many industry associations are taking action to educate members about good risk management practices.

Following are Exhibits 10.17 and 10.21 reproduced in their entirety.

EXHIBIT 10.17 Life in Financial Risk Management (reproduced in its entirety)

Instead of looking at risk management as a roadblock, it should be promoted as part of your culture and viewed as the best way to ensure the firm's longevity.

Life in Financial Risk Management
Shrinking Violets Need Not Apply

When you think of risk management, what comes to mind? Some people think of liability and casualty insurance, some conjure up visions of protecting against computer hackers, while others link the term to the process of ensuring a safe workplace. But this article focuses on financial risk management, sometimes referred to as financial engineering and often involving the use of derivative instruments.

Financial risk management is a global industry that represents a wide array of employment opportunities. As seen in "Various Risk Management Job Categories" on the next page, someone who works in this field may end up dealing with a distinct type of risk, a specific asset class, a particular type of organization, a given function or any combination thereof.

The typical day for an equity hedge fund risk manager is not at all the same as for a corporate treasury professional whose job is to prepare regulatory reports or stress test the exposures of a foreign business unit. Risk classifications aren't universal (e.g., model risk is sometimes categorized as a type of pricing risk while others may attribute it to operational risk).

This makes it virtually impossible to create one boilerplate job description. But the unifying theme is the employment of technology, quantitative analysis and a lot of common sense to balance risk against expected returns. In that sense, it's no different than any other financial decision-making activity.

Susan M. Mangiero, CFA, FRM, Ph.D.
GSM Associates, LLC

(continued)

EXHIBIT 10.17 *Continued*

derivatives diary

Financial risk management is a relatively new field, coming into its own after a few highly publicized debacles involving derivative instruments and the subsequent awareness about the need for controls. New financial reporting rules about derivatives and the regulatory climate have been agents of change as well.

Corporate Culture

Even as firms recognize the need for risk management in some form, there's considerable diversity in their approaches. Organizations that integrate risk management with other aspects of the overall business model acknowledge its potential as a cornerstone of competitive advantage, seeking to capture market share from those firms that do just enough to comply with regulations and little else.

As Rich Apostolik, president of the Global Association

of Risk Professionals, points out, "early adopters have reaped tremendous benefits, especially in the investment management area. There is a distinct trend toward using risk managers as marketers, trotting them out to investors to assure them that the firm has strict policies and procedures in place, and to explain, from an 'independent' perspective, why certain trades and positions are being taken."

Apostolik added that those who fail to see risk management as a strategic tool "are relegating themselves to the back of the pack, not able to differentiate themselves to their clients or even to the regulators who are now taking a more 'active' oversight role."

Organizational mandate is everything because it determines the likelihood of success. A chief risk officer hired and supported by senior management speaks with greater

authority than someone who is viewed as creating extra work for already overloaded staffers. This is even more the case when the risk manager is part of the executive leadership team, reporting to the board audit committee or to the CEO.

According to Apostolik, "A chief risk officer is normally recognized as important as a chief financial officer and is typically given a seat on the firm's management committee because of the wide-sweeping impact of the decisions made about capital allocation and cost of funds. These have a domino effect on the entire organization's profitability and flexibility in responding to new opportunities."

A good risk manager must be seen as a team player and not as an internal regulator who nixes deals without offering appropriate alternatives. But it doesn't stop there. If the risk management function isn't

taken seriously by top officials, few resources will be made available (e.g., historical data, analytical staff, and computing power) and it's only a matter of time before everyone recognizes that changes simply can't be made.

The message is clear: Getting everyone on board is a precursor to putting an effective risk management function in place. And the only way to make this happen is to educate staff about its importance.

Requisite Skills

What type of person would seek out a position in risk management? For one thing, an effective risk manager must feel comfortable asking lots of questions about how revenue is generated and at what cost, in terms of risk.

This is often easier said than done. Documentation may be sparse or non-existent. Original dealmakers may have

Various Risk Management Job Categories

Asset Class	Job Functions	Organization	Risk
Commodity	Auditing	Accounting Firm	Accounting
Credit	Back Office Operations	Bank	Credit
Equity	Brokering	Brokerage Firm	Legal and Regulatory
Fixed Income	Credit Analysis	Corporation	Market
Foreign Currency	Compliance	Endowment	Operational
	Model Development	Hedge Fund	
	Portfolio Management	Investment Manager	
	Research	Pension Fund	
	Sales	Regulatory Agency	
	Trader	Tax Authorities	

Source: Susan M. Mangiero

EXHIBIT 10.17 *Continued*

 derivatives diary

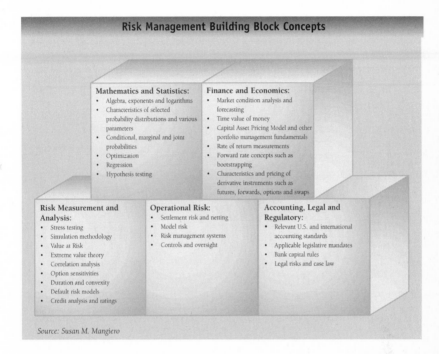

Source: Susan M. Mangiero

left the company or don't remember specific details. Other employees may be unco-operative and refuse to provide information, especially if there's no incentive for them to do otherwise.

Compensation is another big factor. Any firm that pays bonuses for quick fixes to the bottom line without con-sidering the downside is asking for trouble.

E. Daniel Raz, CEO of Ana-lytic Recruiting Inc., describes a risk manager as "someone who can say no to trades with-out alienating the line staff members who work under

tremendous pressure to meet short-term budgetary goals. A talented risk manager will marry together his or her knowledge of the business, along with financial market expertise, to suggest alternatives that do not violate internal con-trols, but can boost revenue."

Taken together, this means that a good risk manager is persistent, diplomatic, creative, knowledgeable and thick skinned. Practically speaking, a likely candidate is someone with deal experience who can adopt a longer-term view, or an oper-ations manager with a strong background in applied systems,

and an appreciation for the cost of making mistakes and the benefits of preventing them.

On the technical side, a risk management professional should feel at home working with numbers, but recognize that a quantitative background is not enough. As shown in "Risk Management Building Block Concepts" above, "must know" building block concepts represent a synthesis of myri-ad disciplines, including math-ematics, statistics, finance, accounting, ethics, economics and law.

The exact background required depends on the type

of risk management position desired. Raz classifies positions as falling into one of three cat-egories:

1) Risk monitoring and reporting
2) Risk measurement methodology
3) Risk management

As displayed in "Risk Man-agement Positions and Required Backgrounds" on the next page, the skill level and educational requirements for these groups diverge. Someone working with mortgage-backed securities needs a strong background

EXHIBIT 10.17 *Continued*

derivatives diary

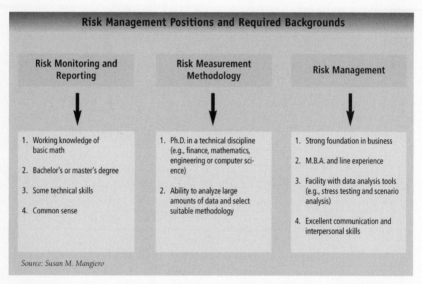

Risk Management Positions and Required Backgrounds		
Risk Monitoring and Reporting	**Risk Measurement Methodology**	**Risk Management**
1. Working knowledge of basic math 2. Bachelor's or master's degree 3. Some technical skills 4. Common sense	1. Ph.D. in a technical discipline (e.g., finance, mathematics, engineering or computer science) 2. Ability to analyze large amounts of data and select suitable methodology	1. Strong foundation in business 2. M.B.A. and line experience 3. Facility with data analysis tools (e.g., stress testing and scenario analysis) 4. Excellent communication and interpersonal skills

Source: Susan M. Mangiero

in mathematical statistics and econometrics to accurately model prepayment rates and other key characteristics. Pricing options or option-related securities typically requires a solid understanding of stochastic calculus. Someone in operations must be fluent with market rules and settlement procedures.

A good risk manager is intellectually curious about what makes markets tick. This is especially true given the complexity of some transactions and the fact that few securities trade in a vacuum.

What happens in the bond market affects price movement in the equity market. What occurs in Europe affects what happens in the United States and so on.

While this "one global market" idea generally applies to most finance jobs, it's even more the case with risk management because things can go awry in such a short period of time. Staying abreast of current regulations is certainly a necessary part of the job, but you must also anticipate changes in the financial and regulatory climates.

Modifying systems, adding and training staff, remixing business activities and the like all take time and careful planning. A risk manager has to look past the obvious. Much like a detective, a critical eye is a precursor to successfully evaluating the evidence, identifying the culprit and reinforcing the rules.

Last but not least, common sense is a key element of the work. Knowing how to strike a balance between restricting seemingly profitable but risky business and giving the green

light to other activities requires a solid understanding of company goals and constraints.

It likewise means being able to detect when something fails the "smell test." Human error is widely thought to be responsible for many of the large and "infamous" derivatives-related losses since their inception. The individual who can reasonably assess the need for a manual override of an otherwise automated process has a chance of preventing mishaps or minimizing damages.

State of the Profession

The field continues to grow, but anemic economic conditions, consolidation in the financial sector and a perceived oversupply of financial engineering graduates have slowed things for now. But this isn't true for

all of risk management.

For example, the explosive growth in collateralized default obligations has led to a high demand for talented people with excellent credit analysis skills. This trend is unlikely to abate anytime soon given the record levels of bankruptcies today.

Raz encourages candidates just starting out to develop both math and computer skills as a way of distinguishing themselves from the competition. Good writing and presentation skills are similarly important. If few people can understand the results of an analysis, it has limited usefulness. A well-spoken risk manager who can explain complex concepts in simple terms to senior executives, board members, employees, clients, suppliers, shareholders, regula-

EXHIBIT 10.17 *Continued*

---

 derivatives diary

tors and the press is invaluable.

[*"Learn More" below provides a partial list of Internet resources if you want to read on about this challenging, fast-paced and always changing industry.*]

Going Forward

Most people recognize the need for thoughtful financial decision-making and the existence of reasonable controls. However, those who want to bet

the house may be forced into better behavior with new risk management regulations that go well beyond generalities.

On the accounting front, this includes Statement No. 133, Accounting for Derivative Instruments and Hedging Activities and IAS 39, Financial Instruments: Recognition and Measurement.

The Sarbanes-Oxley Act of 2002 and related U.S.

Securities Exchange Commission announcements regarding off-balance sheet transactions are additional imperatives, along with the new Basel Capital Accord that determines required capital reserves for banks. [*See "Issues and Updates" below.*]

These developments favorably augur the continued development of the risk management field, and for individuals who

thrive on the challenge, excitement and satisfaction of adding financial value in a meaningful way. ■

Disclaimer: The information provided by this article should not be construed as financial or legal advice. The reader should consult with his or her own advisors.

© *2003 by Susan M. Mangiero. All rights reserved.*

Issues and Updates

On April 30, 2003, the Financial Accounting Standards Board issued Statement No. 149, Amendment of Statement 133 on Derivative Instruments and Hedging Activities. See www.fasb.org for additional information.

See www.iasc.org.uk for additional information about IAS 39 and the International Accounting Standards Board.

See www.sec.gov/rules/final/33-8182.htm for the full text of *Disclosure in Management's Discussion and Analysis about Off-Balance Sheet Arrangements and Aggregate Contractual Obligations.*

See www.bis.org/index.htm for additional information about the new Basel Capital Accord.

Learn More

Here is a partial list of Web sites that offer additional information on financial risk management.

Analytic Recruiting Inc. — www.analyticrecruiting.com

Global Association of Risk Professionals — www.garp.com

International Association of Financial Engineers — www.iafe.org

IRMI – Risk Management and Insurance Information Resource — www.irmi.com

Professional Risk Managers International Association — www.prmia.org

---

Susan M. Mangiero, CFA, FRM, Ph.D., combines many years of hands-on capital markets and risk management analysis with training financial professionals at various money center banks and *Fortune 500* corporations. Her education includes an M.B.A. in finance from New York University, a Ph.D. in finance from the University of Connecticut and post-graduate computational finance work at Carnegie Mellon University. Mangiero is serving her second year as a volunteer member of the FRM® (Financial Risk Manager) committee for the Global Association of Risk Professionals. derivmail@AFPonline.org.

EXHIBIT 10.21   Communicating with the Board of Trustees: MOSERS newsletter (reproduced in its entirety)

"Where Do Returns Come From?"   June 2003
Volume 5 Issue 6

Answering Tough Questions

If you are a parent, you can probably recall the first time your child asked you with the most naïve and angelic face, "Where do babies come from?" We polled some of MOSERS' staff to see how they answered this difficult question, and got some pretty interesting answers. They ranged anywhere from "Ask your Dad," to "My wife handled that," to "Heaven," to "The stork brings them," and some were even brave enough to engage in a lengthy discussion of the birds and the bees. Regardless of their response, one thing everyone seemed to have in common was that it made them very uncomfortable. We in the Investment Department are faced with an equally challenging and discomforting question. Specifically, "Where do we expect investment returns to come from?" Unlike the child's question, there is no set of stock answers from which to choose. The difference between babies and investing is that investing is a very dynamic process with rules that change over time. Luckily for the stork, baby making is a pretty static process. As the investment landscape changes, we believe that a good investment program must adapt to the opportunities that the markets are offering. Historically, the MOSERS investment program was driven by a long-term adherence to rigid allocations. While this type of process is more easily understood and certainly provided excellent results through the decade of 1990s, it appears that the investment landscape and the economic uncertainty that we currently face is not the same animal we were dealing with just a few short years ago. *We believe that to be successful in today's markets, investors must focus more on diversification, the separation of asset class returns from skill-based strategies, flexibility in portfolio implementation, and last but not least, risk management.* In this edition of Value Added, we will explore where

returns came from in the past and the philosophies that worked in that environment. We will attempt to contrast that with where we believe returns will come from in the future and why we believe the tenets starting at the bottom of page 3 will be the successful drivers of our investment program going forward.

Sources of Return: Understanding the Basics

We begin by establishing the foundation for where returns come from. This is the "conception" portion of the equation. In other words, these components of return will never change. What will change is the amount of the total that each component is expected to generate. We will address this in more detail later, but for now we'll just focus on the equation below.

Beta Defined: Another name for beta is "asset class return." Essentially, this is the portion of the total return that we attribute to being invested in a particular asset class. As referenced in the formula, there are two components of beta. They are (i) the risk-free rate and (ii) the risk premium. The risk-free rate is the return that theoretically would be

1

(continued)

EXHIBIT 10.21 *Continued*

earned from an investment that was completely free of risk. Ninety-day treasury bills are most often used as a proxy for the risk-free rate. Currently, 90-day treasury bills will earn about 1% per year. The second component of beta is the risk premium. The risk premium is the excess return an investor expects to receive in order to leave the safety of the risk-free asset and take on risk.

While we would expect returns from the aggregation of the risk-free rate and the risk premium to be positive over very long periods of time, history has witnessed 20 year periods where this was not the case. Various factors, like the

level of interest rates, current prices, and yields all play a role in determining what beta return investors will realize. Investor psychology will also play a role, as it has implications for the various factors just mentioned. Currently, there is a wide range of thinking regarding the risk premium for stocks, with the bearish contention arguing for no risk premium and the bullish folks talking about a return to historical levels of approximately 4%. While the range is wide, there are a couple of points that seem consistent across the spectrum. The first is that we should not expect the double digit beta returns of the 1990s that were in large part driven by investors' irrational

expectations for economic growth and, in the near term, we should expect very little in the way of return from the risk-free component of beta because interest rates are near all time lows.

Alpha Defined: Now that we have discussed beta, we'll turn our attention to the second piece of the return equation - alpha. Alpha is the skill-based component of the return equation, or the return generated through implementation decisions. Stated differently, this is the return that is generated from a manager's ability to select particular investments that perform better than the asset class as a whole. No one

seemed to care much about alpha during the 1990s due to the large returns being generated from the beta component. However, if returns from beta going forward are, as most predict (mid to high single digits for a portfolio of stocks and bonds), then alpha becomes a much more important return driver than in the past. For example, we have historically generated about 150 basis points of alpha in our portfolio. If that 150 basis points is stacked on top of beta returns in the double digits like was commonplace in the 1990s, it represents a much smaller percentage of the total fund return than if it stacked atop a beta return in the mid single digits.

A Look into the Past: Examining the History of MOSERS' Investment Philosophy

A glance back over the decade of the 1990s reveals that the underlying beliefs steering MOSERS' investment philosophy and decisions were much different than the beliefs driving MOSERS' investment program today. Upon reflection, tenets underlying MOSERS' investment philosophy throughout most of the 1990s can be summed up in three main points.

Tenet #1: Buy beta and hold on!

This tenet stems from looking at history which reveals that stocks have outperformed bonds over very long time periods. Because of this belief, and the knowledge that MOSERS (as a public pension system) has an infinite time horizon, seeking the maximum rate of return over the long-term was the objective. Structuring portfolios based on beta, or asset classes that have been known to provide the highest risk premium, became the objective. Thus, rising allocations to stocks among pension funds throughout the 1980s and 1990s became the norm. While we did not get completely suckered by this tenet, it was certainly alive and well in our portfolio. By March 2000, some 72% of our portfolio was invested in equities and nearly one half of that was invested in the S&P 500 (arguably a large-cap growth index at that point in time). Little thought or consideration was given to the short-term volatility or risks associated with this high concentration to equities. In MOSERS' defense, during the 1990s this approach worked very well. As equities went soaring, MOSERS was on board for the ride. While the last few years have been painful, MOSERS benefited, even including the bear market, because of the significant allocation to equities throughout the 1990s.

Tenet #2: Active management is a loser's game, so invest passively and keep your cost low.

As the indices became more and more concentrated through the mid to late 1990s, active managers struggled to keep up. Most active managers create portfolios that are (i) smaller in market-cap than the broad indices and (ii) more equally weighted, whereas the indices are cap-weighted. As a result of these two phenomena, the majority of active managers had trouble keeping pace with the indices through the late 1990s. By the end of the 1990s, the S&P 500 was outperforming over 65% of all active U.S. equity managers. More and more people gravitated to low cost index funds because of this. At one point in the late 1990s, MOSERS was over 80% passive in its management style and our cost structures were among the lowest in the nation.

2

EXHIBIT 10.21   *Continued*

Tenet #3: Develop a long-term philosophy, and build a static asset allocation policy around it.

With the emergence of the practical application of modern portfolio theory, the last 20 years of investment management have been focused on the concept that one should build a long-term investment plan with static asset allocations based upon the investor's time horizon and historical asset class performance. Essentially, portfolio management was based upon fixed views of the future and became something that many believed you could sit down and write a "how-to" book about. Investment decisions became centered around rigid rule-based decisions with very little thought about tactical decisions based upon factors at play within the economy. In addition, very little thought was given to diversification and rebalancing. The realities of the 1990s were that funds which tried to diversify and establish systematic rebalancing policies, were punished by lower returns than had they focused only on equities and let their policy mixes drift. Through this period, at ever increasing levels, risk was generally ignored, as very few contemplated the possibility of a sustained period of poor performance from the equity asset class. MOSERS did a better job than most in diversifying the portion of the portfolio that was not allocated to equities, even taking steps to name it the "Diversification Pool." We added commodities and treasury inflation indexed securities (TIPS) to the portfolio in 1998 and significantly altered the structure of our fixed income portfolio in early 2000 with the objective of lowering the correlation to the equity portfolio. In addition, we initiated a leading-edge rebalancing program with the help of one of our external managers, NISA Investment Advisors of St. Louis. The rebalancing program uses a combination of futures and cash purchases/sales to minimize transaction cost within an acceptable level of tracking error relative to the policy mix.

A Look into the Future: The Evolution of MOSERS' Investment Philosophy

With the downturn in the equity markets over the last three years, it seems that most investors, retail and institutional alike, got a healthy dose of experience (where experience is defined as, "what you get, when you don't get what you expect"). This "experience" has brought about the realization that risk is a four letter word, and given how little we know about the future course of events, diversification needs to be at the forefront of all our thoughts and ultimate decisions. The alternative course is to hold out "hope" that things will get better and that nothing has really changed. We believe that neither the members, nor the state of Missouri are well served by "hope" being the strategy that future retirement benefits rest upon. The question of where returns are likely to come from in the future must be examined and our investment philosophies changed based on our conclusions. Having spent much of the last few years coming to these conclusions about our philosophies, we believe the methods of successful money management in the years and decades ahead will not be the same ones that proved successful through the decades of the 1980s and 1990s. What follows are the tenets that we believe will be critical to investment success in the future.

Tenet #1: Diversification is critical because the future is unknown.

As mentioned earlier, being diversified during the 1990s was not a paying strategy. In fact, the more diversification within a portfolio during the past decade, the worse the performance, as high concentrations to the U.S. stock market, in particular growth-oriented stocks, was the source of the real payoff. With the market's tumble from its highs in March of 2000, diversification seems to be of greater importance today. Diversification, however, seems to have taken on a much broader meaning. It is no longer about holding a variety of stocks, but rather encompasses a much broader array of asset classes, each with characteristics that will perform differently in a variety of economic scenarios. Staff is continually asking whether MOSERS has a portfolio in place that will fair well under a variety of economic situations. During the 1990s, the portfolio was structured well for an economy of rising growth and falling inflation, or disinflation. However, a study of history suggests that other economic scenarios have been common as well - just not in the last twenty years. The decade of the 1970s saw falling growth and rising inflation, a period referred to as stagflation. During periods of stagflation, inflation-hedging or real assets such as real estate, timber, and other commodities would be expected to perform well. While periods of outright deflation, as opposed to disinflation, have not been common throughout U.S. history, they have occurred. Japan knows all too well the havoc deflation can wreak on an economy. For the last ten years, Japan's economy has been stuck in a deflationary rut that has left stock prices 88% below their peak in late 1989. The best performing assets in a deflationary environment are the longest maturity U.S. Treasury securities. There are certainly other types of economic scenarios that history would suggest are not only possible, but are probable over long time periods. The chart to the right helps to identify these scenarios along with the types of investments that would be expected to perform well during those periods. Having a significant allocation to all these types of investments should be our focus, not a bet on one outcome. The future is just too uncertain.

Economic Diversification

EXHIBIT 10.21 *Continued*

As addressed initially within this newsletter, there are two distinct sources of return – beta and alpha. Each investment and asset class within the portfolio mix should be evaluated based on the characteristics they are expected to bring to the table. In addition, a conscious decision should be made regarding the portions of the fund's returns that we expect to come from beta and from alpha. The chart below illustrates the continuum of returns we expect from beta and alpha in the context of our portfolio's asset allocation.

Continuum of Beta vs. Alpha

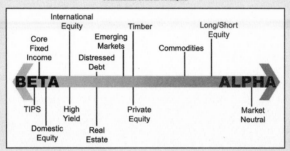

In today's environment of extremely low interest rates, we maintain that one should not expect more than mid to high single digit returns from the beta component of a portfolio split evenly between stocks and bonds. Beta has historically driven most institutional investment programs and MOSERS' is no exception. Beta should be positive over long periods of time, but it is important to understand that the return from beta is based upon the market's views of various risks. Beta is not generated by skill, but rather by exposure, thus when seeking beta it is important to purchase it cheaply and reserve the higher expenses for those areas where skill-based decisions must be made. A classic example of beta exposure within our portfolio comes from our passively managed internal portfolios. Through this implementation decision, MOSERS is able to get returns from exposure to beta at a very low price.

Alpha, the second source of return, should be more of a focus than it has been in the past. We believe finding managers that can produce alpha is a key component to ensuring MOSERS' investment success in the coming years. As returns from beta are harder to come by, finding managers who possess the skills to produce returns above and beyond the asset class returns will be crucial. True alpha should be coveted, and we should be willing to pay up for it. Why do we believe this to be the case? Alpha is a zero-sum game. Simply put, for every winner there is a loser. Thus, just as alpha can provide positive value added to total return, it can also detract from performance. The only way to successfully capture alpha is to select managers who focus on inefficient markets and possess the

skill set to achieve success through implementation of their unique skills. We believe, and our performance supports the notion, that MOSERS is in a good position to capture positive alpha for several key reasons. First, MOSERS' governance policies are structured in such a way that within-class allocation shifts and manager hiring and termination decisions have been delegated to the internal investment professionals and the external asset consultant. MOSERS has amassed a strong team of internal investment professionals that collectively spend about 300 hours per week dedicated to making sound investment decisions. In addition, we have taken the steps necessary to ensure we are receiving independent advice from our external asset consultant. Second, we have been fortunate to experience relatively low turnover among the investment and consulting staff, thus allowing the team to grow and build upon our experiences. We believe this has been the case because the Board and the Executive Director have been willing to provide the necessary resources, both human and technological, to allow for a culture that promotes "outside-the-box" thinking. We are constantly reminded of the John Maynard Keynes quote, "It is better to fail conventionally than to succeed unconventionally." Too many pension funds are focused on following the herd or staying in the middle of the pack. MOSERS is financially better off today because such thinking has not been commonplace here. Third, MOSERS is in a unique position at roughly $5 billion in assets to be big enough to matter, yet small enough to be relatively nimble. Larger pension funds do not have that luxury.

EXHIBIT 10.21 *Continued*

Tenet #3: All asset classes/investments are cyclical, thus flexibility is key.

Economies are cyclical and it logically follows that all asset classes/investments should be as well. Let's look back at the spring of 2000 when money was flooding into technology stocks just before the market took its tumble. Expectations for higher growth rates in "new economy" industries like technology, media and telecom pushed prices of those companies' stocks higher and higher. As prices rose and the market values of those companies increased, those companies found themselves flush with newly minted cash. Management of those companies utilized the cash to build plants, purchase equipment, and hire additional employees with the expectation that it would lead to higher growth and more profits. Because of the seemingly endless opportunities for outsized profits, new players (competition) entered this marketplace with hopes of dipping their hands into the pot of gold. Ultimately the system was sowing the seeds of its own demise. Economics 101 was alive and well --- *"High returns attract capital investments, which generate competition, which leads to lower future returns, while low returns dissuade capital investments which lead to divestiture, bankruptcies, and less competition, which inevitably will lead to better future returns."* It is this cyclical nature of investments that creates opportunities to buy cheap and sell dear.

The within-class allocation latitude granted to the CIO has allowed MOSERS to be more tactical in an attempt to take advantage of these cycles. This is certainly not a slam dunk, primarily because the forces pushing and pulling on these cycles are vast. However, we believe that with a focus on valuation and risk control, our ability to make more right calls than wrong ones is achievable. As Peter Bernstein, a well-known economist recently stated in his <u>Economics and Portfolio Strategy</u> newsletter, "In a volatile world, opportunities and risks will appear and disappear in short order. Flexibility is the watchword." It is important to note that in MOSERS case, this flexibility will be used "at the margin" and only in those instances where valuations are extremely compelling.

Tenet #4: This isn't about return or risk. It's about risk-adjusted returns.

Throughout the 1990s, a great deal of focus was placed on return with little attention to the risk associated with investment in these asset classes. Over the last year, we have spent a great deal of time looking at expected return and risk in tandem in order to maximize the expected return for a given level of risk being assumed. Part of this change in thinking stems from the fact that we now recognize that, despite our infinite time horizon, there are still benefits to pay. In fiscal year 2003, we will pay out some $150 million more in benefits than we will receive in contributions from the state. This is a natural evolution in the aging of our pension fund, however, it does demand an increased focus on shorter-term risks. In the coming months you will be hearing more about our risk management efforts, as we are spending more time examining the risk to the portfolio and focusing more energy on managing those risks.

Finally, it is important to remember that there is no "Holy Grail" or "Silver Bullet" in investing. Investing is a game of survival and is not as simple as following the crowd. In fact, following the crowd will often lead to trouble down the road. As Warren Buffett has stated, "what the wise person does in the beginning for all the right reasons, the fool does in the end for all the wrong ones." Today's investment environment requires independent thinking and independent action. We believe that more time should be spent thinking about what could go wrong (the risk side of the equation) than what could go right (the return side of the equation). While there is still much to learn, the greatest resource we have been given to ensure our success is the commitment by the Board to provide us with the tools needed to pursue and implement our beliefs and to educate ourselves to ask all the necessary questions along the way.

Finding Our Direction: Translating Philosophies from Paper to Practice

The drastic swing in philosophy from the late 1990s to today may lead you to the conclusion that policy portfolios with static asset allocations are no longer relevant. We believe that policy portfolios in today's environment of extremely low interest rates cannot exclusively be expected to provide us with the necessary returns to adequately fund our pension plan. If we are correct in this assessment, we are faced with the following alternatives: (i) continue to depend primarily on returns from beta with the realization that contribution rates will have to go up in the future, (ii) be willing to increase our focus on alpha as a means of increasing returns with the understanding that alpha is a zero-sum game (for every positive alpha, there is a negative alpha) and that net of fees, it is likely that there will only be about 4 winners out of 10 playing

5

EXHIBIT 10.21 *Continued*

the game, (iii) become more flexible in the implementation of our strategies, taking advantage of our ability to be nimble, or (iv) utilize a combination of all of these strategies in prudent doses in order to maximize the diversification benefit that each brings to the table. We obviously think the answer is the combined approach.

One of our biggest challenges is that this new way of thinking forces us to act "un-institutional-like." We will need to abandon our fixed views of the future and rigid rules-based approach to investing and allow for some flexibility being an ongoing component of the process. That is not to say that we should not have a plan. Indeed, an investment plan that provides rules and constraints is important, as long as it provides some flexibility at the fringes to take advantage of opportunities that will invariably present themselves. No doubt, this approach requires us to think about investing differently, and in many instances requires a higher level of expertise and daily monitoring/oversight on the part of those implementing the program.

The good news is that much of the heavy lifting is behind us. In the past year you've challenged the old rules and come to the conclusion that there may be a better way. This is unconventional thinking that is not common in the public retirement universe. The reputational risk of being different is not to be discounted, but, in the end it is not about our reputations, it is about paying benefits to our members. MOSERS has thrown out the traditional road map and replaced it with a new one that thus far has proven profitable. While we will never claim victory based on short time frames, it is certainly nice to get off on the right foot. Since June of 2002 when the new structure was adopted, MOSERS is about $190 million better off compared to where the portfolio would have been if the previous allocation had remained in place.

At the upcoming retreat, we will spend time talking about specific details related to how each asset class has been structured to address a variety of economic outcomes, and what strategic decisions have been made in the last year to capitalize on the factors at play in the economy. We hope this overview of the underlying philosophies guiding the program has given you the foundation for an engaging discussion about our future.

Resources:

Pensions & Investments Magazine, "Engineering Targeted Returns and Risks", Ray Dalio, Bridgewater Associates, January 10, 2003.

Economics and Portfolio Strategy, "Are Policy Portfolios Obsolete?", Peter Bernstein, March 1, 2003.

The Ambachtsheer Letter, "Persistent Investment Regimes' or Random Walk? Even Shakespeare Knew the Answer", Keith Ambachtsheer, April 2003.

This newsletter is produced and distributed in advance of each scheduled board meeting with the objective of educating the Trustees regarding investment issues facing the pension fund. If you have questions or would like additional information on any topic contained herein, please contact Meg Cline.

Notes

Preface

1. *Pensions & Investments* reports worldwide institutional assets as $13,481,975 millions, "Special Report: Money managers directory," May 27, 2002, page 19.
2. See *ShareOwnership2000*. New York Stock Exchange, Table 15.
3. "ISDA Announces 2003 Mid-Year Market Survey Results: Vanilla Swaps Pass $120 Trillion: Strong Credit Derivatives Growth Continues," *International Swaps and Derivatives Association Press Release*, September 23, 2003

Chapter 1

1. Fiduciary Education and Training." Testimony by Donald B. Trone, president of the Foundation for Fiduciary Studies before the ERISA Advisory Council's Working Group on Fiduciary Education, July 17, 2002.
2. Christopher Farrell, "The Problem with Pension Plans," *BusinessWeek Online,* January 11, 2002.
3. Craig Gunsauley, "401 (k) Sponsors Focus on Diversification," *Employee Benefit News,* July 2002.
4. "Seeking to Be Respectable," *The Economist,* April 13, 2002.
5. Various e-mail interviews with Mark Szycher, Director of Research and Chief Risk Officer, Weston Capital Asset Management, LLC.
6. Allison Bisbey Colter, "Pension Funds Have Been Slow to Invest in Hedge Funds," *Wall Street Journal,* April 17, 2002.
7. Robert Clow, "Hedge Funds Jealously Guard Their Investment Strategies and Cannot Always Offer Pensions the Level of Transparency They Seek," *Financial Times,* April 30, 2002.
8. Chris Clair, "Hedge Funds Look Better to Pension Plan Sponsors," *Pensions & Investments,* June 10, 2002.
9. Chris Clair, "Institutional Investors Jumping Big into the Hedge Fund Market," *Pensions & Investments,* February 18, 2002.
10. Jeff Benjamin, "Hedge Funds Go Crazy from Heated Demand," *Investment News,* April 22, 2002.
11. Paul F. Roye, "Risks and Opportunities for Public Pension Plans" (keynote address, Public Funds Syposium, July 17, 2001).

12. Thomas Schneeweis and George Georgiev, "The Benefits of Hedge Funds," *CISDM Working Paper,* June 19, 2002.
13. *Federal Register,* Vol. 65, No. 219, November 13, 2000.
14. "Pension Fund Consultant Survey 2001," Nelson Information, a Thompson Financial company.
15. See http://iafe.org.educate/ for course outlines voluntarily contributed by professors around the world as part of the "Financial Engineering Syllabus Project," sponsored by The International Association of Financial Engineers.
16. Chris Clair, "Derivatives Have Place in Risk Management," *Pensions & Investments,* April 30, 2001.

Chapter 2

1. Judy Ward, "Participant as Plaintiff: Know Your Enemy," *PLANSPONSOR,* April 2002.
2. Richard Phillips, *DCM Pension Track,* DCM Financial Partners, Ltd., Third Quarter, 2001.
3. "More Outsiders Facing Fiduciary Liability, Says DOL Official." Reprinted by Poulton Associates, Inc. with permission from *Employer's Health Benefits Bulletin,* Thompson Publishing Group, Inc., January, 1996.
4. Randy Myers, "The Stakes Are Soaring in Shareholder Lawsuits," *Corporate Board Member,* July/August 2002.
5. Andrew Ross Sorkin, "Back to School, but This One Is for Top Corporate Officials," *New York Times,* September 3, 2002.
6. 590 N.E. 587 (Indiana Courts of Appeals 1992).
7. Randy Myers, "The Stakes Are Soaring in Shareholder Lawsuits," *Corporate Board Member,* July/August 2002.
8. "The Pension Fallout," *Online Newshour,* February 19, 2002. See http://www.pbs.org/newshour/bb/business/jan-june02/pensions_2-19.html.
9. Fred Schneyer, "West Virginia Piles on WorldCom Bond Sale Suit," *PLANSPONSOR,* July 17, 2002.
10. "Florida State Board of Administration Nation's Most Litigious Pension System," *Corporate Governance News,* September 2001.
11. Andrew Osterland, "Better Balance," *CFO Magazine,* June 2000.
12. Fried Frank Harris Shriver and Jakobson, "A Plaintiff Wail: The New Role of Institutional Investors Under the Securities Litigation Reform Act," 1996.
13. Max W. Berger, John P. Coffey, and Gerald H. Silk, "Institutional Investors as Lead Plaintiffs: Is There a New and Changing Landscape?," 2000.

14. New York Stock Exchange, *1999 Fact Book: Institutional Investors.*

15. Lisa Stansky, "Enron Fees: $64 Million and Counting: Firms' Bills to Court Heading Skyward," *The National Law Journal,* July 9, 2002.

16. David E. Brown, "Director and Officer Liability Changes Loom in Post-Enron Proposals," Alston & Bird, LLP, 2002.

17. Tamara Loomis, "D & O Insurance Not a Sure Thing," *New York Law Journal,* August 30, 2002.

18. "D & O Insurance Costs Up Sharply," *Financial Executive,* September 2002.

19. Stephen A. Radin, "Directors Beware: Statutory D & O Indemnification Obligations Do Not Include Fees on Fees," *Business & Securities Litagator,* July 2002.

20. In the survey, approximately 83 percent of survey respondents classified themselves as Corporate/ERISA funds. In stark contrast, only 10.9 percent of funds are classified as public/government and 3.6 percent are classified as nonprofit. Their minor representation may affect survey results because many government funds are defined benefit plans. See http://www.plansponsor.com.

21. According to Investopedia.com, Thomas Carlyle invented the term "dismal science" as a nod to the nineteenth-century Malthusian prophecies of overpopulation and resulting famine. See http://www.investopedia.com/terms/d/dismalscience.asp.

22. Julie Earle, "American Pension Assets Feel the Pinch," *Financial Times,* September 10, 2002.

23. Kara Scannell, "Public Pensions Come Up Short as Stocks' Swoon Drains Funds," *Wall Street Journal,* August 16, 2002.

24. Kathy Chen, "Unfunded Pension Liabilities Soared in 2001 to $111 billion," *Wall Street Journal,* July 26, 2002.

25. Daniel Golden and Charles Forelle, "Colleges Can Feel the Pinch of Shrinking Endowments," *Wall Street Journal,* July 19, 2002.

26. Ibid.

27. David Bank and Martha Brannigan, "Major Donors Slash Gifts to Charity as Stocks Fall," *Wall Street Journal,* July 19, 2002.

28. Nicole Lewis, "Charitable Giving Slides," *Chronicle of Philanthropy,* June 27, 2002.

29. Yuka Hayashi, "Pension Funds Buy Stocks in Bear Market to Balance Portfolios," *Wall Street Journal,* August 8, 2002.

30. Joel Chernoff, "Beware of 'Pension Time Bomb,' Connell Tells Funds," *Pensions & Investments,* August 19, 2002.

31. Ibid.

32. Diane Mix (President, Horizon Cash Management, LLC), in discussion with the author, December 10, 2002.

Chapter 3

1. "Facts from EBRI," Employee Benefit Research Institute, November 2001, page 5.
2. "Opening Statement of the Honorable William J. Coyne, a Representative in Congress from the State of Pennsylvania: Hearing on Retirement Security and Defined Benefit Pension Plans," U.S. House of Representatives, Committee on Ways and Means, Subcommittee on Oversight, June 20, 2002.
3. U.S. Code, Title 29, Chapter 18, Subchapter I, Subtitle B, Part 4, Section 1104.
4. *Harvard College v. Armory,* 9 Pick. (26 Mass.) 446, 461 (1830).
5. Ibid.
6. *Trust Examination Manual,* Section 3 (Asset Administration)—Part C (Prudence in Investments), Federal Deposit Insurance Corporation.
7. Olena Berg, "Letter to Comptroller of the Currency," U.S. Department of Labor, PWBA, Office of Regulations and Interpretations, March 21, 1996.
8. Ibid.
9. Ibid.
10. "29 CFR 2509.75-5—Questions and Answers Relating to Fiduciary Responsibility," U.S. Department of Labor, January 13, 1976.
11. Rafael Chodos, Esq., *The Law of Fiduciary Duties: With Citations to the California Authorities,* Blackthorne Legal Press, 2000.
12. "Public Pay and Pension Plans Policy, Section 4.1 State Role," National Governers Association, Adopted annual meeting 2000 and revised winter meeting 2002.
13. Ibid.
14. "Pension Reform Measures and States," Public Pension and Retirement Savings, National Governers Association, August 2, 2002.
15. Ibid.
16. Ibid.
17. Nicholas Greifer, "Pension Investment Policies: The State of the Art," *Government Finance Review,* February 2002.
18. Ibid.
19. Missouri State Employees' Retirement System, MOSER's web site, "Investments" header, http://www.mosers.org/about/invest.html.
20. Nicholas Greifer, "Pension Investment Policies: The State of the Art," *Government Finance Review,* February 2002.
21. Investment Policy for Missouri State Employees' Retirement System, Adopted by the Board of Trustees in June 1995 and last revised on September 20, 2001, pages 14 and 15.

22. E-mail correspondence on July 15, 2002, from Gary Findlay, executive director of the Missouri State Employees' Retirement System.

23. Office of the Comptroller, Department of Financial Services, State of Florida, *State of Florida Comprehensive Annual Financial Report, Notes to the Financial Statements for the Fiscal Year Ended June 30, 2000,* page 32.

24. Ibid., 33.

25. Texas State Auditor's Office, "Methodology Manual: Financial Modules, Investments: Appendix: Derivatives," February, 1995.

26. Gene Callahan and Greg Kaza, "In Defense of Derivatives," *Reason,* February 2004, pages 32–40.

27. Statements by Honorable Ron Paul of Texas in the House of Representatives, *Congressional Record,* October 2, 1998, that cite the Michigan State initiative.

28. "Learning Lab: Frequently Asked Questions," The Foundation Center web site, http://www.fdncenter.org.

29. "Glossary of Terms in Philanthropy," Donors Forum of Chicago web site, www.donorsforum.org.

30. National Conference of Commissioners on Uniform State Laws web site, http://www.nccusl.org.

31. National Conference of Commissioners on Uniform State Laws, Press Release: "Uniform Prudent Investor Act (UPIA) and Revised Uniform Principal and Income Act: States' Nationwide Need to Adopt Both Acts to Bring Trust Law into Line with Modern Portfolio Theory," Chicago: January 2000.

32. Randall H. Borkus, "A Trust Fiduciary's Duty to Implement Capital Preservation: Strategies Using Financial Derivative Techniques," *Real Property, Probate & Trust Journal,* Spring 2001, Vol. 36, No. 1, page 165.

33. Risk Standards Working Group, "Risk Standards for Institutional Investment Managers and Institutional Investors," 1996.

34. Elizabeth A. Pitrof, "Liability Exposures and Protections for Nonprofit Organizations and Their Directors and Officers: Prepared at the Request of ALTRU, Inc.," October 1997.

35. Ibid.

36. Comments of Jeffrey M. Kaplan, in "To Meet Their Duty Under Caremark to Oversee Compliance, Corporate Directors Should Ask These Questions," *Corporate Governance Report,* The Bureau of National Affairs, Inc., August 5, 2002.

37. *Gilbert v. EMG Advisors, Inc.,* 172 F.3d 876 (9th Cir, 1999).

38. Ibid., citing *Howard, 100 F.3d at 1490.*

39. Dominic Bencivenga, "Parties Argue Over 'Degrees' of Sophistication," *New York Law Journal,* September 1, 1994.

Chapter 4

1. Daniel Altman "Derivatives: Corporate Financial Leverage Wrapped in Enigma," *New York Times,* June 11, 2003, provides some interesting perspectives on financial literacy.
2. "News Release," Fannie Mae, Washington, D.C., July 15, 2003.
3. The "ISDA Market Survey" reports total interest rate and currency notional amounts outstanding 2H 2002 as $99,832.73 billion.
4. The term *notional* expresses the idea that the principal amount—sometimes referred to as the face value—is not exchanged. Rather, a cash flow amount, based on notional principal amount, is exchanged on specified dates or under certain conditions.
5. The OCC is one of several sources of market statistics. Their focus is on derivatives usage by banks.
6. "OCC Reports Derivatives Volume Over $60 Trillion," Comptroller of the Currency Administrator of National Banks News Release NR 2003-45, June 6, 2003.
7. Assets for independent foundations for 2001 are reported as $403.5 billion by The Foundation Center. See *Foundation Growth and Giving Estimates, 2002 Preview,* New York, page 5.
8. "Charities & Non-Profits," *The Digital Daily,* Internal Revenue Service.
9. Elise Ober, Research Coordinator, Development Office, Salisbury School, "Access to Form 990s on the Web: An Ongoing Process," *NEDRA News,* New England Development Research Association, Salisbury, CT, Spring 2000.
10. "GuideStar Posts Private Foundations' IRS Returns," Philanthropic Research, Inc. (GuideStar), 2000. See http://www.guidestar.org.
11. September 2003 e-mail interview with Suzanne E. Coffman, Director of Communications, Philanthropic Research, Inc. (GuideStar).
12. As discussed on the Internal Revenue Service web site, charities and nonprofits that do not complete Form 990-PF must file a variation of the form (unless exempted). Throughout this book, "Form 990" refers to Form 990-PF.
13. "IRS Form 990 Isn't the Whole Story," Williamsburg, VA: GuideStar.
14. April 2002 e-mail interview with Chuck McLean, Vice President of Research, Philanthropic Research, Inc., (GuideStar).
15. *Starting a Private Foundation,* Forum of Regional Associations of Grantmakers, 1999, http://www.givingforum.org.
16. Some plans are exempt and are described in "2002 Instructions for Form 5500: Annual Return/Report of Employee Benefit Plan," Washington, D.C.: Internal Revenue Service.
17. http://www.dol.gov/ebsa/5500main.html.
18. "Form 5500 Filing Tips," Internal Revenue Service web site, http://www.irs.gov.

19. This comment is based on a late 2002 interview with a U.S. Department of Labor official who prefers to remain anonymous.
20. Ibid.
21. This comment is based on a mid-2003 interview with an auditor of a public pension fund who prefers to remain unnamed.
22. Wesley Brown, "Retirement Funds [sic] Owns $650 Million in Harmful Derivatives," *The Morning News,* March 6, 2003.
23. Deciding whether and how much to invest in foreign currency investments should encompass a variety of factors, not the least of which is the risk-adjusted return impact of broadening exposure beyond the United States.
24. March 2003 phone interview with Andrew S. Lang, National Director for Nonprofit Services, BDO Seidman.
25. Statements are based on a mid-2003 interview with the managing director of a large university endowment who prefers to remain unnamed.
26. CCH Editorial Staff, "FASB Seeks Enhanced Pension Disclosures," *Federal Securities Law Reporter, Report Letter No. 2082,* July 2, 2003.

Chapter 5

1. Standard deviation is a measure of absolute risk and considers the variability around expected returns. The coefficient of variation is a relative measure of risk because the standard deviation is divided by expected return. The absolute value of the coefficient of variation is used when expected return is negative, although it is hard to compare investments when one has a positive return and the other does not.
2. Exhibit 5.2 is a simplification for illustrative purposes only. Proper investment ranking should reflect an investor's objectives and constraints.
3. The correlation coefficient for Portfolio 1 is +1.0 and represents perfect positive correlation. The opposite is true for Portfolio 5. With a correlation coefficient of −1.0, perfect negative correlation is said to exist. The 33 percent drop in portfolio standard deviation is computed as 100% times [(4% divided by 6%) −1].
4. Nevin Adams, "Median Master Trust Returns Slide 9% in Q3," *PLANSPONSOR.COM,* October 23, 2002.
5. Eugene F. Brigham and Joel F. Houston, *Fundamentals of Financial Management, Concise Third Edition,* Mason, OH: South-Western Publishing, 2002, page 252.
6. The discussion of diversification does not apply to investors who seek to purposely concentrate monies in an industry, country, or region.
7. A 15 percent loan rate requires a payment of $135 in interest (i.e., $900 loan amount times 0.15).

8. Association for Investment Management and Research, *Update Report of the Leverage and Derivatives Subcommittee as of February 14, 2001,* Charlottesville, 2001.
9. Basel Committee on Banking Supervision, "HLI Report—Anniversary Review," Bank for International Settlements, January 25, 2000.
10. Basel Committee on Banking Supervision and the International Organization of Securities Commissions, "Review of Issues Relating to Highly Leveraged Institutions (HLIs)," Bank for International Settlements, March 2001.
11. A stock's beta is estimated by dividing a stock's covariance with the market index by the variance of the market index, typically using returns rather than prices.
12. Hedging as a way to reduce market risk is not considered here.
13. The estimated regression line for this specific analysis of market index returns vis-à-vis individual company stock returns in known as the characteristic line.
14. When bonds differ in several ways, comparing them by duration is more difficult.
15. Technically, the use of other formulas may mean that the duration for a zero coupon bond is close to but not equal to its time to maturity.
16. Bond yields and prices move inversely. Investors with a higher risk perception about a bond will increase their required return, driving up yields and pushing down prices.
17. For both equities and fixed income, the theoretical construct of a "market" portfolio refers to a broad, well-diversified basket of investments.

Chapter 6

1. Leo Melamed, "Essays & Speeches by Leo Melamed: A Brief History of Financial Futures, Presented at the Seminar on Financial Futures," May 3, 1994.
2. *BIS Quarterly Review,* Bank for International Settlements, December 2002.
3. The Bank for International Settlements reports a $1.2 trillion daily average total turnover in OTC trades that involve spot transactions, outright forwards, and foreign exchange swaps. See "Triennial Central Bank Survey of Foreign Exchange and Derivatives Market Activity in 2001," Bank for International Settlements, March 2002.
4. See Figure 6a, "Most Frequently Used Derivative Type by Underlying Asset Class for Investors," in *1998 Survey of Derivatives and Risk Management Practices by U.S. Institutional Investors* by Richard M. Levich, Gregory S. Hayt, and Beth A. Ripston, October 1999.

5. Various types of margin and other futures-related terms are described in "The CFTC Glossary: A Layman's Guide to the Language of the Futures Industry," January 31, 1997.
6. According to the Chicago Mercantile Exchange web site, the goal of this Standard Portfolio Analysis of Risk® approach is to quantify the worst-case loss for a portfolio of futures and options on the same underlying asset or index. See http://www.cme.com.
7. One source of information is the *Numa Directory of Futures & Options Exchanges.* See http://www.numa.org.
8. Price discovery and other basic concepts are discussed in "A Guide to Understanding Opportunities and Risks in Futures Trading," Chicago, IL: The National Futures Association.
9. The web site for the Financial Accounting Standards Board summarizes Statement No. 133, *Accounting for Derivative Instruments and Hedging Activities.* See http://www.fasb.org.
10. U.S. Treasury bonds and related futures are quoted in units of 1/32 of 1 percent. A quote of 97-24 is interpreted as 97 plus 24 32nds. To convert this to dollars, divide 24 by 32 to get 0.75 and add to 97. For every $100 face value, the bond costs $97.75. Scaling this for a $1 million face value translates into a price of $977,500.
11. The term *cash* refers to the underlying asset.
12. Many futures positions are closed out with offsetting trades before expiration to avoid making or taking delivery.
13. Harry M. Kat, "Managed Futures and Hedge Funds: A Match Made in Heaven," Reading, U.K.: University of Reading, ISMA Centre Working Paper, November 2002.
14. "Managed Futures: Portfolio Diversification Opportunities," Chicago, IL: Chicago Board of Trade, 2002.
15. See "Prize-Winning Research Creates First Benchmark to Measure the Performance of Trend-Following Strategies." This Foundation for Managed Derivatives Research press release, dated April 20, 1999, describes the research work of William Fung and David Hsieh, whose paper won recognition from the International Association of Financial Engineers in 1999.
16. See the web site for Standard & Poor's at http://www.standardandpoors.com.
17. Randy Myers, "Extra Alpha," *PLANSPONSOR,* April 1997.
18. Ibid.
19. Randall Rohn, "Enhanced Index Funds: What's in a Name?," mPower.com, Inc., February 19, 2001.

Chapter 7

1. According to RiskCenter.com, the option on the Kospi 200 stock index, traded on the Korea Stock Exchange, accounts for a "63 percent of the

global increase in trading activity." See "Equity Index, Interest Rate and Energy Derivatives Are the Main Drivers For F&O Record Volume Year," November 7, 2002.

2. The Bank for International Settlements reports a 2001 outstanding amount total for exchange-traded options of $12,492.8 billion, about 15 percent higher than the $10,879 billion OTC options statistic.

3. See Figure 6a, "Most Frequently Used Derivative Type by Underlying Asset Class for Investors," *1998 Survey of Derivatives and Risk Management Practices by U.S. Institutional Investors* by Richard M. Levich, Gregory S. Hayt, and Beth A. Ripston, October 1999.

4. According to *Characteristics and Risks of Standardized Options*, most option writers must adhere to applicable margin rules. (Copyright © 1994 American Stock Exchange, Inc., Chicago Board Options Exchange, Incorporated, New York Stock Exchange, Inc.; Pacific Stock Exchange, Incorporated, and Philadelphia Stock Exchange, Inc.)

5. Refer to the New York Clearing Corporation web site, http://www. nybot.com.

6. Ibid.

7. See the web site for the Option Clearing Corporation, http://www. theocc.com.

8. *A User's Guide to Currency Options,* Philadelphia Stock Exchange, Philadelphia, December 1996.

9. The full ticker symbol is not always the same as the option root, in part because the identifying security symbols cannot exceed three characters. See *Options 101 & Help*, at http://www.quote.com.

10. Refer to the *Options Industry Council Glossary* at http://www. 888options.com.

11. Recall that an American option, which was earlier described, offers more exercise flexibility than a European option.

12. Moneyness is customarily evaluated from the perspective of the option buyer.

13. See http://www.888options.com.

14. See the web site for the Chicago Board Options Exchange, http://www. cboe.com.

15. Interested parties would need to contact each institutional investor for more details regarding if, how, and when options have been used.

16. This same generalized approach can be used for any type of option strategy and any type of underlying security.

17. Derivative valuation models assume the absence of arbitrage. This means that no investor should be able to generate a profit without taking some risk.

18. F. Black and M. Scholes, "The Pricing of Options and Corporate Liabilities," *Journal of Political Economy, 81,* 1973, pp. 637–654.

19. R. C. Merton, "Theory of Rational Option Pricing," *Bell Journal of Economics and Management Science, 4,* 1973, pp. 141–183.
20. Revenue Procedure 2002-13, 26 CFR 601.105.
21. Ibid.
22. The term *intrinsic value* usually only refers to positive intrinsic value.

Chapter 8

1. Recall that a long options position gives the holder the right but not the obligation to act later. In contrast, each party to a swap or futures contract is obliged to meet the terms of the contract.
2. "News Release: Gross Domestic Product and Corporate Profits," Washington, D.C.: U.S. Department of Commerce, Bureau of Economic Analysis, Table 10, August 28, 2003.
3. One exception is the currency swap whereby principal in each currency and possibly interest is exchanged at various points in time.
4. Counterparties to other types of swaps would similarly be entering into a legal contract but could be known by different names. For example, neither party entering into a floating-to-floating swap would be referred to as the Fixed Rate Payer because no fixed rate interest rate swap is involved.
5. The word *payor* is sometimes used in lieu of *payer.*
6. LIBOR can be defined as the Eurodollar loan cost for large bank transactions that take place in the London interbank market.
7. One source of information is the *User's Guide to the 2002 ISDA Master Agreement.*
8. "Remarks by Chairman Alan Greenspan at the 2003 Conference on Bank Structure and Competition," The Federal Reserve Board, May 8, 2003.
9. Ibid.
10. This example ignores the fact that default risk for a floating rate security can differ from the default risk associated with a fixed coupon security even when the issuer is the same entity.
11. Matching the swap settlement dates to the interest payment dates of the floating rate note is one way to mitigate timing mismatch risk. Using the same dates for both the fixed and floating rate legs of the swap is another way to avoid timing issues.
12. Swap settlement dates are negotiated. Quarterly and semiannual settlements are common.
13. Assessing counterparty risk considers an assortment of factors, including but not limited to current and expected creditworthiness, forecasted swap rates, transaction size, and available credit lines.
14. Although not discussed here, bond default risk is directly tied to the terms of a bond and to the many variables that reflect the issuer's ability to repay.

15. According to the *ISDA Market Survey*, published by the International Swaps and Derivatives Association, Inc., credit default swap market size at the end of 2002 was approximately $2.148 trillion.

16. Ian W. Marsh, "What Central Banks Can Learn About Default Risk from Credit Markets," Basel, Switzerland: BIS Papers No. 12, August 2002.

17. Ibid.

18. "Professional Actuarial Specialty Guide: Asset-Liability Management," AA-1-98, Schaumburg, IL: Society of Actuaries, August 1, 1998, page 11.

19. Richard M. Levich, Gregory S. Hayt, and Beth A. Ripston, "1998 Survey of Derivatives and Risk Management Practices by U.S. Institutional Investors," October 1999, Figure 6a.

20. Zvi Bodie and Robert C. Merton, "International Pension Swaps," *Journal of Pension Economics and Finance*, Vol. 1, No. 1 (March 2002): 77–83.

21. "CBOT to Launch 10-Year Swap Futures Friday, Oct. 26, 2001," *Chicago Board of Trade Press Release*, October 25, 2001.

22. "Record Volume in CBOT 10-Year Interest Rate Swap Futures," *Chicago Board of Trade Press Release*, August 28, 2003.

23. Refer to the Chicago Board of Trade web site, http://www.cbot.com.

24. "Board Approves Bonds With Interest-Rate Swaps," *The Board of the Dormitory Authority Press Release*, January 24, 2003.

25. Katherine McManus, Karl Pfeil, and Trudy Zibit, "Guidelines for Effective Uses of Swaps in Asset-Liability Management," *Government Finance Review*, June 2003.

26. "CIEBA of AFP Supports Changes to Pension Funding Discount Rate, *Comment Letter to the Honorable John Snow, Secretary of the Treasury*, February 13, 2003.

27. "Pension Managers Support Quick Action on Pension Funding Interest Rate: Urge Caution on Radical Pension Changes," *Association for Financial Professionals–Committee on Investment of Employee Benefit Assets Press Release*, July 15, 2003.

28. See http://thomas.loc.gov, Bill Summary & Status for the 108th Congress and http://www.whitehouse.gov/.

Chapter 9

1. George A. Mangiero and Susan M. Mangiero, "Correlation and Hedge Effectiveness," *GARP Risk Review*, May 2001, pp. 22–23.

2. "Credit derivatives market 'could reach $4.8 trillion' by 2004, " September 18, 2002 Press Release, British Bankers Association.

3. U.S. House of Representatives member Patrick J. Toomey introduced H.R. 2120 on May 15, 2003, "to revise the banking and bankruptcy insolvency laws with respect to the termination and netting of financial contracts, and for other purposes." See http://thomas.loc.gov, Bill Summary & Status.

4. June 2003 e-mail exchange with Mr. Marc-Henry Chamay, head of eBusiness for Allen & Overy.

5. See "Liability of Broker Dealers for Unsuitable Recommendations to Institutional Investors" by Norman S. Poser for a discussion of investment sophistication and institutional investments, *Brigham Young University Law Review*, 1493, No. 4, 2001.

6. Buffet, Warren E., "Berkshire Hathaway Inc. 2002 Annual Report," p. 13.

7. "Remarks by Chairman Alan Greenspan at the 2003 Conference on Bank Structure and Competition," Federal Reserve Board, May 8, 2003.

8. "Derivatives Use in the 1990's," Remarks by Arthur Levitt, Chairman, U.S. Securities & Exchange Commission, Washington, D.C.: IDB/ISDA Conference, November 9, 1995.

9. "Frequently Asked Questions Regarding the Valuation of Embedded Derivatives in Life Insurance and Annuity Contracts in Accordance with FAS 133," Washington, D.C.: American Academy of Actuaries, June 13, 2002, draft.

10. "Accounting for Derivative Instruments and Hedging Activities, FASB Statement No. 133 as amended and interpreted incorporating FASB Statements No. 137 and 138 and certain Statement No. 133 implementation issues as of December 10, 2001," Financial Accounting Standards Board of the Financial Accounting Foundation, paragraph 12a, page 14.

11. "The Roundtable Discussions on IAS 32 and IAS 39 Introductory Note," IASPlus.com, February 14, 2003.

12. "GASB Improves Derivative Disclosure Requirements," Governmental Accounting Standards Board News Release, June 25, 2003.

13. "US Set to Adopt FRS 17 Model," *AccountancyAge.com*, April 22, 2003.

14. "Testimony Concerning Investor Protection Implications of Hedge Funds Before the Senate Committee on Banking, Housing and Urban Affairs" by William H. Donaldson, Chairman, U.S. Securities and Exchange Commission, April 10, 2003.

15. Ibid.

16. Excerpted from "Speech by SEC Staff: Valuation, Trading, and Disclosure: Three Compliance Imperatives, Remarks by Lori A. Richards, Director, Office of Compliance Inspections and Examinations U.S. Securities & Exchange Commission," 2001 Mutual Fund Compliance Conference, Investment Company Institute, June 14, 2001.

17. "Freddie Mac Reports on Restatement Progress," June 25, 2003, Press Release.

18. Craig Schneider, "Stock Options: How Do You Attribute 'Em?," CFO.com, May 5, 2003.

19. See http://thecorporatelibrary.com/spotlight/compensation/expensing_stock-options.html for some additional resources about this issue.

20. "Bank One Corporation (Successor in Interest to First Chicago NBD Corporation, Formerly NBD Bancorp, Inc., Successor in Interest to

First Chicago Corporation) and Affiliated Corporations, Petitioner v. Commissioner of Internal Revenue, Respondent, Docket Nos. 5759-95, 5956-97. Filed May 2, 2003.

Chapter 10

1. The Charitable Giving Act of 2003, overwhelmingly passed by the U.S. House of Representatives on September 17, 2003, includes new rules for distribution.
2. *Foundation Growth and Giving Estimates, 2002 Preview,* New York, NY: The Foundation Center, 79 Fifth Avenue, New York, NY 10003, www.fdncenter.org.
3. The Foundation Center, "After Holding the Line for Two Years, Foundation Giving Declines in 2003," Press Release, April 5, 2004.
4. Recall that many foundations and endowments use a rolling three-year asset average for giving calculations.
5. "College Endowment Earnings Decline Due to Volatile Stock Market and Weak Economy: NACUBO Study Shows Average Returns Drop Six Percent in Fiscal Year 2002," NACUBO Press Release, January 21, 2003.
6. Ricki Fulman, "Companies Pony Up Billions for Flagging Funds," *Pensions & Investments,* November 25, 2002. Reprinted with permission, *Pensions & Investments.*
7. Susan Kelly, "The Next Big Money Pit," *Treasury & Risk Management,* November 2002.
8. "S&P 500 Pension Analysis Shows Market Decline Continues to Erode Pensions," Standard & Poor's Press Release, April 24, 2004.
9. "U.S. Public Pensions Face Uncertain Times" by Parry Young, Standard & Poor's RatingsDirect, June 24, 2003.
10. "Investment Policy Checklist for Pension Fund Assets," Government Finance Officers Association, Committee on Retirement and Benefits Administration, May 2003.
11. Not every investment policy has the same format or quality.
12. "The Impact of FAS 133 on the Risk Management Practices of End Users of Derivatives: Report of Survey Results," Association for Financial Professionals, September 2002.
13. "Report of the Working Group on Fiduciary Education and Training," U.S. Department of Labor, Employee Benefits Security Administration, April 7, 2003.
14. Ibid.
15. The term *supply chain* is normally used to describe the relationship among suppliers, wholesalers, and retailers.
16. International Federation of Accountants, "International Auditing Practice Statement 1012: Auditing Derivative Financial Instruments, March 2001.

17. Vendor selection can be a time-consuming process and requires extensive homework to determine what questions to ask.
18. E-mail discussion with Chris Lewis, Managing Director, Fitch Risk Management, July 22, 2003.
19. Those endowments, foundations, and pensions that use external money managers will seldom have the same needs as those institutions that perform the investment and risk management work in house.
20. E-mail discussion with Chris Lewis, Managing Director, Fitch Risk Management, July 22, 2003.
21. E-mail discussion with Gary Findlay, Executive Director, Missouri State Employees' Retirement System, July 16, 2003.

Chapter 11

1. This point that no perfect measure exists is the same one made earlier in the book about standard deviation and other risk metrics.
2. Market capitalization is found by multiplying a company's per share market price by the number of common shares outstanding. For example, a company with 10,000 shares outstanding and a $2.50 per share market price has a market capitalization of $25,000.
3. Benchmark selection is a complex process and is not covered here. There are entire books written on the topic.
4. See http://www.investorwords.com.
5. Staffs of the Office of the Chief Accountant and the Division of Corporate Finance, "Questions and Answers About the New 'Market Risk' Disclosure Rules," U.S. Securities Exchange Commission, July 31, 1997.
6. "Speech by SEC Staff: SEC Risk Management and Compliance Examinations" by Mary Ann Gadziala, Associate Director, Office of Compliance Inspections and Examinations, 2003 Fiduciary and Investment Risk Management Association, Richmond, VA: Fiduciary and Risk Management Seminar, February 26, 2003.
7. This approach is problematic if the assumption of normality does not apply.
8. Risk managers look at the part of the distribution associated with loss, rather than both the loss and gain regions taken together.
9. Linearity and optionality are two of the attributes that characterize the complexity of a security (or portfolio). The former describes the extent to which the value of a security changes in proportion to the change in a risk factor. A security that changes in value by the same magnitude as the change in a market index level would be described as having a linear exposure to systematic risk. Optionality is an example of nonlinearity because option values do not change in a one-to-one fashion as the price of the underlying asset changes.
10. "J.P. Morgan Chase & Co. 2002 Annual Report," p. 59.

11. Ibid., p. 58.
12. The RiskMetrics Group was a division of JP Morgan until 1998, when it became an independent entity. See http://www.riskmetrics.com/aboutus.html.
13. This is not an exhaustive list of risk sources in modeling.
14. "Supervisory Framework for the Use of 'Backtesting' in Conjunction with the Internal Models Approach to Market Risk Capital Requirements," Basel Committee on Banking Supervision, Bank for International Settlements, Basel Committee Publications No. 22, January 1996.
15. Interested parties may want to read about the new Basel Capital Accord. See http://www.bis.org.
16. Richard M. Levich, Gregory S. Hayt, and Beth A. Ripston, "1998 Survey of Derivatives and Risk Management Practices by U.S. Institutional Investors," New York University Stern School of Business, CIBC World Markets and KPMG Investment Consulting Group, October 1999, p. 24.
17. Katerina Simons, "The Use of Value at Risk by Institutional Investors,"*New England Economic Review,* November/December 2000.
18. Mary Ellen Stocks and Christopher Ito, "Value at Risk for the Asset Manager," The *Journal of Performance Measurement*, Summer 1997.
19. Ibid.
20. Jorge Mina and Gavin Watson, "Value-at-Risk for Asset Managers," *RiskMetrics Journal*, November 2000, p. 10.
21. The nature of the assumptions will vary by asset class, associated model, and type of data used, among other things.
22. "About CCRO," Committee of Chief Risk Officers web site, http://www.ccro.org.
23. "Stress Testing by Large Financial Institutions: Current Practice and Aggregation Issues," Committee on the Global Financial System, Bank for International Settlements, CGFS Publication No. 14, April 2000.
24. "An Internal Model-Based Approach to Market Risk Capital Requirements, Stress Testing," Basel Committee on Banking Supervision, Bank for International Settlements, April 1995.
25. "J.P. Morgan Chase & Co. 2002 Annual Report," p. 60.
26. Martin Veasey and Mark Benfold, "New Take on Risk," *GARP Risk Review*, October/November 2001, pp. 9–11.
27. Sagging equity market conditions and related funding problems are two of many reasons that account for some serious rethinking about what constitutes an optimal asset allocation mix.

Chapter 12

1. According to the *Pension Insurance Data Book 2002,* published by the Pension Benefit Guaranty Corporation, there are 34.4 million insured participants in single-employer programs and 9.5 million participants in multiemployer programs.

2. "Pension Benefit Guaranty Corporation Single-Employer Insurance Program: Long-Term Vulnerabilities Warrant 'High Risk' Designation," U.S. General Accounting Office, July 23, 2003.
3. It should be noted that regulatory mandates can still occur even when things are running smoothly.
4. Henry Hazlitt, "Economics in One Lesson, 50th Anniversary Edition," San Francisco: Laissez Faire Books, 1996.
5. "NAPF Press Release: New Accounting Standards Puts Pensions in Peril," National Association of Pension Funds, February 12, 2002.

Index

BUSINESS VALUATION ANALYTICS℠

Know What It's Worth – and Why.℠

In today's world, anyone concerned about financial valuation faces an uphill battle to stay abreast of current developments. Deal structures are more complicated, market conditions change quickly, and unexplained numbers can land you in court.

Worthwhile Reading℠ is a bi-monthly newsletter that gives you no-nonsense information about valuation techniques and trends, with an emphasis on relevance and application. Designed for busy people who need to know what impacts their bottom line and why, *Worthwhile Reading*℠ looks at timely topics such as marketability, risk assessment, method selection, and regulatory mandates. Call 203-261-5119 or visit *http://www. bvallc.com* to subscribe.